ROUTLEDGE LIBRARY EDITIONS:
COLONIALISM AND IMPERIALISM

Volume 40

PERSPECTIVES ON
IMPERIALISM AND
DECOLONIZATION

# PERSPECTIVES ON IMPERIALISM AND DECOLONIZATION

Essays in Honour of A.F. Madden

Edited by
R. F. HOLLAND
and
G. RIZVI

LONDON AND NEW YORK

First published in 1984 by Frank Cass and Company Limited

This edition first published in 2023
by Routledge
4 Park Square, Milton Park, Abingdon, Oxon OX14 4RN

and by Routledge
605 Third Avenue, New York, NY 10158

*Routledge is an imprint of the Taylor & Francis Group, an informa business*

© 1984 Frank Cass & Co. Ltd.

All rights reserved. No part of this book may be reprinted or reproduced or utilised in any form or by any electronic, mechanical, or other means, now known or hereafter invented, including photocopying and recording, or in any information storage or retrieval system, without permission in writing from the publishers.

Trademark notice: Product or corporate names may be trademarks or registered trademarks, and are used only for identification and explanation without intent to infringe.

*British Library Cataloguing in Publication Data*
A catalogue record for this book is available from the British Library

ISBN: 978-1-032-41054-8 (Set)
ISBN: 978-1-032-45802-1 (Volume 40) (hbk)
ISBN: 978-1-032-45808-3 (Volume 40) (pbk)
ISBN: 978-1-003-37877-8 (Volume 40) (ebk)

DOI: 10.4324/9781003378778

**Publisher's Note**
The publisher has gone to great lengths to ensure the quality of this reprint but points out that some imperfections in the original copies may be apparent.

**Disclaimer**
The publisher has made every effort to trace copyright holders and would welcome correspondence from those they have been unable to trace.

FREDDIE MADDEN

# Perspectives on Imperialism and Decolonization

ESSAYS IN HONOUR OF
A. F. MADDEN

*Edited by*
R. F. Holland and G. Rizvi

FRANK CASS

*First published 1984 in Great Britain by*
FRANK CASS AND COMPANY LIMITED
2 Park Square, Milton Park,
Abingdon, Oxon, OX14 4RN

*and in the United States of America by*
FRANK CASS AND COMPANY LIMITED
270 Madison Ave, New York NY 10016

Transferred to Digital Printing 2006

Copyright © 1984 Frank Cass & Co. Ltd.

British Library Cataloguing in Publication Data

Perspectives on imperialism and decolonization.
 —(Journal of imperial and commonwealth
 history, ISSN 0308-6534 ; v. 12, no. 2)
 1. Imperialism—History  2. Europe—
 Politics and government—1789-1900  3.Europe
 —Politics and government—20th century
 I. Holland, R.F.  II. Rizvi, G.  III.
 Madden, A.F.  IV. Series
 325'.32'094      JC359

 ISBN 0-7146-3242-2

Library of Congress Cataloging in Publication Data

Perspectives on imperialism and decolonization.

 1. Colonies—History—Addresses, essays, lectures.
 2. Decolonisation—History—Addresses, essays, lectures.
 3. Madden, A. F.—Addresses, essays, lectures.
 I. Holland, R. F.  II. Rizvi, Gowher.
 JV105.P48  1984      325'.32      84-1886
 ISBN 0-7146-3242-2

Printed and bound by Antony Rowe Ltd, Eastbourne

This group of studies first appeared in a Special Issue on
'Perspectives on Imperialism and Decolonization: Essays in
Honour of A. F. Madden' of *Journal of Imperial and Common-
wealth History,* Vol. XII, No. 2, published by Frank Cass & Co. Ltd.

*All rights reserved. No part of this publication may be reproduced, stored
in a retrieval system, or transmitted in any form, or by any means,
electronic, mechanical, photocopying, recording, or otherwise, without
the prior permission of Frank Cass and Company Limited.*

# Contents

| | | |
|---|---|---|
| Editors' Note | | vii |
| Introduction: Freddie Madden | **Michael Brock** | 1 |

### I. PERSPECTIVES ON IMPERIAL HISTORY

| | | |
|---|---|---|
| Can Humpty-Dumpty be put together again? Imperial History in the 1980s | **David Fieldhouse** | 9 |
| Colonialism French-Style, 1945–55: A Retrospective View | **Kenneth Robinson** | 24 |
| Imperial Theory and the Question of Imperialism after Empire | **Ronald Robinson** | 42 |

### II. IMPERIAL EXPERIENCE: SENTIMENT, DEMOGRAPHY AND POWER

| | | |
|---|---|---|
| Thomas Day and the Politics of Sentiment | **Paul Langford** | 57 |
| The March of Everyman: Mobility and the Imperial Census of 1901 | **Colin Newbury** | 80 |
| British Foreign Policy and the Influence of Empire, 1970–1920 | **Paul Hayes** | 102 |

### III. INTERPRETING BRITISH DECOLONIZATION

| | | |
|---|---|---|
| Transfer of Power in India: A 'Re-statement' of an Alternative Approach | **Gowher Rizvi** | 127 |
| The Mediator's Moment: Sir Tej Bahadur Sapru and the Antecedents to the Cripps Mission to India, 1940–42 | **D. A. Low** | 145 |
| The Imperial Factor in British Strategies from Attlee to Macmillan, 1945–63 | **R. F. Holland** | 165 |
| British Decolonization since 1945: A Pattern or a Puzzle? | **John Darwin** | 187 |

| | |
|---|---|
| Notes on the Contributors | 210 |

# Editors' Note

These essays have been collected to mark the retirement of Freddie Madden. The contributors have, at various times, been associated with him either as pupils or colleagues during his four decades at Oxford. Their articles, in the diversity of subject-matter and time-span which they encompass, reflect the catholic historical sympathy which was always Freddie Madden's hallmark as a historian; whilst their coherence around the central theme of the growth and demise of Western empire testify to the vitality of that imperial historiographic tradition which was the pre-eminent concern of his activities both as teacher and scholar.

R. F. Holland
G. Rizvi

# Freddie Madden

## by

## Michael Brock

Every enterprise needs at least one old hand. The Harrowby Papers include an account of the cannonade at the Battle of Fontenoy by a young staff officer. 'Our old officers say,' he wrote, 'there never was so hot work except at Malplaquet'.[1] The old fellows who had been serving since Malplaquet, more than thirty years earlier, were the oracles. There must be someone whose presence reminds the newcomers that today's battle is not the first ever fought, and that today's quirks and fashions will last no longer than yesterday's. In Oxford's Commonwealth Studies since the Second World War this role has fallen to Freddie Madden. He gave first-rate tutorials to the generation who returned in 1945–6 (as the author of these lines has much cause to know):[2] he is giving equally good ones today. His career has spanned a great change in this area of the University's work. Surveying the period from the election of the first Beit Professor in 1905 to 1971, he wrote in *Oxford and the Idea of Commonwealth*:

> There was also for the greater part of this period another mark of Oxford imperial history – a missionary fervour for 'Commonwealth'. Within the University and the curriculum its intellectual force derived more from the Christian humanitarianism of Coupland and Harlow than from Curtis.[3]

The last of the Round Table dynasty cannot have read Kipling's poems with sufficient care; or perhaps they were prejudiced against the poet who had refused to serve on the Rhodes Trust with Philip Kerr.[4] They did not apply to their own plans the message about the impermanence of all such planning with which Kipling comforted himself after the Liberal victory of 1906.

> This season's daffodil,
>   She never hears,
> What change, what chance, what chill,
>   Cut down last year's;
> But with bold countenance
>   And knowledge small,
> Esteems her seven days' continuance,
>   To be perpetual.[5]

These established apostles of the Commonwealth did not know that in a Cambridge pub two irreverent neophytes named Jack Gallagher and Ronald Robinson had begun to look on Britain as a country which was being colonized, and thus to study its imperial past from a wholly different perspective. Freddie had acted as caretaker in the interregnum between Coupland and Harlow. His second caretakership from December 1961 to April 1963 marked the end of an era. With Jack Gallagher's move to Oxford in the latter month a new dynasty acceded to the Beit chair.

This was a revolution in academic style. Add the emotions engendered by 'decolonization', and the result has been a turmoil which would have taken many learned helmsmen off course. It has not shaken Freddie. He accepted that it involved a basic reassessment of the nature and significance of Commonwealth history as this had been taught at Oxford and he incorporated much of the new thinking in his writing and teaching. But his belief in three great truths was not affected: the British Empire and Commonwealth should be studied and judged, first, as a whole; secondly, in the perspective of long periods of time; and, thirdly, as a complex and varied governmental entity. It would be hard to find a less fashionable set of positions. The first two involved working against the academic tide: the third runs counter to some of the strongest popular feelings of our time. Freddie Madden writes:

> In the literature generated after a colony has achieved independence the outlook has tended to be narrowed ... by a zenophobic 'funnel vision' so that one gains the impression that a particular colony existed in a vacuum locked in isolated constitutional combat with the metropolis. This has become more evident recently with the balkanization of imperial history into area, regional, continental, or more absurdly 'Third World', history. But even in mature ex-colonies like Canada and Australia, departments of history regard with evident pride their ignorance of the parallel histories of other colonies within the common imperial experience.

Those remarks are taken from the introduction to the Madden and Fieldhouse *Constitutional Documents of the British Empire*, now being prepared for an American publisher. 'One primary aim' of the editors has been to show the balance of forces in the Imperial scene. The reader is told:

> The documents have been chosen and arranged thematically so that at every stage ideas, policies and actions emanating from England are balanced by those evolving in individual colonies; and by setting together evidence on many of those colonies which shared similar problems it is intended to show how much was in common between them and how much experience in any one of them might affect others.

There have been great gains from this brave resistance to the overspecialization and fragmentation which have become characteristic of much historical study. In the chapter of the *Cambridge History of the*

*British Empire*, Volume 3, which Freddie wrote in Harlow's place (against a deadline in four months), he quotes the Liberal administration's pledge of February 1906 to 'advance the principle of equal rights' in South Africa 'for civilized men irrespective of colour', and points to the attitude of the Australian and New Zealand governments as a key factor in nullifying this promise.[6]

It was equally unusual for an academic historian of Freddie Madden's generation to be concerned with a long sweep of years. Increasing professionalism gave analysis precedence over narrative. The attempt to penetrate the mental world of earlier centuries meant that anyone surveying a long stretch of time would be suspected of improper teleological inclinations. One of the greatest historians of the last generation eschewed, not only all narrative, but any attempt to delineate the development of events. The titles of the two master works which established Sir Lewis Namier's fame are significant. Namier announced *The Structure of Politics at the Accession of George III* as being 'introductory' to a study in detail of 'the four Parliaments of 1761–84'. The latter study was, of course, not written.[7] Namier produced instead *England in the Age of the American Revolution*, which was concerned, like its predecessor, with the 1760s and in which the American Revolution was sparely mentioned. Historians of genius obey their own rules to the general benefit. And they are imitated. The imitations may be less beneficial.

Freddie Madden's determination to range widely in time gave him one of his most important insights. 'The history of governance overseas', he wrote, 'began at home in the British Isles and in Europe: an English medieval empire was the seedbed of forms used later'.[8] The three volumes of *Constitutional Documents of the British Empire* will take the story from the earliest times. It is a story of 'governance'; and herein lies the third feature of Freddie's unfashionable independence. He writes about 'bureaucrats' when nearly 40 years of post-war *dirigisme* have made them the world's leading scapegoats.

Any historical study of complex governmental arrangements must be concerned to a great extent with the ways in which public officials have behaved. The importance of the English medieval empire in Imperial studies lies in the fact, which Freddie Madden has illustrated to such effect, that later officials used old precedents. Except for a fairly short period late in the story these officials had no overriding aim. 'The desire to foster a brood of Westminster models as a legacy of British rule has been', in Freddie Madden's eyes, 'a comparatively recent, even brief and passing, phenomenon in British policy'.[9] Nor were imperial arrangements, even in later times, the stuff from which popular politics were made. The noisy imperialism of the later 1890s was very short-lived; and, as Freddie tells us, with the new century Joseph Chamberlain himself 'had few regrets at the passing of a mood he had often found embarrassing'.[10]

There are few master clues to guide the student across this vast diverse scene. Imperial responsibilities were neither continuously profitable, nor continuously burdensome, to the British.[11] The old hand is the best guide and he should have the last word. In the *Essays Presented to Margery Perham*, 1963, Freddie Madden wrote:

> It has been widely assumed that ... the Imperial power has sought to impose a mould upon colonies so that they should be governed under a constitution as much like that of Britain as possible, and that the colonists asserted their liberty to devise an appropriate form of self-government for themselves .... But ... these labels are neither exclusive nor consistent. For example, in many British possessions it has been the colonists who have demanded nothing less than the British model and the Imperial government which has pleaded for a consideration of alternatives. In any period distance and economy have inevitably provided that the product finally delivered at the frontier is different from the blueprint devised in the department .... So the necessity of establishing government upon the frontiers of empire – to erect a rule of law and a system of control on settlements, conquests and trading stations – has provided ... a rich harvest of variations on a common theme, even in periods when the general purpose of Empire has seemed to be clear .... The institutions communicated have carried within themselves the germ of growth; and no more than their prototypes in Great Britain might they be moulded from without, for the instincts for self-government and liberty were a necessary inheritance from the common impulses of a shared history .... Exact identity with the British model was neither desired nor demanded: it was repudiated as inconvenient or inhibiting by both rulers and ruled. Imperial and colonial politicians quoted British example or precedent only where it was useful to their case.[12]

These are important truths and it has been a noble role to insist on them whatever the wind and tide.

Freddie Madden's writing has been only a part of his work. He has added all kinds of duties to the statutory lecturing and seminar work required of a University Lecturer or Reader. Apart from many years as Senior Tutor to the University's Overseas Service Courses, he has laboured prodigiously in undergraduate tutorial teaching. As an examiner he is variously experienced even by Oxford standards. He was Director of Oxford's Institute of Commonwealth Studies from 1961 to 1968, Vice Chairman of the Modern History Board for five years after that, and then Director of the Hong Kong Administrators' Course. He has spent his leaves strenuously in Visiting Chairs and Fellowships, making sure that his view of the Commonwealth did not become too Oxonian. In his leisure moments he has performed notably on Oxford's amateur stage. He is, as befits an old Oxford hand, 'a college man', who has served Nuffield College long and faithfully. He was its Dean of Degrees for 15 years, and the Chairman of the Senior Common Room for almost as long; and he has 'stood in' for more than one Domestic Bursar. Perhaps a friend of many years and near contemporary may quote to the 'old hand' who has not cared for fashion, and whose *magnum opus* has not yet reached the publisher, a verse from a not-too-fashionable poet:

> Grow old along with me!
> The best is yet to be,
> The last of life, for which the first
>     was made:
> Our times are in His hand
> Who saith 'A whole I planned,
> Youth shows but half; trust God:
>     see all, nor be afraid.[13]

NOTES

1. Edward Wortley Montagu to John Gibson, endorsed 12 May 1745; Lady Mary Montagu Mss., Vol. 5, f.77 and following. The writer was Lady Mary's son. For this and accompanying letters see the edition by C. T. Atkinson, *Journal of the Society for Army Historical Research*, XXVII (1949), 160-70.
2. They were given on the second floor in the Hawksley Room. Jean Van Der Poel's *Jameson Raid* (Oxford, 1946) had recently been published and the room seemed ill named. No reminder was needed about the withholder of the 'missing telegrams'.
3. Frederick Madden and D. K. Fieldhouse (eds.), *Oxford and the Idea of Commonwealth* (London, 1982), 27. Reginald Coupland (1884–1952) became Beit Professor in 1920. His successor in the Chair, Vincent Todd Harlow, died in office in December 1961. The passage quoted continues: 'This does not mean that all shared their optimistic faith: Wheare and Williams remained detached; even Harlow's evangelism was curbed by disciplined scholarship.'
4. See C. Carrington, *Rudyard Kipling* (London, 1955) 487-8.
5. 'Cities and Thrones and Powers' heads one of the stories in *Puck of Pook's Hill*. The verses appeared first in *The Strand* and *McClure's* in May 1906, the book being published in October 1906.
6. Ch. 10, p. 370. The pledge was given by the Under-Secretary, Winston Churchill.
7. Namier apparently said that he had shrunk from taking the story into the 1780s as this would have involved dealing 'with that detestable man Charles Fox'. For a penetrating analysis of his historical method see Isaiah Berlin, 'Lewis Namier: a Personal Impression', in M. Gilbert (ed.), *A Century of Conflict, 1850–1950* (London, 1966) 228-30.
8. J. E. Flint and G. Williams (eds.), *Perspectives of Empire*, London, 1973), 10.
9. Kenneth Robinson and Frederick Madden (eds.), *Essays in Imperial Government Presented to Margery Perham* (Oxford, 1963), 2.
10. *Cambridge History of the British Empire*, III (Cambridge, 1959) 366.
11. See D. K. Fieldhouse and A. F. Madden, *The Balance Sheet of Empire: Governors and Governed* (London, 1973).
12. *Essays in Imperial Government* (Oxford, 1963) 1-2.
13. Robert Browning, *Rabbi Ben Ezra*, the opening verse.

# I. Perspectives on Imperial History

# Can Humpty-Dumpty be put together again?
# Imperial History in the 1980s*

by

David Fieldhouse

Imperial history is commonly said to have been born as a defined field of study when J. R. Seeley, Regius Professor of History in Cambridge, gave his famous lectures, later published as *The Expansion of England*, in the early 1880s. The subject was given institutional life, and therefore respectability, with the endowment of three chairs a generation and more later: the Beit Chair of Colonial History at Oxford in 1905, the Rhodes Chair of Imperial History in London and the Vere Harmsworth Chair of Naval History (not converted into 'Imperial and Naval History' until 1933), both in 1919. Those who established and held these chairs presumably believed that imperial history existed and knew what it was about. What did they, and their contemporaries, understand by the term?

So far as one can generalize from the work of the early practitioners, imperial (or 'colonial') history described a double process by which the more developed states of Europe first established political and economic control over most parts of the less developed world; then incorporated these regions into new aggregates, commonly described as 'empires'. More important, this process was commonly thought to be organic and irreversible, changing the character of world history. Once established, empire became the dominant and determining fact in the life both of the metropolis and its dependencies. It was unhistorical, now, to think or write of 'England' in isolation from its empire: it had become part of 'Greater Britain' and its whole history had to be reinterpreted, teleologically, in relation to that fact. On the other side of the relationship, the dependencies also lost their historical autonomy. India, for example, had been incorporated into British imperial history. Her past had obviously been tending in that direction, her present and future would be moulded by the imperial factor, though Seeley warned that this would not be in the same way as the settlement colonies. Thus the function of the imperial historian was, first, to explain how and why the metropolitan states had grown from small European societies into world powers; then to analyze what significance this expansion had for metropolis and dependencies alike. In doing this he would also be studying the most important single dynamic force in modern world history, for empires were the logical and inevitable outcome of the process of nation- and state-building that had created the world system of the later nineteenth and early twentieth centuries.

The reason why a question mark now hangs over imperial history of this type is, of course, that such simplistic assumptions lost most of their compulsion some time ago. On the one hand, empire no longer seems the ultimate destiny of European states, as Seeley claimed it was for England and as their native historians did later for most continental states. Decolonization, and the fact that these metropolitan states were then able to survive and prosper without their enveloping empires, destroyed the teleological concept of an 'imperial destiny'. European historians, therefore, turned inwards again and studied their own countries as individual nation states, whose destiny lay in autonomous evolution or in a regional European association. Conversely, at the other end of the imperial relationship, historians of and in the one-time overseas colonies rejected the imperialists' assertion that alien rule had totally reconstructed these dependent societies, or was even the most important formative influence on their character. In place of imperial history they rediscovered (and in many cases virtually created) autochthonous local histories, relegating the imperial factor to the margins of causation. Thus European and 'Third World' historians combined to break the tablets on which the traditional imperial history had been written. My question, therefore, must be whether anything is now left. Can the fragments of the old imperial history be put together again into new patterns which are intellectually respectable? Or is it condemned to share the midden of discredited academic subjects with, say, astrology and phrenology?

Before passing judgement on this question, however, it is necessary to look carefully at the subject-matter of the traditional imperial history and consider what alternative methods there are of studying the same things. Put simply, can the hard core of its subject-matter now be disaggregated into discrete elements – that of the metropolis and individual dependencies – in such a way that each is fully coherent in isolation. If so, then imperial history can be buried. But if not, if there exists a lump of historical material which cannot properly be put into any other conventional historiographical pigeon-hole, then the need for imperial history, even if in a new form, may be said to remain. My argument is that there is such a lump and that it can be defined as 'the area of interaction' between the component parts of imperial systems.

I

It has been suggested above that one might, in principle, be able to break down the subject-matter of the traditional imperial history into two basic elements: the history of the metropolis as it expanded, and that of one or more overseas dependencies. Let us now examine each in turn, defining its basic concerns and asking the question: is this fully explicable in isolation, ignoring possible exogenous influences? First, then, how does imperial history stand as part of the domestic history of a European state such as Britain?

If one adopts a sufficiently narrow metrocentric view of things, it is indeed possible to treat the making and running of empires as an integral part of metropolitan history under four main heads.

First, the reasons and motives behind European expansion. This involves analysis of any aspect of the social, economic, political, religious or ideological life of the imperialist state and society which may be thought to have made for empire-building. Expansion overseas might be expected to occur if the mix of endogenous factors happened to be right at a particular time. Too many people, not enough wheat, potatoes or jobs might result in settler colonization; declining exports coupled with surplus capital in the acquisition of other territories. A weak, possibly defeated, state looking for self-esteem, especially if it had irridentist ambitions, might settle for land overseas irrespective of its intrinsic value. Such imperial arithmetic takes little account of what lay at the other end: like the owl and the pussy-cat, the imperialists just sailed away in a beautiful pea-green boat, propelled exclusively by methane generated in the country they left. And, of course, many of them did just that.

The second head concerns the process or mechanics of empire-building. Here we are in a world inhabited by 'discoverers' (that most arrogantly Eurocentric of all concepts), by 'navigators', conquistadors, colonizing companies, missionaries, frontiersmen and so on. They are all European and they too act from internal compulsion. Some of their motives are high, some low, and many mixed. But the home country must take full responsibility for what they did overseas because they are intrinsic to its domestic history.

Third, there is the organization of empire. This is the realm of colonial offices or ministries, of the sophisticated metropolitan bureaucrat with his intricate system of moving papers round his department, between offices in the metropolis and then round the world. It is also the milieu of the proconsul in Calcutta or Lagos and the district officer in the bush. Under this head, again, one studies concepts such as 'sovereignty' and the transfer of metropolitan institutions and legal principles overseas. Although, if it is to be done properly, this involves knowledge of conditions in the colonies to see how metropolitan systems operated on the ground, and how techniques of what were once called 'native administration' were devised, the traditional imperial historian could go a long way without detailed study of the host societies.

Finally, the costs and benefits of empire. This is an old game, played since the earliest days of European colonization, and still intellectually attractive because no answers are conclusive. Were imperial states richer than they might otherwise have been? Did empire raise them in the hierarchy of great powers? Who, in the metropolis, gained and who lost? Was there an 'aristocracy of labour', subsidized by colonial exploitation?

These topics have been defined somewhat flippantly, but they are, and always have been, the essential stuff of imperial history. In the first half century of its existence such issues were central to Seeley's *Expansion of England* (1883), to H.E. Egerton's *Short History of British Colonial Policy* (1897), to the three general volumes of the *Cambridge History of the British Empire*, planned in the early 1920s. In an increasingly modified shape they have continued to form the basis of most modern studies of empire; and rightly so. Even if, as treated by some earlier writers, these themes might sound jingoistic or, in the hands of later Oxford professors such as Coupland and Harlow who believed in the Commonwealth as a teleological ideal, pietistic or messianic, it would be impossible to deny that these things constitute an important field of study. Why then did imperial history of this sort lose some of its one-time intellectual validity?

The main reason, as has already been suggested, is that some of its practitioners claimed too much for it. Reduce the claim; state that this segment of imperial history is primarily part of the domestic history of the metropolitan states and does not purport to be the history of the overseas territories, and you are left with intellectual bed-rock. It needs no apology and remains a thriving academic industry.

How, then, should we approach the history of the overseas dependencies, which were regarded by the earlier imperial historians as intrinsic to their field of study? This is where the main change has occurred in the last three decades. No one, whether in Europe or overseas, would now claim that, in treating these countries merely within the framework of European expansion, the imperial historian was telling anything like a complete or satisfactory story. It is now axiomatic that the study of any colony must lie within the four corners of that society; that it must start with the earliest available evidence, which may date from centuries or even millenia before Europeans arrived; and that alien rule must be seen as merely one of many forces contributing to the evolution of the modern postcolonial nation-state. That is the basis of modern regional studies. That is why imperial history, central to the history of Europe, has become marginal to that of the 'Third World'; why, in its original form, it has fallen from its pedestal; why some are concerned to see what can be done with the pieces.

The key to the problem lies in the concept of marginality. What, precisely, is the marginal role in Third World historiography to which imperial history has been demoted? Is it the same for all one-time dependencies? And how serious would it be for the history of the 'Third World' if the imperial factor slipped off the page altogether? It is important to answer these questions, because in this way it is possible to define that third area of 'interaction' between metropolitan and overseas history which was mentioned earlier and which, as it will be suggested, should be joined to the study of European expansion to form the subject-matter of a new and reconstructed imperial history.

It is obvious at the start that 'the imperial factor', to use Cecil Rhodes's phrase, was not the same for all types of colony. I shall therefore divide all the one-time dependencies into two broad groups (though in fact the dividing line is very indistinct): white settler communities and non-settler societies. Seeley made precisely the same differentiation.

First, the settler colonies, which, in the modern period I take to include all of Latin, Anglophone and Francophone America, together with South

Africa and Australasia. It is important to remember that the original imperial history was constructed to fit this type of dependency; so that Seeley, for one, found it difficult to fit India into his typology of an organic British empire. It would, therefore, be surprising if no single aspect of the traditional subject-matter of imperial history now seemed relevant to the autonomous history of these settler colonies: and, in fact, one can see that the native historians of these countries, particularly those writing of their earlier years, talk much the same language as the metrocentric imperial historian, and for the same reason.

The reason, of course, is that, if one ignores the earlier history of the indigenous inhabitants of these places – Amerindians of many ethnic groups, Maoris, Australian aborigines, Bantu, Bushmen and Hottentots in the Cape – (which is admittedly bad history and is now discredited), the history of these settler societies was originally simply an extension of that of a metropolis. Settler history thus starts as imperial history and remains structurally connected with it for a considerable length of time. Thus, for 150 years after the first British colonies were founded in North America, the third and fourth of my categories of imperial history subject-matter (the organization of empire and the benefits obtained from it by various parties) still remained central to colonial history, and never more so than in the last two decades before independence. The same is true of the Iberian colonies for some 300 years and of the South African and Australasian colonies for perhaps 100 years. That, of course, is one main reason why the early British imperial historians believed that imperial history was leading towards imperial federation: if the history of societies that were so dispersed geographically had remained more or less congruent for so long, surely their ultimate destinies were convergent.

This, of course, was to push a good point too far. What these writers forgot was that one could, as historians now commonly do, write histories of most aspects of even early settler societies, with little or no reference to the metropolis. American colonial historiography has now diverged from the four basic themes which I defined as the core of imperial history and the same trend can be seen everywhere else. In short, while the native historian of these one-time colonies must always be aware of the metropolitan influence, because it was always there, it has become increasingly marginal to his basic preoccupation with the evolution of his own society and state.

If this happened to the historiography of settler colonies, it was even more likely to affect the history of non-settler dependencies in the 'Third World'. Their peoples did not come from Europe; their past stretched far behind the first 'discoveries'; and, however much they may have been affected by the period of alien rule, the very fact that they eventually became independent was proof that they had not been permanently absorbed into the same historical process as the one-time imperial state. So why did historians and others attempt to fit such places into an 'imperial history' framework that was originally constructed for the settler colonies? Why was there a subsequent reaction which virtually took them out of that framework? And, finally, what significance, if any, may a reconstructed imperial history have for the history of 'Third World' ex-colonies?

Probably the main reason why dependencies such as India, or colonies in Africa, were treated simply as part of European imperial history was that those Europeans who first attempted to write their history knew little or nothing of what had happened before the Europeans arrived; while Asians and Africans, who knew quite a lot, even if only from oral tradition, had no concept of 'history' as Europeans understood the subject. The general (though not universal or uniform) tendency among European historians of these societies was, therefore, to treat everything that happened before European 'discovery' as 'prehistory' or mythology. History proper began when a 'backward' society became hitched to the progressive West, thus being absorbed into 'imperial history' and becoming part of a new organic process.

There is irony in the fact that this arrogant approach to the early history of non-European countries, which is obvious in most European literature until quite recently, should have been given its most dogmatic expression by historians of the Marxist-Leninist school. Ignorance was again largely to blame; but there was also dogmatic belief that 'history', in the accepted nineteenth century sense of a dynamic process of change whose motive power was dialectical, simply could not have existed in societies which lacked the dynamic forces generated either by capitalism or the modern western state. As an example of this genre (though it would now be regarded, even in Marxist circles, as a caricature) we may cite a passage from a book published in 1966 by Endre Sík, an Hungarian, under the title *The History of Black Africa*:

> Prior to their encounter with Europeans the majority of African peoples still led a primitive, barbaric life, many of them even on the lowest level of barbarism. Some of them lived in complete, or almost complete, isolation; the contacts, if any, of others were but scattered skirmishes with neighbouring peoples. The *State*, taken in the real sense of the word, was a notion unknown to most African peoples, as classes did not exist there either. Or rather – both existed already, but only in embryo. Therefore it is unrealistic to speak of their 'history' – in the scientific sense of the word – before the appearance of the European invaders. More exactly, the study of this early history of the African peoples belongs in the province of ethnography rather than of historical science.[1]

Sík goes on to argue that the study of African history after the arrival of the Europeans has significance in two main ways: I am here conflating his four points into two.

First, he suggests, one should approach the history of Black Africa 'a part of general historical science':

> The history, say, of the rise of capitalism in Europe, the history of

the primitive accumulation of capital, cannot be grasped without a full understanding of the role of Africa in that primitive accumulation. The history of the rise and growth of industrial capitalism in Europe and America cannot be comprehended without a survey of the colonial policies and colonial activities of industrial capital at that time, particularly in Africa.[2]

It also, he says, 'brilliantly substantiates and most vividly illustrates a whole series of theses maintained by Marx, Lenin and Stalin in the field of historical science ...'.[3]

Second, African history constituted a treasury of cautionary tales – 'monstrous crimes committed by world capitalism over long centuries, from the time when it was still in the womb of its mother – feudalism';[4] and these examples could be used to stimulate African freedom fighters to struggle for liberty.

The whiggish Dr Sík need not detain us and it may be thought I have set him up as a mere Moscow-indoctrinated man of straw. He is certainly well outside the spectrum of respectable African historians; yet that sort of argument does qualify him for membership of the club for imperial historians of the coarsest variety. It also provides a convenient antithesis for examining the post-colonial and anti-imperial historiography of the present 'Third World' or 'regional' historian, who has reacted against precisely that sort of Eurocentric arrogance.

A typical representative of the generation which first publicized a new approach, in this case to the African past, is the Nigerian Dr J. F. A. Ajayi, a pioneer of the view that African history is an autonomous field of study which cannot be written within the framework of 'the expansion of Europe' or of imperial systems. In a well-known passage from an essay first published in 1968, 'The continuity of African institutions under colonialism', he argued as follows:

> In any long-term view of African history, European rule becomes just another episode. In relation to wars and conflicts of people, the rise and fall of empires, linguistic, cultural and religious change and the cultivation of new ideas and new ways of life, new economic orientations ... in relation to all these, colonialism must be seen not as a complete departure from the African past, but as one episode in the continuous flow of African history.[5]

Others, of course, were already arguing along the same lines; and since then many have gone much further, pushing the European and imperial element in African history to the outer rim of their analysis. Such attitudes were the inevitable consequence of the development of serious historical and anthropological studies undertaken in the overseas dependencies, much of it done after 1945 with the growth of the first generation of colonial universities. Scholars now tended to look outwards from each dependency, seeing the imperial factor, to an increasing extent, as external and transitory. Nationalistic impulses accentuated the trend. As the new, post-colonial states were created, it became imperative to write about them as 'nations', each with its own unique and autonomous history, no longer as mere provinces of distant empires. For the 'Third World' countries at least this was the solvent of the old imperial history.

## II

In the metropolitan states also erosive forces were at work in these decades after about 1950. The intellectual unity of imperial history had been built on the assumption that the imperial impact was irreversible, so that colonial self-government would lead, not to fragmentation of empire, but to strong post-independence associations (the Commonwealth, the French Union etc.). This proved largely false: empire led, at least in the British case, rather to overt declarations of total separation tempered by the rhetoric of Commonwealth. In this way the fundamental message of the old imperial history was discredited, and along with it what many had regarded as its basic function. If empire led nowhere, why bother to study an evolutionary process which had failed the test of natural selection? Clearly the proper unit of research and analysis was the individual society in the process of becoming a nation, not the colony being laboriously prepared to qualify as a Member of the Commonwealth. This was the starting point for regional studies as a substitute for imperial history. Linguistic considerations, of course, accentuated the trend: expatriate scholars naturally tended to concentrate on the country or region whose public and social life were conducted in the particular language they had studied; though South Asian historians were able to penetrate a long way into indigenous politics through the fortunate fact that the Indian and Ceylonese political classes corresponded largely in English. In this way and for these and other reasons, the overseas component of imperial history gradually broke into regional fragments.

The growth of specialized regional studies is not to be regretted. This writer began academic research as a regional historian, in New Zealand; and it seemed at the time that there was a basic fallacy in the assumption that colonial societies could only be studied in an imperial context. Yet now that we stand at the far end of this historiographical revolution, the time has come to face the fundamental question: is 'Third World' or 'national' history enough? When one has atomized the traditional unities of imperial history into 'metropolitan' and 'overseas' has anything of importance to either side been lost? Or, in terms of my original categorization, does there remain a third field of study, the 'interaction' between the two, which is intrinsic to the histories of metropolis and ex-colony alike?

We may start by providing a crude definition of my 'area of interaction' between metropolitan and colonial history, and then refine and defend it. An imperial state, such as Britain or France, was necessarily different from a non-imperial state such as Switzerland or Norway, and also from what it might have been had it not had an empire, because, and to the extent that, possession of colonies had measurable effects on its development. These effects were not total: that is, the history of England was not, as Seeley in effect argued, dominated by or coextensive with the history of its overseas expansion; large segments of English (and later British) history may have been unaffected by its imperial activities. Yet other important segments were significantly affected, so that it would be impossible to tell a true story of British history without taking some account of the imperial factor. The same is true of the one-time colonies. Even if the imperial impact on the indigenous societies was less than Europeans liked to think (or in some cases feared) and small in relation to the domestic forces at work, that impact was certainly measurable and probably important. These two segments therefore constitute that 'area of interaction' which is the special subject-matter of imperial history as it exists in the 1980s.

That, of course, is mere assertion. To support it one must ask three questions; first, why the subject matter of this 'area of interaction' cannot properly be subsumed into the domestic history of a particular metropolis or a one-time colony, so doing away with the need to study imperial history altogether; second, what is special about the imperial historian's approach to his field; and finally what equipment he must possess and what problems now face him.

The basic reason why there are elements in the history of all imperial states and all ex-colonies that cannot be absorbed into their domestic histories is, of course, that some at least of the historical forces that produced these elements lie elsewhere. It would be impossible briefly to define all these things: but examples may be offered at both ends of the relationship.

First, in the metropolitan states, it is obvious that the nature of the economy, the patterns of foreign policy, even the character of the armed forces, were necessarily influenced by the fact of possessing colonies. The colonial trade, and the re-export trade in colonial products, were both central to the growth of the British economy before the early nineteenth century: major ports such as Bristol, Liverpool and Glasgow survive as archaeological evidence of this influence. The expansion and survival of certain key British industries during the nineteenth and early twentieth centuries, notably the Lancashire cotton industry were, to some extent, contingent on colonial markets and declined when these ceased to be available. Patterns of capital investment in Britain, particularly from the mid-nineteenth century, were affected by the opportunities provided by the colonies for capital export. During and after the Second World War sterling, as an international currency, was heavily dependent on the dollar-earning capacity of colonies such as Malaya. And so one could go on in this and many other important areas of metropolitan life, in France, Belgium and other imperial states as much as in Britain. Thus, while no one would now accept Seeley's argument that empire was the dominant factor, or the 'essence', of British history, it would be equally unrealistic to exclude it entirely. Again, while the purely domestic aspects of such things are the province of the metropolitan historian, it is the function of the imperial historian to pinpoint and explain those influences which stemmed from the existence of overseas empire.

To invert the standpoint, the same is necessarily true of the one-time colonies. The modern trend has been to provide these new nation-states with autonomous histories, and this has involved attempts to domesticate what were previously assumed to be exogenous factors. Thus expatriate officials, once regarded as all-powerful agents of the imperial state, are shown to have been heavily dependent on, and perhaps manipulated by, indigenous 'collaborators'. The once common assumption that cash crops, markets, overseas trade, specialization and other typical features of the modern economy were introduced by the imperialists is discredited by evidence of more or less sophisticated pre-European systems of production and exchange. Stress is placed on the resilience of indigenous moral, social and religious traditions in the face of alien attempts to 'modernize'. Thus the imperial impact becomes increasingly insignificant.

All this can be taken too far, and probably has already resulted in distortion. How, for example, could one explain the political culture and administrative system of modern India except in terms of imported and imposed British institutions, the initial purpose of which can only be explained in terms of imperial intentions? What might the political map of West Africa, or its commodity structure, look like if the region had not been divided between Britain, France, Germany and Portugal, and then developed (or, as some would say) underdeveloped, so as to become complementary with their own economies? The list is endless and does not need to be spelt out. The point is simply that the influence of empire on dependencies cannot be totally digested by their local historiographies, simply because the roots of much causation lay outside the dependency. Like the grain of sand in an oyster, its effects can be partially domesticated by indigenous secretion; but its presence is explicable only by reference to its external origins. That explanation lies within the limits of imperial history, because that alone is concerned with both ends of the story.

### III

To turn to the second and consequential question: what is peculiar about the way in which the imperial historian of the 1980s approaches the study of those elements which are common to the history of both a metropolis and its colonies? The peculiarity lies in his standpoint, his centre of gravity, which is different from that of both metropolitan and 'Third World' historians, and also from that of the older imperial historians, with their metrocentric orientation. All these have a single territorial and conceptual base, seeing the world from inside Britain, or France, Senegal or Sri Lanka, as the case may be. The modern imperial historian, unlike, say, Seeley, has no territorial base or, for that matter, loyalties. He places himself in the interstices of his subject, poised above the 'area of interaction' like some satellite placed in space, looking, Janus-like, in two or more ways at the same time. It is his duty, as an in-between man, to give equal weight to what happens in a colony and in its metropolis, and to be intellectually at home in both. That, as will be suggested later, creates serious technical problems, because of the sheer quantity of information it requires. But it also explains the importance for the imperial historian of two among other tools of his trade: the use of 'comparative' and 'contextual' history, for both are central to the concept of an 'area of interaction'.

The value of 'comparative history' is, of course, strongly disputed. Against it is the danger that one may draw false or strained analogies between essentially unrelated events, much as compilers of Bibles used to link superficially related ideas over very long periods, on purely verbal grounds, by cross-referencing them in the margins. Conversely, in favour of comparative history is the proposition that genuine similarities or contrasts illuminate both sides. In the case of imperial history, comparisons between institutions and ideas are very often valid because they may flow from common roots in the same metropolis or, as between different imperial systems, from the same west-European culture.

If validly made, such comparisons constitute one of the most useful interpretative tools in the equipment of the imperial historian, providing a third dimension to the significance of things which are likely to escape the purely regional historian. An imperial people could only bring with it what it already possessed; but it always brought it, though often in different forms, to all its dependencies. How much of this baggage survived transfer depended partly on local conditions overseas. In some places it was buried under the dominant indigenous culture, in others it overlaid it. Yet, where it can be detected, it is particularly valuable because, in studying the fate of the same alien inputs in different host societies, the historian can achieve a deeper understanding of both the imperial impact and the indigenous stock at this point of interaction. In much the same way a pathologist may insert or inject a foreign substance into living tissue, because the reaction will tell him something about the condition of the host organism. To illustrate this, two examples of the use of this technique may be mentioned, both by Cambridge imperial historians.

First, there is the concept of 'collaboration', rationalized and publicised in a paper, first given in 1969 by Professor R.E. Robinson, but already a fully-fledged idea in imperial history.[6] All colonial rule depends on collaboration by some at least of the ruled. But why should some societies, and some elements in any one society, be willing to collaborate, and others not? Since the aims, and to a large extent the methods, of the imperialists were similar as between one colony and another, colonial reactions must have been the main variable; and the study of these reactions, on a comparative basis, has been fundamental to the modern school of 'resistance' studies. Such studies depend to a considerable extent on knowledge of the common stock of imperial practices in different countries.

Or, in quite a different context, there is one fundamental premise of the 'Cambridge' school of South Asian historians who, if I understand them correctly, see the evolution of Indian nationalism as a response, in part at least, to the changing character and methods of British rule. But Indian reactions differed widely, and comparative study of how they responded to identical stimuli can help to explain this. Buried deep in the heart of Christopher Bayly's Allahabad[7] or Baker and Washbrook's Madras[8] lay that most typical of British institutions, exported, in different forms, to virtually all dependencies; the representative and more or less elective council – town, district, provincial or national. For these and other historians such councils constitute vital bugging systems, sending out messages about the character of very different Indian societies as they reacted to new imperial challenges. One can compare their reactions because there was genuine common ground. With less assurance one can also compare Indian reactions to elective political institutions with those in other dependencies: for example, in African colonies in the 1950s and early 1960s. Knowledge of such similarities and contrasts adds greatly to the historian's understanding of individual societies or states. Conversely, to write as novice research students commonly do, in their ignorance of the wider world of their subject as if what they found in a particular place was unique, is to miss a vital dimension of imperial history.

This leads us to the concept and use of 'context' in imperial history. It might, of course, be said that the context of any brand of history largely determines its content and I have already suggested that the main definitive feature of modern imperial history is that it concentrates on those intermediate subject areas which the others cannot reach. What one sees depends to a large extent on how one looks at it; and there are usually several alternative ways of looking at subjects in which the imperial historian may be interested. Thus, a 'Third World' country may be studied in a strictly geographical context; as part of, say, the Islamic world; in terms of ethnic groups, climatic zones, language or other defined characteristics. It is as if one were to draw a large number of excentric circles, each of which linked a particular territory with others with which it shared some, but by no means all its characteristics; and how these lines are drawn may significantly influence how one sees it.

An empire is only one of these circles; and it would be perverse to suggest that it is necessarily the most important: that was the mistake made by too many imperial historians in the past. Nevertheless empire is usually a context of the first importance; and this assertion finds support amongst Marxist and neo-Marxist writers such as Immanual Wallerstein, Samir Amin and André Gunder Frank, whose primary concern is to account for what they describe as the 'underdevelopment' of the 'Third World'. For Wallerstein at least the crucial fact in modern history was the creation, starting from the sixteenth century, of a 'world economy' with three main components: 'core', 'semi-periphery' and 'periphery', each clearly distinguished by the extent of its dependence on other parts of this new 'world system'; and its development can only properly be understood in the context of imperial expansion.[9] Although the new 'world system' was never coextensive with any one imperial system (because of intra-European rivalries and the fact that capitalism does not at all times require political empire to achieve its aims), the actual historical process involved the mobilization of European power through the medium of the imperial state. Colonialism enabled two obstacles to the 'peripheralization' of areas such as West Africa – indigenous resistance and competition from other Europeans – to be overcome and the region to be incorporated into the 'periphery' of the 'core' economy. Once that had been achieved, formal empire could be wound up, leaving the mechanism of 'neo-colonialism' to maintain the core-periphery dichotomy; but even so, one can only understand its genesis and character by studying the history of imperialism. Clearly imperial history performs a vital contextual role in this new world of dependency theory; and, following the example of Sir Winston Churchill in 1941, it would be wise to welcome allies from across an ideological divide.

## IV

I come now to my final question: what tools and types of knowledge does the contemporary, reconstructed, imperial historian of the 1980s need? How much can be expected of him?

At the risk of seeming to prevaricate, it must be said at the start that it is no longer possible to design or define an all-purpose, standard model. Thirty years ago it could still be done. The imperial historian who accepted Seeley's concept of his subject, knew about the expansion of his own country and, in rather general terms, about the expansion of other European states. He studied their reasons for colonization, how colonies were governed, what economic relations were established between them and the metropolis, and why, regrettably, some colonies had broken away from their parent states. If he was British he was apt to applaud Latin American independence as an escape from tyranny, while regretting that the United States had not waited until the British had developed the modern Commonwealth (another of the central topics in imperial history) as the ideal means of correlating empire with liberty.

Now this model will just not do in the 1980s because it lacks two important dimensions. First, it was too insular and nationalistic, even patriotic: British, French or any other expansion was seen in near isolation, as the special expression of that nation's essence. Expansion must now be seen in the two contexts of European history and the creation of a 'world system'. So the compleat imperial historian would have to be very familiar with the whole process of modern imperialism, as much at home with, say, sixteenth-century Spanish as with eighteenth-century British or nineteenth-century French imperialism. Given the quantity of published work of high quality since the early 1950s, this is no longer possible in detail: you read the book reviews and keep a good card index.

Second, I have suggested that the development of regional studies has made it possible, and therefore essential, to see imperialism as a double-ended process, in which the colonies played as dynamic a role as the metropolis, and must therefore be studied in their own right, not merely as provinces of empire. The result is that the imperial historian can no longer get away with knowing about the techniques of colonial government or with the formal relations between colony and metropolis. To understand the nature of imperialism he must study the colonies from within or, placing himself between the core and periphery, look at both from the same distance simultaneously.

To say this is, of course, to admit that no one person can now fully satisfy all these requirements. There were too many imperial states, far too many dependencies, and empire lasted too long a time. Only an Arnold Toynbee might now have the confidence to operate on so global a scale; and, even then, the result would necessarily be distortion through excessive categorization and simplification. Imperial history has grown beyond the competence of any one man: there can no longer be a compleat imperial historian.

In practice the result is that there are now perhaps three loose, and overlapping, categories of specialists working within this broad field. First, there are those who are primarily concerned with the metropolitan end of empire, and thus approximate most closely to the older model, though now without the nationalistic or teleological prejudices of the past. Their main preoccupation is with the power that created and controlled imperial systems. Second, there are those who study more general themes and concepts, such as theories of imperialism or dependency, capital investment, trade and migration within and between imperial systems. Finally, there are the regional specialists, who study the history of one or more overseas dependencies during the colonial period, and for so long after decolonization as the influence of empire remained significant. All three are linked by common awareness of the formative influence of overseas empire on Europe and colonies alike, and on the character of the modern world order. All share a common vocabulary which enables them to compare and understand developments within different parts of the broader field. Imperial historians can, therefore, perhaps best be regarded as a loose federation with indeterminate boundaries rather than a unitary state. There have been secessionary tendencies and some unilateral declarations of independence; but in this empire at least the centre has been able to hold.

Imperial history is very different from what it was three decades ago. There was, indeed, a great fall and many doubted whether the bits could, or even should, be put together again. My argument can be summed up by saying that they were because they had to be; indeed that they came together spontaneously, because the essential subject-matter could not be satisfactorily absorbed into the autonomous history of any one component element. Imperial history survives in new and still evolving forms because if it did not exist it would have to be invented.

NOTES

*This paper was first given as an inaugural lecture in Cambridge in 1982 at which Dr Madden was present. It reflects our common views after 24 years of collaboration in Oxford.

1. Endre Sîk, *The History of Black Africa* (Budapest, 1966), I, 17.
2. Ibid., 18.
3. Ibid., 19.
4. Ibid., 19.
5. T. O. Ranger (ed.), *Emerging Themes of African History* (Nairobi, 1968), 194.
6. 'Non-European Foundations of European Imperialism: Sketch for a Theory of Collaboration' in R. Owen & B. Sutcliffe (eds.), *Studies in the Theory of Imperialism* (London, 1972).
7. C. A. Bayly, *The Local Roots of Indian Politics* (Oxford, 1975).
8. C. J. Baker, *The Politics of South India, 1920–1937* (Cambridge, 1976); D. A. Washbrook, *The Emergence of Provincial Politics: the Madras Presidency 1870–1920* (Cambridge, 1976).
9. I. Wallerstein, *The Modern World System*, I and II (New York, 1974, 1980).

# Colonialism French-Style, 1945–55: A Backward Glance

## by

## Kenneth Robinson

During the nine years when Freddie Madden and I were colleagues in Oxford, from 1948 when I succeeded Margery Perham in what was then called the readership in colonial administration until 1957, when he succeeded me in what had now become the readership in Commonwealth government, much of my research and writing were concerned not with the administration of British colonies or with the Commonwealth, but with what since 1945 had been called the French Union[1] and with what we can now see was the final phase of French (as of British) colonialism, at any rate in the sense of the maintenance of French jurisdiction over almost all of what had once been the French empire. This concern with the French Union was a consequence of the post-war re-establishment in Oxford of training courses for colonial civil servants. Whitehall considered that those on what was called the 'second course' – for men with some years' experience in the colonies – should study, among other things, 'British colonial aims' and 'comparative colonial administration'.[2] It fell to my lot to undertake the teaching of French colonial administration as part of this course. For this my qualifications were slight. In November 1945 the Colonial Office and the Ministry of Overseas France had initiated a programme of technical cooperation in Western Africa.[3] I had been the secretary of the British team at the initial talks in London, had taken part in almost all the subsequent meetings in Paris and London, and had been present at the earliest of the specialist meetings in West Africa, on veterinary problems in Dakar in May 1946 and on medical cooperation in Accra in the following November. I had also made very brief visits to Senegal and French Togo. In the course of all this I made the acquaintance of many French officials, both in the Ministry in Paris and in Africa, of some of those in the academic world in Paris, who had overseas interests and experience, and had met some French ministers, including Marius Moutet and René Pleven. But if I was to teach British colonial civil servants something about French colonial administration I must obviously try to learn for myself 'on the ground'.

Accordingly I spent the first three months of 1950 studying the day-to-day work of *chefs de subdivision* (district officers) in the Ivory Coast, Upper Volta, the French Sudan and Senegal. I spent some ten days in each of several administrative divisions reading the files, attending the courts, meeting the *chefs de canton* and others with whom the administrator had business, visiting schools and dispensaries and studying the activities of 'provident societies', compulsory cooperatives of which all cultivators were obliged to be members and essentially an arm of the administration.[4] I also visited the territorial capitals (except that of the Upper Volta) and met departmental heads, senior administrators and the governors, reading as much material as I could that it would not be possible to take away. But the very facilities so readily given me by the French authorities distanced me not only from African political leaders and their organizations but even from Africans generally. Only at the territorial centres of the *Institut français d'afrique noire,* directed from Dakar by that most learned and witty polymath, Théodore Monod,[5] did I meet French-speaking Africans informally (and sometimes, through their kind hospitality, occasionally meet others). After all that I had been told and read about the close and easy relations the French had with educated Africans by contrast with the arm's length at which, it was said, they were kept by the British, this was a surprise, more especially as my first wartime stay in Ghana had been at Achimota and I had begun lasting friendships with Yao Adu and Kofi Busia and met many others in the homes of my friends.

There was, of course, a more particular reason for this isolation from Africans who might well have distrusted an Englishman so closely associated with the administration. It was one of which I only gradually became aware. In the Ivory Coast and to some degree in the French Sudan and Upper Volta, the administration had for some time been carrying out a steady campaign to emasculate – even destroy – the *Rassemblement Démocratique Africain* (RDA), an interterritorial political movement created at Bamako in the French Sudan in October 1946. The aim of the founders had been to translate into a united mass movement, solidly based in all the French tropical African territories, the campaign undertaken in the Second Constituent Assembly by the Parliamentary *Intergroupe* of all the native deputies to restore the reforms included in the earlier draft constitution of April 1946 but discarded or watered down in that of October 1946. The Socialist Minister of Overseas France, Marius Moutet, successfully dissuaded those African leaders who belonged to the French Socialist party from joining in this initiative. The RDA thereupon made what was to turn out to be the mistake of affiliating for parliamentary purposes to the Communists. Although some thought that the National Assembly elections of 1946 would result in a Communist government in France and the Communists did emerge as the largest single party, their ministers in the tripartite government then formed voted against it in May 1947 and were accordingly dismissed, to remain in opposition until 1981.[6] The war in Indochina began in earnest in December 1946; there was an insurrection in Madagascar in April 1947 for which the Malagasy nationalist leaders were held responsible; the cold war was increasingly virulent and General de Gaulle continued to denounce 'the system'. Particularly after they left the government, the Communists strongly supported RDA claims and grievances. All this made it easy to stigmatize as communist, (or what, in most French eyes, was even worse, 'separatist') any political groups which sought to secure for the natives of French colonies the substance of such rights – social as much as political – as they had supposedly acquired in the post-war dispensation.

As I left the Ivory Coast, in January 1950, the administration's attempts to destroy the RDA and even to arrest Houphouet, in defiance of his parliamentary immunity as a deputy, provoked a new series of 'incidents' culminating in riots in which 13 Africans were killed and some were injured. The French government was compelled to agree to a Parliamentary enquiry. Its report was, however, never debated by the National Assembly because some months before it was presented, Houphouet disaffiliated the RDA from the Communists, after discussions with François Mitterrand, then Minister of Overseas France (from July 1950 to August 1951) who undertook to make things easier for the RDA if the party supported the government. Mitterrand later argued that he had been impressed, after a visit to Accra, by the effect which British policies there might have on Houphouet, who was of the same ethnic group as Nkrumah.[7] Mitterrand had certainly asked me some searching questions about Ghana when I met him at a small private dinner party during my visit. Although the RDA, after abstaining in various Assembly votes, did support the Pleven government on a vote of confidence in December 1950, Mitterrand was unsuccessful in securing the compliance of the colonial administration which, especially in the Ivory Coast, but elsewhere as well, falsified the elections with the result that the RDA had only three members from West Africa after the National Assembly elections of 1951.[8] Although Mitterrand lost his post as Minister of Overseas France in the new government, the RDA nonetheless formally affiliated to his party in January 1952, when he was minister of state for North African Affairs. This party, the Union Démocratique et Sociale de la Resistance, was a very small group, nearly half of whom were now overseas deputies. It was, however, very close to the centre of gravity of French politics and by 1956 Houphouet was a minister in the French government, as he remained not merely until the end of the Fourth Republic but even in that of de Gaulle.

But in the early months of 1950 all this was in the future. The outlook for any acceptable regime in West Africa was meanwhile sombre. Nothing seemed so striking as I continued to study that regime at the local level, as how little, in spite of all the post-liberation discussion and reforms, it had changed since Robert Delavignette (by this time Director of Political Affairs in the Ministry of Overseas France) had described it in his brilliant book *Les vrais chefs de l'empire,* published in 1940.[9] Forced labour, the manipulation of which had been at once a source of power for the African chiefs and a major source of hostility to them, and which Delavignette had denounced, had been abolished, though it was not until 1950 that the use of conscripts for the army, even on public development projects, was prohibited. But this was the only major change. The uniformity of the administrative structure from the Governor-General to territorial governor, *commandant de cercle, chef de subdivision, chef de canton*, to *chef de village* broken only by the occasional recourse to grouping several cantons under a *chef de province*, all except the village, artificial units of French administrative design, concealed very few concessions to African society, in contrast to the extraordinary patchwork of 'native authority' units to be found in British West Africa. In the choice of the *chefs de canton*, the essential link between the French *commandement* and their African subjects (there were some 2,000 cantons in 1937), a varying emphasis had been placed at different times between 1910 and 1945 on the importance of their belonging to chiefly or at least 'notable' families, and increasingly on their educational standard and assumed willingness and capacity to work with the French. They were organized within 20 salary grades, given marks (recorded on their personal files) for various qualities by their administrative bosses, and had even formed, in several territories, organizations to watch over the interests of what were still described as *chef coutumiers*. But they were, in practice, a special type of civil servant and were, it was claimed, being organized as the basis of new *partis de l'administration* with notable success in Upper Volta, Niger and Northern Dahomey. But, as was generally agreed, their authority had been greatly weakened (though to a varying degree in different territories) by their utilization for many unpopular tasks of the administration: the maintenance of tax registers and the census, the collection of tax (and the additional tax for which until forced labour was abolished labour service could be commuted), the collection of recruits for conscription, the operations of the Provident Societies, the collection of their subscription known as the 'little tax', the distribution of seed, the allocation of loans, the collection of 'interest' on loans in kind, the maintenance of seed reserves; in all these operations the chiefs, who were generally the majority of members on the management committee, played major parts. They were even sometimes its chairman, an office usually filled by the *commandant*.

This close connection of the French administration with the production of cash crops had a long history in West Africa, and it was intensified during the Second World War (as it had been in the First). It represented a much more visible and direct pressure of the administrative apparatus on the daily life of the peasant than existed in this sphere in British territories where, moreover, there was no legal military conscription. But if the heaviness of administrative control in every-day African life was one noticeable characteristic of these arrangements, another was the virtually complete absence of any form of local government, even in most urban areas, let alone the countryside. There was no equivalent of the Native Authority Treasury which, in British West Africa, sometimes offered scope for financing small local development projects, even if it did not permit the provision of services on the scale of the larger authorities in Northern Nigeria. In these circumstances, the considerable resources often available to the Provident Society offered an alternative source of funds for small local works or equipment under the effective control of the local French administrator; 'a more flexible instrument', Hailey wrote 'than would have been supplied by recourse to grants from the colonial budget'.[10]

Nor were the *conseils de notables*, theoretically established in every *cercle*, in any way effective organs of African opinion. Their powers were purely advisory, their membership nominated by the *commandant*, who presided when they met. His *chefs de cantons* were often among the members though they were his subordinates. There were few towns with even a nominated town council, and most of them had an official as mayor, except in the four old communes of Senegal where municipalities elected by universal suffrage on a common roll were more or less comparable with those of metropolitan France, though subject to supervision by the Governor of Senegal in regard to the police functions undertaken by similar metropolitan municipalities.[11] When I tried to assemble my impressions of these months in French West Africa I could not recall any occasion on which administrators had so much as mentioned the existence of the *conseils de notables*, or any local councils except the Senegalese communes. This absence of representative local authorities or, so far as could be told, any concern on the part of French administrators to see them developed, was especially noticeable at a time when British West African governments were beginning to implement the famous despatch of 25 February 1947 in which Arthur Creech-Jones urged them to secure active African cooperation in the 'programmes of political, social, and economic advancement on which we have now embarked' by developing an 'efficient and democratic system of local government'.[12]

Unlike Native Authorities in British territories, the French *chefs de canton* had no responsibilities for the administration of courts of customary law. Although the post-war reforms had decreed that all Africans would in future be subject to French law in criminal matters, and this would be administered by French judges, not, as in earlier times, by courts presided over by administrators, the old system remained for civil cases which were brought before courts in which the judge was the *chef de subdivision* or the *commandant de cercle* assisted by two assessors. While the decisions of Native Courts in British West Africa were subject to review by the administrative officers, they were much less involved than their French counterparts in such court work which, as I was able to see for myself, took up a considerable part of the French administrators' time. But such courts were quite unlike the Native Courts of British territories; they were French courts of a special kind dispensing what they understood to be African customary law. Even in 1950, the reform of 1946 which made criminal charges against Africans subject to the French Code and to be adjudicated by French *magistrats* had not been fully implemented owing to the lack of enough trained *magistrats*. Various expedients had been applied for some years but the delays in dealing with cases continued.

Two other aspects of French colonial practice were less often remarked by British observers. The first was the frequency with which not only governors and other senior officials but even those in the districts were identified with metropolitan political parties. I was often told by one of them that his colleague was a socialist or a Gaullist. It was hardly surprising that political motives were frequently attributed to them, particularly when the party to which they belonged was also represented by territorial politicians and parties and, still more, given the long established French practice of 'making the elections'.[13] The politicization of the administration was naturally more pronounced after the fall of France, the division of the French colonies between the Vichy regime and supporters of de Gaulle, and the Liberation. The second aspect was that there was a sizeable number of metropolitan French in French West Africa (and indeed the other French territories in Tropical Africa). There were nearly three times as many Europeans in French, as in British West Africa though the African population was little more than half that of the British territories. This was not, except in the Ivory Coast, a planter or *colon* group, and even there planters were a small part of the white residents. Large numbers of metropolitan French were employed in posts which in British West Africa were usually filled by Africans (or in East Africa by Asians): clerks in banks and in government offices, primary school teachers, shop assistants, and many others in relatively humble work requiring no very elaborate skills. Although about half of them lived in Senegal, where there was no separate electoral roll for *citoyens de statut français* (not all of them were Europeans of course), there were in the rest of the French West Africa such separate electorates for elections to the territorial assemblies, in which they were accorded representation quite disproportionate to the number of such citizens in the territory. Since the senators of the Council of the Republic were elected by the territorial assemblies (together with the deputies), separate representation was also provided in that body. Such separate electorates also returned deputies to the National Assembly from Equatorial Africa, Cameroon and Madagascar. Much comment, often favourable, has noted the political skills which African political leaders acquired during their membership of such metropolitan bodies. It is less often realised that, on the other hand, the separate representation of what were really very small European electorates contributed greatly to the filibustering, especially in the Council of the Republic which delayed so many of the reforms attempted in the decade from 1947 to 1956 in colonial matters.

In his essay[14] on 'the Commonwealth, Commonwealth history and Oxford' Freddie Madden has noticed the readiness of many of the Imperial historians there (and he could well have added those concerned with the economics and government of empire) to offer prescriptions of policy and advice to governments and politicians; some, he says, were 'proconsuls manqués'. Twelve exciting years in the Colonial Office had largely immunized me from such ambitions. I had not left Whitehall to take pot shots from the wings but in the hope of arriving at a better understanding of the dynamics of the colonial situation. Since my return to Oxford I had somewhat vociferously contended that 'colonial studies' – as they were then called – must not be regarded as an examination of an esoteric technique by practitioners who kept themselves in a little world of their own, but as an integral part of the relevant major disciplines: history, politics, economics or sociology. My attitude was indeed that expressed some years later in an often quoted dictum of Thomas Hodgkin:

> It becomes necessary to study African political institutions in precisely the same way as British, French or American institutions are studied – as interesting in themselves whatever may happen to European power.[15]

That my attention should be focused so much on the institutions and structure of French colonial government and even on day-to-day problems of administrative practice was therefore something of a paradox. It was not merely a reflection of the teaching needs that occasioned my involvement in this work, nor even, I hope, of the habits of mind that I had no doubt brought with me from Whitehall but rather of an assumption, more general then than it is now, that there were significant differences between the colonialisms of the different powers and that these differences might be expected to have long-term consequences.[16] Authentic information about French colonial doctrines, institutions, and practice was thus essential to the increasing numbers of students wishing to examine African, Asian or Caribbean problems, and not only those with the professional interests of colonial civil servants. But in this context it seemed to me that comparisons, whether of policies or institutions, too often resulted in misunderstanding of the elements specific to the French colonial situation and should await a more complete knowledge of both terms of the comparison.

In an address to the Royal Empire Society in January 1951 I tried nonetheless to summarize my judgement of French policy in West Africa. For its success, I said, 'it surely demands a willingness to endow the essentially local government institutions which it seeks to provide in overseas territories with the widest powers and scope' but I thought this was so contrary to deep-seated French habits of mind that 'I cannot feel any conviction that French policies will in the long run in French West Africa avoid the emergence of separatist and nationalist feeling such as one finds elsewhere in the colonial territories. But it must be admitted that at present these policies seem relatively successful.'[17] But by the time I made my next attempt to study French administration overseas, in November 1952, when I spent a month in Madagascar, the likelihood of French success in containing African nationalism seemed considerably more problematic. The extent to which the administration had intervened to falsify the election results in overseas constituencies for the National Assembly in 1951 was more widely publicized, the inability of the metropolitan governments, constantly a prey to party manoeuvres, to control their representatives in Indochina or North Africa more evident, the military brutality in the suppression of the Malagasy insurrection and the revolting tortures to which the *sûreté* in Madagascar had resorted, to incriminate the nationalist leaders were becoming better known, though their exploitation by metropolitan communists tended to encourage scepticism.[18]

My purpose in arranging to visit Madagascar was mundane. I hoped to see what progress was being made with a project, launched after the insurrection, to establish in selected villages or groups of villages what were called – how ponderous it sounds! – *collectivités autochtones rurales* (CAR). These were intended to enlist the rural Malagasy in a village project for community development. All Malagasy residents in the selected area and over 18 were compulsorily members of the CAR, and elected a council of not less than eight 'notables' who themselves elected a President and a Treasurer. They had certain funds, could borrow from a central fund for approved development works – such as rural roads, irrigation canals, and equipment – and might finance various welfare measures. It may be that my studies this time were more superficial; I read the files, discussed the problems with the *chef de district* (the terminology was different but the chain of administrative control virtually identical except that each district was divided into *gouvernements* which grouped several *cantons*) and visited the work in the fields or the roads. Many of those I talked to regarded the whole idea as a waste of money and time; others were clearly using it as another device for direct administration. Some told me that the 'nationalist politicians' saw it as an instrument for more effective administrative control and a cover for reintroducing forced labour and collective punishments. Many of the projects I was shown seemed to me grandiose and unlikely to be remunerative. Part of the area where I worked had been in the hands of the insurgents but most of it had been unaffected. I did not think the future of these experiments hopeful: a complacent administration and an apathetic population seemed unlikely subjects for such ventures.[19]

On the other hand I had come to Madagascar from Kenya just after the declaration of a state of emergency in connection with Mau Mau and the arrest of Kenyatta on 21 October 1952. Mau Mau was, like the insurrection in Madagascar, largely limited to particular areas, and it was the murders of Europeans and what might be called 'establishment' Africans or Malagasy that produced so strong a reaction among Kenya settlers, as the insurrection did among Europeans in Madagascar. In both there was a widespread use of oaths to ensure the obedience and continued participation of those enrolled in the secret organizations which mounted the campaign; in both the governments alleged that the movements were in fact instigated and controlled ('managed' was the word used in Kenya) by the existing political movement of a nationalist kind, the Mouvement Démocratique de la Rénovation Malgache and the Kenya African Union, in both there was a generally held view that these were not so much social revolutionary movements as a psychological phenomenon. Mau Mau was depicted as an atavistic rejection of modernity. The insurgents in Madagascar were also depicted as constituting the rearguard of the Malagasy civilization doomed to disappear. Both were the subject of psychological accounts by local psychiatrists or psychologists. While it is still uncertain whether fully satisfactory accounts and explanations of either of them will ever be arrived at, the most plausible in each case seems to be that they represented a split in the nationalist ranks which the leadership did not wish to precipitate into action but of which it lost control. In both cases, there is much that is deeply disturbing in the actions of the colonial power. In Madagascar it has been argued that the revolution which in 1972 brought the fall of its first independent head of state, Philibert Tsiranana, had its origin in a peasant revolt in 1971 led by one of the leaders of the two 'secret societies' implicated in the insurrection of 1947.[20]

There has been some discussion in recent years of whether there was any decisive 'turning point' in the period of decolonization. My short stay in Madagascar in 1952 was certainly a decisive point in my own assessment of the probability of a peaceful decolonization of the remainder of the French empire. It would not be easy to point to any reason for this. I recognized French difficulties and I understood their deep distrust of *merina* nationalism and their conviction that to allow its leaders the autonomy within the French Union that they claimed in 1946 would represent the restoration of *merina* domination over the many other ethnic groups in the coastal regions of the island. But in a world moving steadily towards a proliferation of 'sovereign' states which had no ethnic unity or any consciousness of a common past or any measure of linguistic unity – all of which Madagascar had to some degree – to seek to thwart in every way Malagasy aspirations for a national independence was, I thought, not merely misguided but simply wrong. The French were not willing to permit even that autonomy within a French union that they proclaimed as their purpose – let alone national independence – although there in Madagascar the preconditions were surely more favourable than in most colonies. Yet when Philibert Tsiranana, President of an independent state of Madagascar, received me there in 1960, French policy seemed to have been vindicated, for all the usual accusations of neo-colonialism. All the more so when two of the three MDRM leaders who had not been allowed to return to the island since their conviction for their alleged part in the 1947 insurrection had accepted Tsiranana's invitation to join his government.

Nonetheless I ceased to study the structures of French colonial government or its methods except when this was a clearly necessary part of the examination of some more general political problem. For example, French electoral law and procedures both in France and overseas clearly had to be elucidated in connection with my investigation of the elections to the Senegal territorial assembly in March 1957.[21] But my next visit to parts of overseas France was made with a similar purpose. One of the few relatively unambiguous decisions of the post-liberation discussions of the future of the French empire was that the four 'old colonies' – Martinique, Guadeloupe, French Guyana and Réunion – should be fully integrated with metropolitan France as Departments of the Republic. Even so there had been an unsuccessful attempt to ensure that metropolitan laws would not apply automatically to these Departments but only if expressly so stated. In fact it was finally agreed that the opposite should be the case and special provision was also made for the application within a specified period of such earlier metropolitan legislation as had not already been applied. This integration of a colony with the metropole was, of course, the traditional objective of earlier French colonial policy and in many ways the four old colonies had already gone quite far in this direction before the war. But one result of the provisions of Chapter XI of the UN Charter was 'a marked unwillingness to agree that people may cease to be non-self-governing not only as a result of securing international recognition as constituting an independent state but also as a result of incorporation in a larger unit'[22] more especially, one might add, if that larger unit was a colonial power. The UN nonetheless accepted in 1953 that a colonial relationship might be terminated in this way and a statement of the factors 'indicative' of such an association was approved by the Assembly. It was with these considerations in mind that I visited Martinique and Guadeloupe in the autumn of 1953 and concluded, after examining the arrangements made in these two Overseas Departments, that:

> Assimilation has in fact been carried through very completely in political and juridical matters. 'Departmentalism' is not a means of maintaining a disguised form of 'colonial' government. The real problems and uncertainties arise partly in respect of the working of these political institutions in a social and economic milieu which differs in many important respects from that of metropolitan France but also from the implications, hitherto largely unconsidered of 'assimilation' in respect to the social service activities of the modern welfare state, in relation to which these social and economic differences assume even greater importance. How these latter problems will be resolved is not clear but meanwhile the mass of the population would have something to lose and little to gain from ending the close association of Martinique and Guadeloupe with France. It is within such an association that they will continue to seek those changes in the social order which some of them passionately and many of them obscurely desire.[23]

Twenty years after that was written, no one would contend that integration is not completely effected in formal legal and political institutions even if the application of metropolitan social welfare benefits was delayed – only in 1980, for example, were metropolitan rates of unemployment benefit introduced in Réunion. But departmentalization is criticized on similar grounds to those advanced in respect of other parts of larger countries. Their distinct cultural features are not recognized as, for example, in Brittany just as much as the Antilles. Some consequences of departmentalization are claimed to be disadvantages: metropolitan personnel fill too many posts in public services, especially the more senior ones; metropolitan encouragement of higher birthrates is absurd in countries that are overpopulated (this was said even in 1954); there is nothing for the unemployed to do except emigrate (and of course integration facilitates this). Lack of local control of the economy, especially inability to encourage industrialization by protection, and above all, the impossibility of any radical change in the social order, also feature in the indictment. All the familiar arguments are there. The branches of the French Communist Party which in 1946 led the demand for full departmentalization have been transformed into local parties claiming 'autonomy' and there are even some which want 'independence'. What autonomy seems to mean in this case is not only a long-term commitment to maintain a certain level of financial aid, but local control of the way such monies are spent.[24] Furthermore, whilst dissidents emphasize the low turn-outs, support for government candidates remains strong, and some politicians, such as Martinique's veteran deputy and best-known son, Aimé Césaire, have built up a solid personal constituency. So, while it is not easy to assess support for such anti-departmentalist forces, the 'colonial' problem has not altogether been eliminated, any more than it has in Corsica.

Retrospective analyses of the terminal period of western European colonial rule have often drawn a contrast between the comparative facility of British withdrawal and the stubborn struggle of the French to remain, with its disastrous accompaniment of major colonial wars. In drawing this contrast some point to a continuing British experience of the development of self-governing states in their colonies of white settlement and later in India and Ceylon. This, it is contended, exercised a decisive influence in what came to be described in that terminal period as the 'transfer of power', with its implication of deliberate contrivance.[25] A surprisingly different terminology had been employed by J. A. Hobson in that seminal work *Imperialism* when he assured his readers in 1905 that 'the trend of British colonialism has uniformly been towards internal self-government or practical independence'. Whatever weight may be given to that experience in determining British attitudes in the 1950s, it was undeniable that it had no analogy in French experience of empire. On the contrary, in that experience, empire had been presented first, in the last quarter of the nineteenth century, as a vital element in the restoration of France's position as a major power, and after the First World War and again after the Second, of recovering and maintaining that position.

Nowhere was the determination that whatever evolution of the colonial peoples might take place it could only be within the French *bloc* made more explicit than in the Constitution of the Fourth Republic. Amidst all its ambiguities and contradictions the character and role of the new French Union was made explicit by the deliberate removal of any reference to the 'free consent' of its constituent parts. The French Republic which now included not only the new Overseas Departments but also the Overseas Territories (that is, those colonies not made departments), was one constituent of the Union of which the others were those parts of the French empire which had been brought into relationship with it by international treaties (that is, the former Protectorates in Indochina and

North Africa) described as Associated States and the former mandated territories (Togo and Cameroon) described as Associated Territories, but for all other purposes treated as Overseas Territories. These components pooled all their resources to guarantee the defence of the Union and the Government of the French Republic 'assumes the coordination' of these resources and the 'direction of the policy apt to prepare and ensure' the defence of the Union. In the 'conduct of the Union' (an even more general phrase) the French government was to be assisted by a High Council composed of the French Prime Minister, four other French ministers *ex officio* and such other members as the French government might decide to add for each meeting, while the Associated States would each have such representation as might be provided in the 'acts which defined their relation to France'. In other words, the Constitution reaffirmed ultimate imperial control, if not domination, of the Union which it sought to impose. It was, in this respect, a reaffirmation of the unity of the French empire, and one enshrined in a Constitution which included the greater part of the colonial territories proper in a Republic 'one and indivisible'. But even the second constituent Assembly had to relegate one part of the French Empire to a separate statute to be enacted later: Algeria, in respect of which it papered over the cracks even more outrageously than elsewhere.

The details of the post-liberation settlement of these colonial issues were embodied not merely in the Constitution but in numerous separate laws and decrees. It was not difficult to show that their purported federal character was bogus, that the French Union Assembly (composed of equal numbers of members representing metropolitan France on the one hand, and on the other, Overseas Territories, Departments and Associated States) had only advisory functions and, except in so far as the French government or the French National Assembly might seek its advice, these were limited to legislation relating to the Overseas Territories, or that the representation the Overseas Territories secured in the National Assembly and the Council of the Republic was not proportionate to their populations, not elected by universal suffrage, and unduly weighted in the representation of metropolitan Frenchmen. All this should not blind us to the remarkable fact that the Overseas Territories obtained what proved to be significant representation in the French Parliament. Another consequence, whose ultimate implications were quite far-reaching, was that future changes in respect of the Overseas Territories in practice were to be made in a form which applied to all of them, though not necessarily uniformly. Far more complete accounts are now available of the devious manoeuvres of the members of the two Constituent Assemblies and their significance in regard to their colonial provisions than could be pieced together in 1949 when I attempted a detailed analysis of the Public Law of Overseas France which, I now realize, is not without its *naivetés*.[26]

It was a consequence of the disintegration of the Third Republic and the occupation regime that a new Constitution was required and the course of events in which the Free French established themselves in some of the French colonies that made it inevitable that that Constitution should attempt a restructuring not merely of metropolitan France but also of the Empire. We may for a moment consider the question of what might have appeared in any similar public British statement. And, as it happens, in May 1947, Prime Minister Attlee initiated some discussion of the 'existing status and interrelationship' of the 'constituent parts' of the 'British Commonwealth and Empire'. He wrote:

> Theoretically there is a broad division between the self-governing states, Great Britain and the Dominions on the one side and the Colonial Empire, the former group having equality of status defined by the statute of Westminster. This Dominion status is regarded as the final stage of evolution already reached by some and to be reached ultimately by other of the constituent parts of the Empire. In fact however this pattern has already been broken. Eire is in an anomalous position as an independent republic. The Dominions, notably South Africa and Canada, dislike the term Dominion Status. India which only twenty years ago clamoured for Dominion Status now demands independence. Ceylon and Burma both ask for independence either within or without the Commonwealth. It is I think clear that while there is strong evidence of the reluctance of many leaders of political opinion in the Asiatic countries to leave the Commonwealth, the phrase if not the content of 'Dominion Status' is not now attractive.

'The critical position in India, Burma, and Ceylon', Attlee thought, made a review urgent. What was needed, he said, was 'a formula which will enable the greatest number of independent units to adhere to the Commonwealth without excessive uniformity in their internal constitution or in their relationship to Great Britain, the Commonwealth and one another. Some such phrase, for instance, as the Associated States of the Commonwealth might provide an umbrella under which a number of independent states might be brought together'. He instanced besides Britain and the existing Dominions, Eire, Rhodesia, India 'whether single or multiple', Burma and Ceylon. Other colonies and dependencies which 'for military reasons cannot have exactly the same degree of freedom as a Dominion might also be brought in'.

In the Colonial Office brief for the Secretary of State on the proposed discussion,[27] Attlee's ideas were summarized as envisaging

> the creation of a new form of relationship ... with the two-fold purpose of (a) including under this umbrella states, such as an independent India, which for political reasons might be unwilling to accept allegiance to the Crown; (b) providing also (and this lies mainly in the future) for small colonial territories such as Malta which may achieve full internal self-government but which primarily because of their size would not be able (and probably would not want) to manage their own external affairs and defence.

The office saw no objection from the colonial point of view to the creation of the suggested new umbrella so long as the group of 'White Dominions' was included under it and it was not intended to be an 'additional relationship' since 'it is important that the status of an independent member of the Commonwealth should be open to any of the present constituent parts of the Commonwealth as soon as it is qualified politically to attain that status'. 'Dominion status' might well, they thought, be dropped but not allegiance to the crown which 'is the central feature, and in the case of the present Dominions the only formal feature of Commonwealth unity'. There was a real danger that 'any departure from insistence upon allegiance to the Crown would in the long run have a disintegrating effect so far as the territories now colonies are concerned'. The right way of providing for places such as Malta would be for the UK to continue to conduct their external affairs and for their governments to have access to the UK government (and move so far as necessary) other independent governments of the Commonwealth through some form of organized consultative machinery 'the development of which has already been under recent consideration in the Colonial Office. On this basis the Commonwealth would consist of National States responsible for their external affairs and Associated States whose external affairs are conducted by the UK'. The 'consultative machinery' to which the office referred was that discussed in the paper on the General Political Development of Colonial Territories annexed to the report of the Agenda Committee which under the chairmanship of Sir Sydney Caine had been producing papers to be put before the conference of African governors to be held in November 1947. One of the topics it considered was 'Is it practicable to devise arrangements for closer association of colonial peoples in the broad lines of policy?' This, the officials observed, was

> in some sense the crucial one for the future of the Colonial Empire as a political organisation. Unless machinery can be devised which will substitute links of consultation for present links of control there is a very real danger of the ultimate dissolution of the colonial parts of the British Empire.

The Committee considered the recently promulgated French arrangements, and recognized that direct colonial representation in Parliament would be a 'constitutional revolution but is not therefore wholly impracticable'. But it thought that if such representation was not proportionate to population it would be 'open to the criticism that the colonial members have no real voice, while in fact, as recent French experience suggests, it may well lead to a state of affairs in which "colonial members" exercise a decisive voice in purely UK affairs like the Irish members in the late nineteenth century. The possibility of creating a special body of representatives of the legislatures of the UK on the one hand and of the colonies on the other, preferably in equal numbers, was more attractive but it would need very careful consideration.' Some difficulties were aired but 'a joint body of this kind might be of great value in dealing with matters of joint concern to the UK and the colonies notably in the sphere of external affairs and defence; it might, in particular, be used as a means of securing satisfactory representation of the UK and the colonies in international organisations'. Alternatively, and less ambitiously, 'more informal methods of periodical consultation in conferences' such as that envisaged in 1948 might be more practical, might be associated with a secretariat, and include technical conferences on special subjects.[28]

This paper accompanied that about Constitutional Development in Africa which has been much discussed and even described as 'revolutionary'.[29] Yet there was no constitutional proposal in that paper which had not already been put into practice somewhere in the colonial empire. When the papers were submitted to the Secretary of State, the Permanent Under-Secretary thought the only one he might wish to discuss with the Prime Minister or submit to Cabinet was that discussing this very tentative suggestion for a consultative machinery. The Secretary of State decided neither was necessary but he observed:

> The manner in which the British Empire has stood the shock of the post-war changes justifies the British philosophy I think as against the French. Yet there may be small territories incapable by themselves of independence and also essential to Imperial strategy, such as Gibraltar whose true destiny may be incorporation in the United Kingdom. The number of Members they would send would not upset the balance.[30]

The situation in Indochina and Algeria presented France, Tony Smith has written, with 'problems that Britain was simply fortunate to escape [at least until Suez]'. I wonder whether such a judgement takes into account the British withdrawal from Palestine or their long and determined fight to remain in Egypt which, especially after the transfer of power in India seemed more essential to Britain's position in the world. But, on the other hand, I find it difficult to suppose that withdrawal from India or indeed many of the events in the inter-war period that preceded it, could have taken place had it been French. What I have been trying to suggest is that in the politics of the colonial situation, no less than in other spheres of political action, habits of mind are important even if 'policies' are not.

NOTES

1. The term 'French Union' was first used officially on 24 March 1945 in the announcement of the French government's intention that 'the Indochina Federation will form with France and other parts of the community, a French Union whose external interests wil be represented by France'. For the significance of this statement see D. B. Marshall, *The French Colonial Myth and Constitution-making in the Fourth Republic* (New Haven, 1963), 134-5; for its origins, see P. Mus, *Le Destin de l'Union Français* (Paris, 1954), 82-5.
2. *Post-War Training for the Colonial Service: Colonial No. 198* (HMSO, 1946), para 19. (There were similar courses in Cambridge and London universities.)
3. For the Anglo-French conversations, see my Callander Lectures at Aberdeen Uni-

versity, *Memoirs of a Colonialist* (to be published in 1984) and for a contemporary view my 'Europe in Africa', *The Spectator*, 1 April 1949. A more objective assessment, based on French and British archives, is M. Michel, 'La Coopération intercoloniale en Afrique noire 1942–51: Un néo-colonialisme éclairé?', *Relations Internationales*, 34 (1983), 155-71.
4. See K. Robinson, 'The "Sociétés de Prévoyance" in West Africa', *Journal of African Administration*, 2 (1950), 29; and D. B. Cruise O'Brien, *Saints and Politicians* (Cambridge, 1975), 123-25. Dr O'Brien writes 'The Providence Society was the dominant institution in agricultural administration throughout the colonial period', a statement corroborated in detail for Senegal in A. Auchnie, *The Commandement Indigène in Senégal, 1919–47* (Unpublished Ph.D. thesis, London, 1983), 189-212.
5. See his fascinating book of talks given on Radio Dakar *L'Hippopotame et le Philosophe* (Paris, 1946).
6. As a member of the first Constituent Assembly, the RDA leader, Félix Houphouet-Boigny of the Ivory Coast did not, unlike many African members, associate himself with the French socialists but with a small group of 'fellow travellers', the Mouvement Unifié de la Résistance, closely allied with the Communists. See Marshall, 167-8. For the harassment of the RDA see E. Mortimer, *France and the Africans* (London, 1969), 105-10, 122-5, and 137-45.
7. F. Mitterrand, *Présence française et Abandon* (Paris, 1957), 171-200. But Mitterand is in error in his reference on p. 172 to Kwame Nkrumah who was not in prison in 1949 nor was he the head of government in the Gold Coast in 1950 nor, for that matter, an Ashanti.
8. For the falsification of the 1951 elections in West Africa, achieved by methods familiar in metropolitan France, see A. R. Zolberg, *One Party Government in the Ivory Coast* (Princeton, 1964), 13-18 and Mortimer, *France and the Africans*, 166-7. Senghor noticed in 1952 that 33 of the 36 elected seats in the Gold Coast parliament had been won by the 'Anti-British' party and observed that the British preferred 'authentic representatives'.
9. As published in 1940, the book was so badly mutilated by the French wartime censorship that Delavignette gave the restored text, republished in 1946, a new title, *Service Africain*. The International African Institute published an English translation, *Freedom and Authority in French West Africa* (London, 1950) at which time Delavignette was Director of Political Affairs at the Ministry of Overseas France. For Delavignette's place among what have been called the 'colonial humanists' of the 1930s, see R. Girardet, *L'Idée Coloniale en France 1871–1962* (Paris, 1972), 184-90.
10. Lord Hailey, *An African Survey: Revised 1956* (London, 1957), 1478. An interesting account of the use and abuse of the Provident Societies from the point of view of an administrator is in M. Méker, *Le Temps Colonial* (Dakar, 1980). This also provides an instructive account of the position of the *commandant de cercle* (in this case a Socialist) in relation to African members of the Territorial Assembly, introduced in 1947 (and in this case RDA).
11. K. Robinson, 'Local Government Reform in French Tropical Africa', *Journal of African Administration*, 8, (1956), 179-85 provides a detailed account of the various bodies and issues arising in attempts to legislate on this subject, ending in the law of 1956.
12. Much of the despatch is reprinted in A. H. M. Kirk-Greene, *The Principles of Native Administration in Nigeria* (London, 1956), 238-45.
13. This is illustrated in many passages in H. Deschamps, *Roi de la brousse*. See pp. 173-78.
14. F. Madden and D. K. Fieldhouse (eds.), *Oxford and the Idea of Commonwealth* (London, 1982), 7-28.
15. T. L. Hodgkin, *Nationalism in Colonial Africa* (London, 1956). A further comment (p. 16) is much to the point: 'Indeed there is some advantage in ceasing to regard Africa, as it has sometimes been regarded in the past as a kind of "thing in itself", the private preserve of *Africanistes*'.
16. G. Balandier, in whose work I first learnt of the concept of the colonial situation ('La

Situation Coloniale: approche theorique', *Cahiers Internationaux de Sociologie*, 11, 1951) emphasized that it was 'par rapport à ces doctrines et aux politiques qu'elles impliquent que réagissent différement les peuples colonisés du même type'. The doctrines to which he refers are those of *politique indigène* and he has no doubt that in West Africa 'les élites noires des térritoires britanniques et celles des térritoires français ont manifesté des comportements différentiels très révélateurs à cet égard: la colonisation n'a pas eu le même signification pour celles-ci et pour celles-la', *Sociologie actuelle de l'Afrique noire* (Paris, 1955), 13.

17. 'French West Africa', *United Empire*, 43 (1951), 63-7. A similar view in 'French Colonial Administration in Africa', *Progress*, 42 (1951), 16-21.
18. P. Mus, *Viet-Nam: Sociologie d'une Guerre* (Paris, 1952); J. Rous, *Tunisie... Attention* (Paris, 1952); P. Devillers, *Histoire du Viet-Nam* (Paris, 1952); C.-A. Julien, *L'Afrique du Nord en marche* (Paris, 1952). Mus and Julien both lectured for me at Oxford. P. Mannoni, *Psychologie de la Colonisation* (Paris, 1950) and H. Casseville, *L'Ile ensanglantée: Madagascar 1946–7* (Paris, 1948) provide contemporary documentation.
19. A report on these projects is in G. Condominas, *Fokon'olona et collectivités rurales en Imerina* (Paris, 1960), 155-94. I did not however study them in Imerina but in the more southern provinces of Fianarantsoa and Tulear, inhabited by other ethnic groups.
20. J. Tronchon, *L'Insurrection malgache de 1947* (Paris, 1974), 176. This remarkable assessment of the evidence now available includes a collection of contemporary documents the provenance of which is carefully discussed. Probably the best contemporary account is that by an anonymous administrator 'L'insurrection malgache' *Bulletin des Missions*, 24 (1950), 255-76. For the trial of the MDRM leaders and the accusations of torture P. Shibbe, *Justice pour les malgache* (Paris, 1954) closely based on the records of the trials where Maître Stibbe (and the veteran Senegalese lawyer, Lamine Gueye) appeared for the defence. I can vouch for this as, after I had been informed by the Ministry of Overseas France that they were 'not available', he kindly allowed me to study them in his Paris flat. Pierre Stibbe was a communist lawyer as was D. N. Pritt, the English QC who defended Kenyatta. For the 'psychological' interprettions, see J. C. Carrothers, *The Psychology of Mau Mau* (Nairobi, 1954) and for Madagascar, Mannoni, *Psychologie* (English translation *Prospero and Caliban*, London, 1956). There is an excellent summary of the events leading up to the Madagascar insurrection and its aftermath in M. Brown, *Madagascar Rediscovered* (London, 1978), 265-271.
21. W. J. M. Mackenzie and K. Robinson, *Five Elections in Africa* (Oxford, 1960), 281-390.
22. K. Robinson, 'The end of Empire; another view', *International Affairs*, 30 (1954), 186.
23. Ibid., 195.
24. Two interesting discussions of these issues are J. Houbert, 'Reunion II: The Politics of Decolonisation', *Journal of Commonwealth and Comparative Politics*, 18 (1980), 325-344, and R. D. E. Burton, 'Nationalist Ideologies in Contemporary Martinique', *Collected Seminar Papers No. 29* (Institute of Commonwealth Studies, University of London).
25. When I wrote this, I was thinking of the arguments summarized in T. Smith, 'A Comparative Study of French and British Decolonisation' in P. Gifford and W. R. Louis (eds.), *The Transfer of Power in Africa* (New Haven, 1982) with whose general thesis I agree though I think he underestimates the persuasive influence of 'le système'. I developed some at least of this thesis about British experience in *The Dilemmas of Trusteeship* (London, 1965), 3-13. It is summarized and criticized by D. Austin, 'The Transfer of Power: Why and How' in W. H. Morris-Jones and G. Fischer (eds.)., *Decolonisation and After* (London, 1980).
26. Mitchell provides the best account. K. Robinson, 'The Public Law of Overseas France', *Journal of Comparative Legislation* (1950), 37-56.
27. PRO CO 967/34. Prime Minister's personal Minute M221/47 of 14 May 1947, and Colonial Office brief for the Secretary of State (Quotations from Crown Copyright material in the PRO are made by permission of the Controller of HM Stationery Office). Incidentally the use of the term Associated States by Attlee antedates by more than five years what D. J. Morgan, *The Official History of Colonial Development*

(London, 1980), V, 66 saw as its first use. It is unfortunate that he does not tell us what were the several grounds on which this was 'generally opposed'.
28. CO 847/36/47238/47 Appendix II.
29. J. W. Cell, 'On the Eve of Decolonisation: The Colonial Office's Plans for the Transfer of Power in Africa', *Journal of Imperial and Commonwealth History*, 8 (1980), 245.
30. CO 847/36/47238/47. Minute of 5 June 1947.

# Imperial Theory and the Question of Imperialism after Empire

by

## Ronald Robinson

The paradox of imperialism after empire raises questions for the historian that are not usually asked, because they are too difficult to answer. For instance, did imperialism end with the disappearance of Europe's colonial empires? Or has it continued under new management? Is what is called imperialism today more or less the same thing as the imperialism of the colonial era? Or, has a world of superpowers and new states, cold war and the World Bank produced a beast of an altogether different species in a revolutionized habitat? And if this is so, has the imperialistic element in international relations increased or diminished? In the light of the continuities and discontinuities it may be that some parts of imperial theory, for example, those of capitalist imperialism, informal empire, or neo-colonialism apply *a fortiori*, or it may be that foreign intervention in the affairs of weak states has changed character to the extent that imperial descriptions are now anachronistic. At its simplest, this is the issue raised for discussion in this article.

It is a problem of definition, but a more elaborate entry in the dictionary will not serve the purpose, since the historian has to define imperialism working through time in hypotheses representing his materials. In this sense, definition is a matter of general theory, and theory at the moment is in confusion, even for the years 1850 to 1960. Until it can be reformed, the post-colonial problem can hardly be formulated. This article revises a well-known definition of imperialism along 'Excentric' lines, (not, incidentally, peripheral) and goes on to reflect on its implications for the post-colonial era.*

I

The excentric idea is an extension of classical theories, but moves away from their Eurocentric perspectives. They were often theories about European society, rather than theories of imperialism. In mercantilist analysis, for example, empire is incidental to state-building in Europe; in classical Victorian economic theory, the colonial theory is deduced from first principles of European capitalist economics – and these two incidentals combined when the classical, pre-war theorists hung their central analyses of politics, capitalism and war in Europe incidentally on the African and Asian partitions. Imperialism as a result tended to be defined

---

* This is a draft presented to the *Deutsches Historisches Institut* conference on 'Imperialism after Empire' at Bad Homburg, September 1982.

almost exclusively in terms of European motives, as a simple projection of European state-power, strategic rivalry and industrial economy overseas. It is clear that imperialism has something, but not everything, to do with these components. Without taking other continents into account, it is not easy to see why they took imperial form in some countries, and not in others.

Imperialism has to be redefined in theory against the background of how the imperial, economic and strategic arms of European expansion were connected overseas. Their relationship to each other was remarkably asymmetrical during the nineteenth century. From the American Revolution onwards formal empires were contracting in the European colonized world where the metropolitan economy was expanding, while in Africa and Asia, where colonial rule was being extended, relatively little trade or investment preceded or followed the flag. India alone entered significantly into the workings of British industrial expansion; but long after, and then, as a result, not a cause, of the imperial establishment. The sub-continent was conquered largely for the sake of the inter-Asian trade, its military forces, and land revenue which also generated an informal trading empire in China. In South and East Asia the power and capital required was not exported from Europe, but was extracted substantially from Asia. Later, tropical Africa shows the widest discrepancy between metropolitan and imperial thrusts. Here, the British annexed an empire of almost supreme irrelevance to expanding economy, and abandoned it when its value was at its greatest. These, and many other incongruities, suggest that colonial empire is not a necessary function of industrial capitalism. They also suggest that much of the wealth generating Europe's overseas expansion, like most of the power behind her empires, was not projected from Europe. By far the greater part was supplied or extracted from local resources in other continents.

How then did the strategic thrusts of Europe relate to imperial expansion during the Asian and African partitions? Although strategic rivalries projected from Europe played a major role, the imperial significance has been exaggerated. With some exceptions, the various national interests involved in these areas had co-existed for decades past under international consular protectorates without necessitating partition. In the Ottoman and Chinese cases, and to a large extent in Africa, partition stemmed, not from new strategic or imperial drives from Europe as such, but from local crises which drove the Powers to stake pre-emptive territorial claims round their major national interests. But, when all the diplomatic excitement and scrambling was over and done with, they had conceded each other's interests substantially, and in most of these vast areas, the partition remained on paper. In most cases new imperial ambitions had not inspired these treaties. They were governed by overriding considerations of national security within the European balance, and their significance is this: all the major powers eventually agreed that a European war was not worth fighting for the sake of more Afro-Asian colonies. They continued, with few exceptions, to act on this principle, which meant that they gave each other a free hand in dealing with these territories thereafter. Up to 1939 they could normally rely on international non-interference in their Afro-Asian colonies. A kind of collective security system for colonial empires was built into the European concert, an indispensable condition for their continuing without prohibitive demands on the European taxpayer, and unacceptable risks to national security. Significantly, as soon as this requirement was missing, colonial empires proved too expensive, too vulnerable to be worth keeping any longer.

The asymmetrical relations between the imperial and the other arms of expansion suggest certain revised theses toward a redefinition. Firstly, the object of imperialism was not to export wealth and power from Europe, but to deploy minimal quantities where they would return dividends at least risk. Imperialism was only worthwhile if it could be had on the cheap. Secondly, the imperialists, therefore, drew the necessary influence, finance, military forces and administrative authority largely from local resources and institutions in the countries imperialized. Thirdly, they achieved this through local intermediaries. Without local cooperation resources could not be transferred, commerce protected, strategic interests secured, or xenophobic resistance contained cheaply. Consequently, the scope and penetrative depth of imperialism was determined, not only by European drives, but also by local collaboration and resistance – the relative strength or weakness of political and social organization in different countries overseas, and their ability to undergo institutional and economic change without foreign control. Accordingly, expansion has not taken imperial form in many countries, but in others has ranged from informal paramountcy to colonial rule, and eventually back to external influence. On these assumptions, imperialism has to be re-defined in terms of the interconnections between its European and its overseas components.

At the local level, it is defined in the nature of the collaborative arrangements – the unequal bargains struck between the imperialists and the imperialized in different countries from time to time. The exploitation of inequality which decided those forced contracts is an indispensable condition for successful imperialism. During the late imperial age, the European lead in technology and national organization over Afro-Asian society was probably at its longest, and local contractors were easily attracted or conscripted. The balance of terms decided both the possibilities of collaboration and resistance, and the costs and benefits of imperialism on both sides. The greater the European resources committed to a collaborative system the less mediators were required, but the less local mediators were employed the more the balance sheets of empire were overdrawn. While the Europeans could not usually do without intermediaries, the intermediaries had no alternative but to negotiate with the intruders as best they could on behalf of their constituents before rival leaders did so. Hence two sets of connections were involved in local collaboration; one between European agents and their local mediators; the other between the mediators and their people. Each set of bargains had to be acceptable in terms of the other, if a local crisis was to be avoided.

It was these connections that governed the local working of imperialism. At the outset, the presence or absence of effective mediators decided the possibility of a European break-in. The breakdown of informal connections in a local crisis in many instances led to the transition to an imperial take-over. During the ensuing formal phase, the choice of local collaborators normally determined the organization, depth and character of colonial rule. The administration institutionalized the local economic and political alliances on which it depended for control. Subsequently, when anti-colonial movements eventually succeeded in detaching mediators from the colonial regimes, and formed a united front of non-cooperation, the imperialists either chose to leave or were forced to go. They had run out of collaborators, and the running out decided the timing of the transfer of power. Since nationalism had triumphed through inverting the colonial collaborative arrangements, the successor party governments projected a kind of mirror image of the previous system into the first few years of independence.

Two different models are suggested for the working of these overseas connections; the first for the British white colonies which attempts to explain why in these cases colonial rule contracted with economic expansion (this may be of special interest from the standpoint of informal empire in the post-colonial period); the second, for Afro-Asia, which explains why colonial rule extended there, without economic expansion.

After the initial stage of colonization under Downing Street rule, the Australasian, Canadian and South African colonies enjoyed self-government under democratic constitutions. They were notably nationalistic, and anti-imperialist politically, yet, normally they cooperated loyally within the empire. The model suggests that their continuing economic and political collaboration stemmed essentially from their growing and mutually profitable business connections with the United Kingdom. Economic attraction was in some sense a substitute for colonial rule, on one vital condition which has disappeared in the post-colonial period. Up to 1914, they had no alternative to the mother country as an export market and investor of long-term capital. Consequently, their export-import sectors tended to govern the speed and direction of their economic growth in ways that complemented the needs of the British industrial economy, and influenced their domestic politics in favour of political collaboration with London. Whether the terms were so unequal as to justify the term 'capitalist imperialism' is a question; but, in any event, the colonial merchant, wheat farmer, sheep-drover and cattleman voted empire-loyalists into office who could keep capital flowing in. The Cape Dutch and the French Canadians were no exception. Unemployment and defeat at the next election were the penalties for letting colonial prosperity sag and government patronage run dry. Economic inputs were sufficient to establish imperial affiliations and so British economic expansion was translated into local cooperation, in spite of the withdrawal of imperial rule.

The reality of informal empire of this kind has been questioned, and it is true that British capital was small in proportion to the local capital invested; but the colonies required capital from London for railways to set local capital and labour working. It is not surprising, therefore, that colonial politics were largely railway politics. The loans which came from the British private sector, moreover, went to colonial governments and so supplied the patronage which often won elections. Populist leaders in these colonies proved as susceptible to railway politics as the barons of the export-import sector, and equally eager to embark on sub-imperial expansion on railways projected to annex sub-continents into the commercial and political empire of Greater Britain. The collaborative equations of informal empire normally worked easily and constructively, so that by 1919 these colonies had taken off into virtual economic and political independence.

The connections of imperialism in Africa and Asia worked very differently. In the informal phase of this model, the Europeans tried to lever Afro-Asian regimes into cooperation from outside, and reshape them through commerce; but the institutional barriers to reform of this kind proved intractable; European economic inputs as a result remained puny and indigenous commercial mediators could not be brought into power. Cosmopolitan export-import sectors meant little to these military or bureaucratic regimes, and so the agents of informal empire had no choice but to rely on the political arm, finding mediators in ruling oligarchies and quasi-feudal elites. The Europeans succeeded in infiltrating the export-import sector without influencing or reforming their governments, which tended to divert foreign loans to non-productive purposes. Sooner or later these states cracked under a combination of bankruptcy, foreign intervention and autonomous instability. In many instances, the terms of cooperation imposed by Europe helped alienate the rulers from their traditional constituencies, leaving them impotent in the face of anti-foreign rebellions. Local crises of this kind overturned informal collaborative systems over much of Africa and Asia, and as they broke, the imperialists had to choose between scrapping their interest or reconstructing local collaboration through taking over their government.

In the formal phase in Afro-Asia the affiliations of imperialism remained essentially political, although economic connections played a part. The first priority of the proconsuls was to avoid rebellion and keep control, and, as the use of metropolitan men and money was frowned on except in emergency, they normally had sufficient power to manipulate indigenous politics, but not to abolish them. The substance of ruling authority had to be extracted from subjects. During the colonial stage, the pro-consuls distributed administrative patronage so as to draw the weightier elements of social leadership into cooperation. The indigenous political arenas in India were urban and provincial, in tropical Africa, ethnic and local, and above and between the divisions, the central administrators rang the changes on the bargains with zemindars, pashas, emirs, chiefs, and the enclaves of European-educated elites. The permutations constituted the true genius of colonial administration, and in the bargains with these intermediaries, the imperialism was largely defined. They, for their part, competed for official patronage on behalf of their followings against other factions and communities, or to improve their opportunities in the modern sector. Hence the less the proconsuls demanded of their mediators by way of reform, the safer they were, and the more they tried to develop society into modern, secular shapes the harder the equations of cooperation became. So long as local and provincial leaders remained traditional, and retained their hold on the peasantry against nationalist agitators from the schools and towns, colonial administrators could easily keep control. But as soon as nationalist organization transcended local and provincial levels, united an urban elite with peasant discontent, and reached for central power, the terms for collaboration turned increasingly against rulers. To keep control of a colony now required more and more sharing of governmental power, or an increasing metropolitan effort. Either way, costs and risks soon outweighed the dividends of colonialism until it was no longer worthwhile.

II

Imperialism, however, is not to be defined by its local component alone. To define its overall character, the European components have to be added. It was once said that 'imperialism is a sufficient political function of integrating new regions into the expanding economy, and acts as its strategic protector'. But, looking at imperialism as a system, this distinction between its economic and political arms seems unreal. Taking the local standpoint into account, and Continental with British examples, imperialism was also a necessary function of extracting strength from new regions, of mobilizing, expressing, and demonstrating world power. After 1870, economic expansion was directed to serve the aims of imperial strategy just as much as imperial strategy was aimed at economic expansion. For instance, the British government loans were directed to consolidating a Canadian conferation from the Atlantic to the Pacific in order to forestall American westward expansion, just as German railway loans were intended to tighten Turkish defence against Russian expansion. The famous debate as to whether imperialism is economically or politically motivated, whether the statesman or the banker is to blame, is ultimately futile. A strong case could be made for thinking that British free trade imperialism possibly, and the protectionist imperialism of the Continental Powers probably, was as mercantilist in terms of state-building through projecting territorial monopolies abroad as anything seen in the previous century.

The case for regarding British free trade imperialism in this way rests on a model for informal empire, which may well be even more relevant as a measure of post-colonial imperialism than it is to the nineteenth century. It is defined in one or more of the following connections between an expanding and a receiving political economy: coercion or diplomacy exerted for purposes of imposing free trading conditions on a weaker society against its will; foreign loans, diplomatic and military support to weak states in return for economic concessions or political alliance; direct intervention or influence from the export-import sector in the domestic politics of weak states on behalf of foreign trading and strategic interests; and lastly, the case of foreign bankers and merchants annexing sectors of the domestic economy of a weak state. British imperialists achieved several of these connections during the nineteenth century, but quasi-monopolistic conditions were required for their success. At the time British merchants dominated trade outside Europe, the City of London was the main exporter of long-term capital overseas, and both developing and poor countries were chronically short of it. These contracts of informal collaboration, like those of formal empire, could be made and enforced only under conditions of high inequality and no alternative European supplier or protector.

Any revised theory of imperialism must extend from rise to fall, and prove the analysis of the one in accounting for the other. From this point of view a few ideas for a model of colonial empire may be suggested.

The transfers of resources necessary for the making of colonial empire may be thought of in terms of the notional contracts for mobilizing these resources, and distributing their costs and benefits. The first of these was at international level, in the agreements which insulated colonies from interference from other great powers, and so removed what might otherwise have been extremely high imperial risks and costs. The second was at metropolitan level, in contracts between the European government and its proconsuls overseas on the basis of empire on the cheap in return for support from home in an emergency. The third set of contracts is found at local level, in the forced contracts of collaboration, which extracted the colonial administration's recurrent costs, provided its subordinate authorities and, in many cases, placed large armies at the disposal of the imperial Power, without expense to the metropole. Colonial economic exploitation is notorious, but equally remarkable is the colonial extraction of force from empire for purposes of imperial strategy and European wars.

The terms of these local contracts were so exorbitant that they could not have been imposed or accepted, except under conditions of monopoly, which depended on conditions of high inequality between rulers and subjects, and at the same time exaggerated it. The rulers' monopoly tended to be, but was not necessarily, economic. More critically, it was a monopoly of a colony's international relations, of its territory, and above all, of a colonial state with a monopoly as the supreme arbiter in local politics between factions and communities which had yet to achieve a national organization.

Formal empire was neither possible nor profitable, except under these conditions. Without monopoly at local and international level costs rose

IMPERIALISM AFTER EMPIRE 49

swiftly out of all proportion to benefits; and when that monopoly was eventually breached, the system fell.

The accommodations at various levels were essentially interdependent. An alteration of terms at one level involved an alteration of contracts on the others, and cost-benefits were re-distributed accordingly throughout the system. At metropolitan level, the tolerances varied with the financial and military cost of colonial upkeep, the supposed economic benefit, and the balance of imperial and anti-imperial sentiment. The commitment of men and money in the metropolitan contract affected the colonial administrator's bargaining power with resisting subjects, and the degree of colonial resistance in turn tested metropolitan willingness to coerce or concede. At local level, the problem for rulers was one of how to distribute patronage, how much power to share with subjects in exchange for their cooperation; for the subjects, the question was how much non-cooperation would elicit the maximum share of power. Between the two extremes, the outcome depended not only on the metropolitan commitment, but also on the depth of colonial intervention in peasant affairs: the demands for development, land, labour, taxes, and the resistance thus provoked. In this way, the existence of colonial empire depended on the possibilities of translating its contracts on one level into terms acceptable on the others.

The task became more and more intractable from 1940 onwards, and the model went into reverse. With the shift of world power from Europe, briefly to Japan in the Far East, and thence permanently to the US and USSR, the European collective security for colonial empire disappeared. Rhetorically at least, the Americans called for a swift approach to colonial self-determination, which encouraged nationalists in the colonies to demand the same. The imperialists' monopoly of their colonies' international relations was at an end. At the same time in South and South-east Asia, national organization, which the British had suppressed in India and the Japanese had promoted in Indo-China, Burma and Indonesia for example, during the war, was strong enough to break the imperial monopoly of central arbitration in local politics. To keep colonial control now required either a virtual concession of power, or a prohibitive metropolitan military effort which, in India and Burma at least, the war-weary British public and the Labour government could not tolerate. They transferred power precipitately, or resigned from retrieving it, in fear of impending anarchy and civil war. In the Indian case, it was the local contract for continuation that could not be translated into metropolitan and international terms any longer.

In the transfers of colonial power in tropical Africa, however, it was an improved metropolitan contract designed in the light of new international conditions, that could not be translated eventually into colonial terms. In 1947 nationalist organization had barely begun in the British tropical African colonies; the imperial monopoly of central arbitration appeared to be intact, although discontent with inflation and shortages left over from wartime mobilization was seething. Alarmed at a riot in the Gold Coast, the British began to prepare their colonies for democratic self-government, and introduced the ballot box in West Africa on the theory that liberal concessions would prolong colonial rule. In any event, after India and Palestine, the British electorate, and doubtless the Americans also, wanted no more colonial troubles. The attempt to democratize colonial government gradually from below swiftly manufactured popular national movements, and after breaking their own monopoly of arbitration in colonial politics, the imperialists could not have stopped the transfer of power had they wished to do so. Hence a metropolitan 'new deal' in local collaboration for purposes of developing the colonies economically was translated into terms of political independence. Considering international circumstances and British opinion, it appeared that nationalism would accomplish the purposes of imperialism by cheaper, and far more effective, means. (A question for post-colonial theory is whether the British, or any other Power has achieved informal empire of this kind.) But, on this model, it would be foolish to debate the question of whether either colonial freedom fighters, or European opinion, or the Americans brought about the fall of colonial empire.

### III

Coming at last to the possibilities of imperialism after empire in theory, it seems reasonable to conclude that the model of formal imperialism is irrelevant to the post-colonial era, at least for the time being. There is, of course, Afghanistan, but it is not likely that it has been occupied for the sake of empire on the cheap. Until the great Powers agree on new partitions, which is a possibility, the conditions for creating the international and local monopolies required for the unequal contracts of colonial empire do not exist. Nor do the great Powers, which are now so much greater than they were, have any need of the comparatively insignificant increments of wealth and power to be extracted from colonial empire. They may yet embark upon it involuntarily as the Europeans often did, but if they do, the cost-benefits will look ridiculous. And, since the word 'imperialism' is associated in theory with formal empire, a more precise definition of whatever is still going in the post-colonial era, is required.

Those historians who doubt the existence of an 'imperialism of free trade' may be wrong as to the nineteenth century, but right as regards the years since 1950. (It is ironic that its originators associated the concept with the Marshall Plan for the reconstruction of Europe.) How far is the model of informal imperialism suggested above relevant to the post-war years? One of its essential elements was the use of gun-boats to open countries for free trade, to enforce loan repayments and protect European merchants and concessions. Although gun-boat diplomacy goes on, it is no longer required, as it once was, to integrate new regions into the international economy; but it may still be needed to integrate the

'Southern' regions into the Eastern socialist or the Western economy.

The use of foreign loans and military aid to weak states in return for commercial concessions and political alliance – another element in the informal model – obviously goes on manifold. On the other hand, the virtual European world monopoly of overseas trade and investment that once made foreign free trade contracts so imperialistic in effect, has perhaps, no parallel today. It could be argued that, since there is competition in the foreign aid market, weak states have a choice of creditors and foreign alliances, and even, non-alignment; and this is true. The grossly unequal contracts of the old monopolistic type of informal imperialism no longer apply. Nor are the political and potentially imperialistic dividends as sure or as enduring. It could be argued that foreign aid represents a genuine transfer of resources for purposes of constructing the economy of the recipient country, not for extracting wealth from it. Again, many weak states have their own internal resources of capital, and so are less dependent than they were in the nineteenth century. It is said that the great powers are embarked in competing to give aid, on a struggle for the hearts and minds, not the economic resources, of the 'South'. At bottom, however, that was exactly what the imperialism of free trade was all about.

On the other hand, a good case for defining foreign aid as a type of informal imperialism can be made. In spite of the competition, the United States is by far the largest capital exporter. Without its contributions, the international aid agencies would be much the poorer; in the case of large development loans, the Western alliance negotiates with weak states in consortia; almost all loans have explicit economic and implicit political conditions attached; and they are normally intended to create collaboration in the domestic politics, foreign and economic policy of the recipients. Weak states can choose between the West, or the East, whose conditions are equally stringent, and whose objects are the same.

Like the foreign loans of Europe to the Ottoman and North Africa, aid is accompanied by financial, technical and military advisers, and since its scale dwarfs that of the nineteenth century, it tends to influence and corrupt administration and politics in weak countries to a correspondingly greater extent. One other comparison with the age of imperialism may be made. Then, the channels of international investment normally proceeded from the private investor through European stock exchanges to overseas governments in search of private profit; now, the bulk of the international transfers pass from donor government to recipient government. Hence, the opportunities for using foreign investment for purposes of informal imperialism have increased enormously. A considerable proportion, however, is also transferred by multinational companies who presumably do so in the old-fashioned way. In so far as the international capitalist system can be identified with the Western alliance, it appears to show manifest imperialistic tendencies of an informal type. The same could be said of its world rivals. If this thesis holds good, it may well be that new scrambles for the South are now in process in sporadic fashion, though much more marginally perhaps than the old ones.

The great Powers, nevertheless, have had comparatively little success in intervening directly in the affairs of weak states by means of military coercion or economic sanctions compared with Powers of smaller stature with a comparatively strong position in the various regional balances of power. This suggests that the lack of accommodation between American, Soviet and Chinese strategies ensures that none of them dominate the regional balances as effectively as the European concert once did. It also suggests that in spite of vast nuclear inequality, the technological gap between strong and weak states in conventional capabilities, like the institutional gap in national organization, has narrowed, compared with disparities between Europe and the South in the imperial age. The reduction of these inequalities together with political independence has increased the costs and risks of direct foreign intervention enormously. By the same token the bargaining position of weak states in international relations generally has greatly improved. On the other hand, it could be argued that the successful interventions of such states as Israel, South Africa, Vietnam, and Cuba, if not those of India, are cases of sub-imperialism.

Existing theories of imperialism for the post-colonial period have fundamental defects from a historical point of view, particularly those of neo-colonialism, and the imperialism of the international capitalist economy. They all assume the continuation of imperialism from the colonial period; and thereby, they imply that it is of the same kind. The assumptions are interesting; but in projecting the classical theories which were designed to explain the rise of European empire into the post-colonial era, they take no account of the fall of colonial empire or the triumphs of colonial nationalism.

Any revised theory of imperialism must incorporate a theory of the colonial state with a theory of colonial nationalism, and so account for the coming of independence. Only then can it be extended into the post-colonial period. The excentric hypothesis suggested above is one of the first attempts to approach this task.

The basic idea is simple. Imperialism is conceived in terms of the play of international economic and political markets in which degrees of monopoly and competition in relations at world, metropolitan and local levels decide its necessity and profitability. In an integrating world containing gross inequalities of wealth and power, comparatively weak societies need the help of a 'Big Brother' for their domestic economic development and external protection, even if they do not want one. During the classic age of imperialism, the Powers of Europe were able to work the international balance in conjunction with the expanding economy to ensure that every little brother had only one 'Big Brother'; and so long as little brother collaborated, the big brother could take over his domestic affairs and foreign relations, where it was profitable or necessary to do so. Imperialism was a relatively marginal activity of Europe's competing national business and state systems in the world at large; but from the standpoint of little brothers, it involved colonial state-building in some form or other, which eventually projected his countervailing national organization, and his takeover of the colonial states.

Little brother was able to do this during sweeping changes in the international balance of wealth and power, and as a result, he now has a choice of several big brothers. He is more or less in a better position to exploit his choices in the world's economic and political markets. These are still dominated by even more powerful systems of expansion; but the South is much more marginal to the continental systems of East and West than it was to the old European world system. Big brothers have relatively less need to exploit little brothers than formerly. The competition between big brothers, moreover, means that independent little brother's affairs are no longer at the disposal of the effective national monopolies that made the old imperialism profitable, except at unacceptable risk and cost.

These fundamental alterations in the bargaining position of weaker societies as compared with the colonial era, suggest certain conclusions. Firstly, if nationalism is indeed the continuation of imperialism by other means, it is imperialism of an altogether different species. A continuation of the previous beast in the revolutionized habitat seems unlikely. Secondly, the competing world systems of the post-colonial era tend to consolidate the political and economic independence of weak states, rather than undermine it, because where one expanding world system aims at destabilizing their independence, there is usually a competing world system striving to stabilize it. To fail in consolidating little brother's national organization and economic growth, opens the way for the other side. Thirdly, it is said that the international capitalist economy has developed an imperialism of its own, and this is true, both in the use of the transfer of resources for purposes of informal imperialism, and in the sense of 'World Bank imperialism', of proliferating the principles and institutions of good capitalist management into little brother's organization. But there is enormous resistance, not to say inertia; and very few, if any, economic planners of either East or West have succeeded for long in dictating his policies or controlling his independence for foreign purposes. Many little brothers are not so little any more, many big brothers are not so big any more, and so, though it survives, this type of informal imperialism is usually very expensive, and its dividends, except in stabilizing independence, highly problematical.

Fourthly, what is much more significant, is that this kind of economic imperialism can no longer be exploited as an instrument of any one national world strategy. In this sense, the expanding international economy has become detached from the expansive power strategies of rival world systems, whereas, in the comparatively monopolistic European world system of the colonial era, national expanding economies more often than not, served the purpose of extending national world power. Lastly, from the standpoint of the South, it must be obvious that the element of imperialism in their international relations has diminished out of all recognition in comparison with the colonial era. Significantly, the only successful example of colonial imperialism in the post-colonial decades has occurred in the Falkland Islands.

# II. Imperial Experience: Sentiment, Demography and Power

# Thomas Day and the Politics of Sentiment*

## by
## Paul Langford

Thomas Day (1748–89) is rarely remembered for his political activities and writings.[1] If his name means anything at all it is probably as the author of a celebrated work for children, and as the designer of a somewhat bizarre experiment in social engineering. His book *The History of Sandford and Merton*, published in three volumes between 1783 and 1789, enjoyed considerable success. It was essentially a collection of fables incorporated in a morally edifying account of the adventures of two boys, one a spoilt product of privileged background, the other a humbler child of innate goodness whose example had an appropriately improving effect on his young friend. Like Mrs Barbauld and Mrs Trimmer, Day tapped a rich vein of contemporary interest in the education of children and provided generations of Victorians with a suitable grounding in juvenile morality. *Sandford and Merton* was still popular with parents more than a century after its first appearance. Interest in its author's youthful experiment has survived even longer. His intention, nothing less than a practical essay in sentimental education, was unusual rather for the lengths to which he took it than for its inherent originality; attempts to practise at least some of Rousseau's precepts in *Emile* were not uncommon among bourgeois parents in the 1760s and 1770s. But Day's scheme, executed jointly with his friend John Bicknell, required the upbringing of two female orphans, who were expected to develop as perfect examples of enlightened education, and in due course, perhaps, provide proper partners for their mentors. The experiment turned out far less badly than it might have done. One of the girls was discharged at an early stage with suitable financial provision for her marriage. The education of the other, named by her guardians Sabrina Sidney, ran its full course. Day's standards of femininity proved higher than she could attain even under his own tuition, but she eventually married Bicknell, and lived to be embarrassed, though not, it seems, mentally scarred by her experience.[2] Day's reputation was unmarred by anything worse (or better) than impractical high-mindedness, and the whimsical annals of late eighteenth-century sensibility gained only an additional instance of eccentric virtue.

I

Day himself would doubtless have been dismayed by the narrow and perhaps prurient interest of posterity in his work. According to his friend

Richard Lovell Edgeworth, 'he valued, in preference to his other writings, certain political tracts; but these, though finely written, full of manly spirit and classical eloquence, have passed away and are heard of no more'.[3] The tracts in question were probably those published between 1782 and 1785, *Reflexions upon the Present State of England, and the Independence of America* (1782), *The Letters of Marius* (1784), and *A Dialogue between a Justice of the Peace and a Farmer* (1785).[4] None of them has survived in the literature of politics. Nor did the causes which they favoured benefit much by Day's attention. The *Reflexions* represented an attempt to push British public opinion towards recognition of American independence. It did not stand out from the great mass of contemporary polemic produced by the peace negotiations of 1782 and 1783, and as will be seen it was misconceived in intention if not mishandled in execution. The *Letters of Marius* were somewhat rambling observations on what Day saw as the corrupt tendencies of Whig politics at the close of the American War. The *Dialogue*, a mock debate between a reactionary country gentleman and a supposedly untutored tenant farmer was still more diffuse. It seems to have aroused little attention, and had no perceptible effect. Day's other ventures were also ultimately unsuccessful. In the public agitation associated with the reform movement between 1779 and 1784 he played a not unimportant part initially, but eventually became discouraged by the divided counsels and doubtful prospects of the reformers.

His final political piece, *A Letter to Arthur Young Esq. on the Bill now depending in Parliament to prevent the Exportation of Wool*, published in 1788, a year before his death, was a bitter denunciation of the woollen manufacturers for their selfish attempts to restrict the market of English wool-producers. It evidently did little to deter Parliament from legislating in defence of the cloth industry. In fact, of all Day's concerns, only slavery, which he passionately opposed, can be supposed to have borne the mark of his political career. Though he did not live to see even the first of the statutes designed to improve conditions in the slave trade, Dolben's Act of 1789, his poetic onslaught on slavery was commended by prominent anti-slavers, and earned him the applause of female poets like Anna Seward and Mary Robinson.[5] Even so his place in the history of agitation against the slave trade must be a small one. The poem on which it was largely based, *The Dying Negro*, was originally published in 1773, and went largely unremarked at the time. In any case it is doubtful whether he should receive the credit for such impact as it made. Substantial portions of *The Dying Negro* were written by his friend John Bicknell.[6] In this as in other respects it is clear that Day's historical interest lies more in what he represented than what he did, more (paradoxically in one who prided himself on his originality and individuality) in the contemporary attitudes which he embodied than in those which he shaped.

To a great extent, no doubt, his failure was the result of personal deficiencies. His impracticality and his naive idealism, his faith in the persuasive power of the pen, and his utter neglect of political manoeuvre and manipulation made him seem a singularly ill-equipped politician. Even his closest friends were conscious of his unsuitability in this respect. Edgeworth, for instance, was struck by his deep pessimism about human nature. 'It was in particular a favourite opinion of my friend, Mr Day, that people never profit by advice.'[7] Day's surviving correspondence is marked very heavily by this sense of disappointment in his fellow creatures. It is summed up by his weary remark to his American friend Henry Laurens, concerning the ungrateful 'nature of mankind, according to my own experience of their character, particularly the constant habit which they seem to have of abusing every good they possess'.[8] Edgeworth mildly admonished Day for this gloomy view of human nature. Others went further. Anna Seward, who was well acquainted with Day, but was not an uncritical admirer, was provoked by the laudatory obituaries which appeared immediately after his death to publish a severe stricture on his misanthropy. Even his charity, she pointed out, was dispensed as it were by a recluse who shunned his own class and gave only within a restricted circle of neighbouring poor: 'society is the proper sphere of action for the benevolent virtues'.[9] No doubt this characteristic pessimism, which certainly formed a major element in Day's make-up and which in his last years seems to have become chronic, could be attributed to a naturally melancholic temperament. But it was also as much a part of his intellectual history as of his genetic inheritance. As Edgeworth implied, Day's extreme cynicism in middle age could be seen as the inevitable successor of his excessive generosity in youth.[10] If this were so, his failure as a politician casts light, not merely on his personal limitations, but also on the inherent flaws in contemporary intellectual fashion.

Day's first steps in politics correspond well with the superficial, even naive, view of public life which he adopted at an early stage. His youth was spent in a way which was strongly to colour his political career but which reveals in retrospect the insubstantial nature of his political education. In part this may have been the consequence of his mother's choice of Oxford, presumably on the advice of his instructors at Charterhouse. Oxford in the mid-1760s basked in the sun after many years in the shade. George III's accession and the royal approbation which it brought to the university contrasted strikingly with the proscription which Oxford and Oxford men had suffered during their years of suspected Jacobitism under George I and George II. The political tone was markedly complacent and there is no reason to suppose that Day's college Corpus Christi, a conventionally Tory college under a conventionally Tory head of house, varied from the general pattern.[11] Had he gone like so many young men of Whiggish background to Cambridge, the result could have been very different. There the mid-1760s was a period of intense strife within the academic community: the election of a High Steward in 1764 divided the university down the middle, bore on party and personal conflicts in Parliament, and became a matter of national controversy.[12] The younger dons and many of their charges were later stimulated by this atmosphere into a major campaign for reorganization of the examination system.

Such activities did much to galvanize a whole generation of Cambridge-educated reformers, whose characteristic concerns combined rational dissent, tending towards unitarianism, with an authentic interest in constitutional reform. Typical was John Jebb, later to be a leading metropolitan radical and for a while a close colleague of Day's. It is difficult to believe that Day would not have been attracted by Jebb's views had he been fully exposed to them as an undergraduate. As it was he arrived at most of them by another route. But the contrast between Oxford and Cambridge has important implications for the precise mapping of his intellectual journey towards radicalism. His religious opinions, for example, seem to have been quite close to those of the Cambridge radicals. Anti-clericism surfaced frequently in his political writings.[13] His markedly deistic tendencies and his belief that the truest proof of a divine intelligence lay in the mechanical complexity and scientific coherence of the physical world can be matched very closely with the views which Jebb was preaching in Cambridge and which added to the latter's celebrity as a lecturer.[14] But Day seems never to have formally declared for unitarianism; in his religious views there is usually more of Rousseau's lofty but imprecise theism than a rational dissenter's uncompromising materialism. It is difficult to believe that Day's college years were not influential in this respect. Oxford in the new reign was not deficient in intellectual energy and critical rigour but innovative theology had no more appeal within its walls than did political subversion.

Both at Oxford between 1764 and 1767, and in the course of his subsequent wanderings, Day plainly read widely in history, politics and philosophy, as well as in the literature of 'sensibility' which was to affect him, like many others reaching manhood in the 1760s, so powerfully. The impact which this reading made upon him may be judged by the way in which it provided a protective layer against the enthusiasms of some of his closest friends and connections. His place in the Lichfield group, which was to form the nucleus of the Lunar Society, is well known.[15] But the fascination of Erasmus Darwin and his colleagues seems chiefly to have lain in the general stimulus it gave to intellectual enquiry (and perhaps especially in the female society which it offered among the daughters and friends of those involved) rather than in its pioneering interest in science. Darwin himself was after all a distinguished physician, Matthew Boulton a pragmatic businessman, and James Keir a celebrated chemist; even Edgeworth, through whom Day became acquainted with the Lichfield group, was well known for his mechanical ingenuity and inventions. Day was capable of being teased about his lack of aptitude for mechanics, at any rate by Edgeworth; but when Boulton solemnly remonstrated with him in similar terms, his response was a priggish assertion of his preference for the 'study of man'.[16] He was, in fact, making a considerable intellectual investment in political and social theory, as yet unaffected by practical experience. In France in 1769, at the time when the Middlesex Election had raised English politics to fever pitch, he lamented the Frenchman's lack of interest in such matters.[17] Yet he showed little inclination to become more directly involved himself and the temptation to read back into these years later views must be resisted. Painted by Joseph Wright of Derby in his Lichfield period, he appears in the predictable guise of a young searcher after truth; his pose elegant but casual, his manner serious, even abstracted. According to Anna Seward this portrait clearly displays the 'politics of the original'; the column on which Day leans is inscribed to Hampden and the book from which he reads is open at his oration against ship-money. The enthusiasm for Hampden is not implausible but there is in fact nothing in the two original versions of this portrait to substantiate it: the column is not inscribed and nothing connects the book with ship-money. More recently the critic of the slave trade has been glimpsed in Wright's portrayal, but there is no evidence that *The Dying Negro* was penned until 1773, three years after the painting was completed.[18]

II

All this was to change in the mid-1770s when Day was given an opportunity to apply his principles to political issues. There can be little question that this was a result of his immersion in the less elevated but equally passionate politics of the metropolis. Day had been entered at the Middle Temple Inn in 1765 but had shown little sign of pursuing his legal studies.[19] His residence was erratic, and though called to the Bar in 1779, he never practised. However, in terms of his political education, there is no doubt of the importance of his legal studies. The Inns constituted a kind of political hothouse in which the proximity of rabid City politics, the influence of a controversial London press, and the coming together of ambitious young men from diverse backgrounds, offered opportunities for ideological debate and activity which went far beyond what Day had experienced at Oxford or in Lichfield. A particularly volatile element in the chemistry of the Inns was the presence of young Americans receiving their legal education. Most of them were from Southern families of wealth and influence, and many of them were ill-disposed towards a government which had already during the Stamp Act crisis threatened to set America aflame from New Hampshire to Georgia. One, John Laurens, son of a prominent American merchant and patriot, struck up a close friendship with Day and the little group of old Charterhouse contemporaries and Oxford friends with whom he mixed, a friendship which was to have significant consequences later in Day's career.[20]

Appropriately for one of Day's sensibility, his political blooding took the refined form of a series of poems published between 1773 and 1777. All concerned the two great contemporary themes which cried out to friends of nature and humanity in the 1770s. The vision which they presented was not remarkable for its originality. His objections to slavery as unnatural, inhuman, and impious, were typical of the revulsion which swept over middle-class opinion at a time when the activities of Granville Sharp were bringing moral arguments against the slave trade before the public and the legal case against it before the law courts. His sympathy with 'the American cause, as the cause of human and of British liberty' was equally conventional.[21] In fact, the most striking feature of Day's work was the passion with which he invested it. The pathetic plight of the dying negro was evoked in powerful language which plainly expressed Day's disgust at the institution of which he was a victim. Similarly intemperate was the language of his *Fragment of an Original Letter on the Slavery of the Negroes*, a systematic denunciation of slavery which he did not publish until 1784, and in which slavery was described as a 'crime so monstrous against the human species that all those who practise it deserve to be extirpated from the earth'.[22] Those thus extirpated would have included many of the colonial sons of liberty whose own struggle against British oppression he so strongly supported. Like many of his contemporaries on both sides of the Atlantic, Day was shocked by the hypocrisy of men who demanded freedom for themselves but not for their dependents. Perhaps for this reason he preferred to concentrate on the folly and iniquity of America's oppressors rather than the justice and consistency of England's victims. His *Desolation of America* was the work of a sentimental pen. Violent and improbable scenes of horror, evoked with heavy-handed reliance on sexual pathos, offered a grim picture of the brutality of the British troops, 'cruel soldiers' wielding a 'reeking blade'. At the height of this effusion Day tested the poetic limits of his theme of outraged womanhood in the space of six lines:

> The cries of wretched mothers, that in vain
> Lament their fate, and mourn their children slain;
> The virgin's shriek, who trembling in the dust,
> Weeps the pollution of a ruffian's lust.
> The mangled infant's wail, that as he dies,
> Looks up in vain for pity to the skies.[23]

This order of poetic politics would not have raised Day to the first rank of radical writers. But with the appearance of something like a national reform movement at the close of the decade he was given an opportunity to develop a harder core of political commitment than the florid outpourings of the mid-1770s might have suggested. Like Sharp he could claim to have been drawn into the reform campaign by the twin causes of abolition and American liberty.[24] Like Sharp, too, he chose to exercise his talents outside Parliament, as a self-appointed tribune of the people rather than their elected representative. There is a plausible story that in the general election of 1780 he seriously considered standing for the borough of Southwark, but was deterred by the reflection that even in a populous and open constituency of this kind he would be compelled to adopt 'the common manners of the bought and buying tribe'.[25] An open invitation to accept a seat without expenditure was not forthcoming and his friends were left to lament his inability to 'plead the cause of America and Africa' in Parliament.[26] However, Day applied himself in the extra-parliamentary movement. He attended the Cambridgeshire meeting in March 1780, gave a powerful address to those present, and was elected to the committee formed to press the county's demands for reform. He repeated the performance in the county in which at this time he resided, Essex, and also appeared at the Berkshire meeting. At the same time he was a founder member of the Society for Constitutional Information, the most prominent of the radical clubs in the capital.[27] Land purchases in Surrey, where he was shortly to establish a new residence at Anningsley in Chertsey, brought an entrée to the most radical of the county committees outside London.[28] At the joint meeting of associated deputies which took place in the London Guildhall on 3 March 1781, he was one of five delegates from Surrey.[29] The names of the other four suggest something of the influence which Day exerted or perhaps the vitality which he displayed, given his lack of established authority and experience. Sir Francis Vincent was a former county MP of a well-known Surrey family; James Trecothick's father had sat in Parliament for the City of London and could fairly be described as a figure of national importance; John Budgen was the son of a Surrey knight of the shire and representative of a long-established gentry family; if the fourth, Mr Nicholls, was (as seems likely) John Nicholls of Ockley he was destined soon to become MP for Bletchingley and an influential member of the Foxite party. Compared with these, Thomas Day was indeed a parvenu whose sudden appearance suggests more than ordinary vigour. His interest in committee meetings lapsed soon afterwards, but there can be little question that continued commitment would have made him a substantial force in the reform movement.

Day saw himself in this period as a political philosopher of weight and originality; it is not a verdict supported by posterity, but his interests do reveal some of the most characteristic trends in the thought of his day. Insofar as his fundamental position can be identified it seems to have been a predictable late eighteenth-century version of Locke filtered through Rousseau. Twentieth-century scholarship has tended to diminish the role of Locke in eighteenth-century radicalism, but in the late 1770s his supposed function as the true progenitor of Whig constitutionalism was the subject of controversy. It is significant in this respect that the nearest Day came to a systematic exposition of the basis of his political thought was provoked by a powerful attack on Lockian principles made by the Dean of Gloucester, Josiah Tucker, in 1778. Tucker was well known as a controversialist, though his onslaught on Locke has rarely been remembered in Lockian scholarship. He evidently regarded it as an important and arduous undertaking himself, for it was initially published in a restricted edition which he sent to various friends for preliminary comment before he committed himself to a definitive statement of his views.[30] Day must have seen this first version for he told his friend Erasmus Darwin, junior, of his intention of confuting a work, 'written', he said, 'with all the contractedness, ignorance and dogmatical impertinence of an orthodox divine'.[31] In fact it was left to the radical Unitarian divine, Joseph Towers, to answer Tucker at length.[32] It is reasonable to suppose that Day would have known Towers, like himself a familiar figure in the metropolitan reform movement, whose pamphlet on the law of libel he recommended in his own *Dialogue* of 1785. He also included in the *Dialogue* a substantial section rebutting Tucker, a section which seems likely to represent the thoughts which he had originally intended to print as a separate work.[33]

Like Towers, Day's principal concern was to demolish the claim that government was founded on evolution rather than compact. Both admitted that it was unnecessary to prove the existence of an actual historical compact; the swelling body of contemporary evidence drawn from semi-anthropological descriptions of primitive peoples in remote parts of the globe made caution in this respect prudent. Even so, Day seems to have been reluctant to abandon the idea of such a formal arrangement. Three or four of the governments in the known world that were free (he presumably meant Britain, the United Provinces, and the United States of America) had such compacts in their recorded past even if (a hit at Britain) they chose to deny it.[34] The same stress on contract emerges from the four letters which Day's nephew, Thomas Lowndes, published in 1806 and in the *Fragment of an Original Letter on the Slavery of the Negroes*.[35] Such explicit consent on the part of the governed he saw as the only acceptable basis of legitimacy, by contrast with Tucker's belief in prescription. Towers had stressed this point. 'The great aim of Dean Tucker's book seems to be, to support ancient systems because they are so.'[36] Interest in prescription is an obvious and outstanding feature of late eighteenth-century thought. Hume (whom Day condemned for his intellectual treachery in this respect), had admitted its legitimizing effect, Tucker made great play with it, and Paley and Burke were to draw it into the forefront of political debate.[37] For Day it was altogether inadmissible when set against the great principles of politics. 'There can be no prescription pleaded against truth and justice.'[38] At issue, of course, was the threat to natural rights theory posed by those like Tucker, who argued for the essentially 'natural' quality of even corrupt and inequitable systems of government. For Day as an enthusiastic reader of Locke, Rousseau and Price, the subject possessed an inalienable right to change a government which abused its authority, a right based on the ultimately consensual relationship of ruler and ruled. The citizen owed obedience, he remarked, in a revealing set of analogies, in the same way that a sick man owed obedience to his physician, a traveller to his guide, a mariner to his pilot; that is to say, in the spirit of a necessary but revocable trust which could be cancelled the moment it was considered to be exercised against the interest of its beneficiary.[39] With this went a typically late eighteenth-century suspicion of the very nature of government, a suspicion which was to reach its fullest expression from the pen of Godwin, and which even in Day's writings suggested an extreme distaste for the business of ruling men. 'A government signifies a certain set of men, that whenever they please hang up all their neighbours, burn their houses, eat their victuals without paying, and kick their breech to warm themselves in cold weather.'[40] Day believed that government in his own day was becoming ever more interventionist, particularly in respect of the manifold taxes and associated sanctions introduced. 'The most innocent, the most necessary actions of life, are made the subjects of penalties and prohibitions.'[41] The last decades of the eighteenth century are not generally seen in such a light; but Day's very concern on this point is itself strong evidence of the naive individualism and optimism which marked the progress of liberal economics. His *Letter to Arthur Young* stressed the 'natural rights of all the species, that of selling the produce of his labour to the best advantage'.[42] Placed alongside a matching faith in the 'natural, eternal, unalienable rights of the species' to a free choice of government, a matter on which Day approvingly quoted the testimony of his friend William Jones, it is not difficult to see what economic tendencies such a vision of liberated man would have encouraged.[43]

Behind this scepticism about the inevitable propensities of government there lay, of course, a mass of assumptions, the most important of them drawn directly from Rousseau, whose *Emile* was cited by Day as the most valuable book after the Bible.[44] Day was a thoroughgoing individualist, envisaging social harmony as a virtually lost cause in the contemporary world; 'every numerous society is but an assemblage of jarring interests'.[45] His psychological theory, if banal, fitted neatly. He saw life as a constant battle between reason (especially his own) and folly (that of his fellow human beings). He sought 'some principle fixed and unchangeable in its own nature, never fluctuating with eternal accidents, nor governed by the opinion of others. That principle was Reason; leaving the Multitude to steer their course by the weathercocks of Fashion, and Custom, I resolved to pursue the determinations of common sense.'[46] This faith in reason was given free rein in the poems, sometimes with aerial metaphors (in his own epitaph, originally written for his mentor, William Small, he rises on reason's boldest wings) sometimes with much emphasis on the uncomplicated nature of 'reason's plain and simple way'.[47] Irrational social conventions came in for predictable censure. In the pieces published after Day's death by his nephew, there is a mock 'Trial of A.B. in the High Court of Fashion' satirizing the absurdities of taste.[48] The natural life of less artificial beings was also praised in appropriate terms, particularly when it was soundly based on those instincts which were intended by the Law of Nature as the true guides of human conduct.[49] No doubt there was in much of this a youthful enthusiasm for newly fashionable ideas. Actual acquaintance with the natural state could be disillusioning. It is difficult after a reading of Day's passionate platitudes not to relish the slightly malicious tone of Edgeworth's account of Day's first encounter with Irish peasants. 'Mr Day's deep-seated prejudice in favour of savage life was somewhat shaken by this view of want and misery.'[50] At this stage in his life he was cultivating a neglect of social arts and manners which proved far in advance of what most of his contemporaries found engaging, as Edgeworth's story of his father's response to his eccentric friend testifies.[51] A short-lived attempt to adjust this posture, brought about by disappointment in love, seems merely to have made him more ludicrous than ever.[52] Day's fundamental faith in artlessness was never really abandoned. His years of withdrawal at Anningsley in the 1780s were marked by sobriety, solitude and scepticism, and make clear the extent of his hostility to conventional living. *Sandford and Merton*, written during this period, has frequent observations in tune with such hostility, ranging from derisive mockery of Ranelagh, to a citation of Red Indians as examples of 'the savage grandeur of man in his most simple state'.[53]

Distrust of government fitted readily into the individualist framework of the late Enlightenment. But in the case of Day and many other English radicals it also had distinctively English undertones. If the British constitution seemed weak when judged by the eternal principles of nature, it could also be shown to have flimsy historical credentials. In this respect the slogans of the parliamentary opposition to government in the 1760s and 1770s can be misleading. The so-called Toryism of the new king and his ministers was doubtless the object of much loathing, but it did not follow that their predecessors on the throne and in office were better loved. Only parliamentary Whigs fully subscribed to the belief that Whig government before 1760 had been mild, benevolent and libertarian. For others the history of governments from the Glorious Revolution was at best a catalogue of missed opportunities, at worst something much more sinister. What had been erected since 1688 was, in Day's view, not a reformed system of government, but a 'new fabrick of oppression'.[54] His litany of grievances, recited in one of the speeches which he made at county meetings in 1780 and reiterated in his *Dialogue* of 1785, included the game laws, the Riot Act of 1715, the repeated extension of excises, the standing army, the Triennial as well as Septennial Act, the ever-growing National Debt (squandered on futile foreign adventures) and the gradual elimination of legal safeguards for the Englishman's liberty, including the alleged restriction of jury rights in libel cases.[55] This list of misdeeds closely resembled the criticisms of old-style Tory and country opposition in earlier reigns. In fact it was very similar to the last great Tory protest under George II, John Shebbeare's *Letters to the People of England*, the publication of which had led in 1758 to Shebbeare's punishment and stigmatization as a Jacobite.[56]

There were intriguing ironies here; Day's own forebears were of impeccably Whig background. His father had held the lucrative post of Deputy Collector (Outwards) of Customs in the Port of London, and the fortune which now made Day independent had been accumulated by an enthusiastic supporter of successive Whig regimes. Thomas Day senior, the son of a Huntingdonshire draper, had been brought up to serve the great ducal house of Manchester whose seat lay in his native parish of Kimbolton.[57] He had acted as the financial adviser and agent of two successive Dukes, the second and third, and as trustee of the former's will had laboured long over its complex financial provisions and suffered much indignity at the hands of the second duke's unmanageable widow, the Dowager Duchess.[58] His own post in the customs was held from the

Dukes who possessed a hereditary patent to the Office of Collector Outwards but much of the substantial wealth which he acquired must have derived from his involvement in Manchester family affairs, and more particularly from the considerable sums of money which his patrons placed in his hands.[59] If ever a family's fortune was made from the patronage of Whig oligarchs, it was that of the Days. Yet the son was unforgiving in his resentment at seeing 'the very man that had deposed one king for attempting to invade their liberties, resigning their liberties, without a struggle, to his successor; and founding the public security upon the glorious basis of mercenary troops, a national debt and general corruption'.[60] The note of bitterness, even of personal betrayal, which can be found in such a denunciation is perhaps significant, for it represents the attitude of many who felt that the inheritance of Hampden and Sidney had been abused. Jebb, another radical son of a conventional Whig, confessed that he actually found Tories less objectionable than certain Whigs: 'Prostitute Whigs offend me more, and the slumbering Whigs most of all'.[61] Such attitudes had considerable play in the radical movement and did a good deal to weaken its prospects of success in cooperation with milder men.

Initially Day was more or less prepared to take the parliamentary Whigs at their own value. In his *Ode for the New Year*, 1776, he praised a string of Whigs: Richmond, Savile, Camden, Chatham, Sir Charles Saunders, and most of all the defenders of the Hanoverian Whig tradition, 'Mild, but determin'd, Rockingham', and 'Burke ... great exemplar in a venal age'.[62] But this faith in parliamentary Whiggism did not last long. It was a standard radical fear from the time of the Middlesex Election that the campaign against influence and corruption might well succeed in reducing the power of the Crown without giving power to the people. In 1770 when Burke put forward the classic defence of mainstream Whiggism in his *Thoughts on the Causes of the Present Discontents*, Catherine Macaulay had claimed that the true beneficiaries of Burke's politics would be a selfish aristocratic clique dominated by his friend Rockingham. Such fears were magnified by the obvious gulf which separated the Rockingham Whigs from the metropolitan radicals. When the Association movement emerged in 1779–80, most of Rockingham's energies seemed devoted to restraining the enthusiasm and supposed extremism of the extra-parliamentary agitators. The consequent tensions brought forth renewed complaints. For the Society of Constitutional Information, William Jones warned lest 'by reducing the Regal power to its just level we raise the Aristocratical to a dangerous height'.[63] By this time Day had entered fully into the campaign against overmighty subjects. 'I have never yet heard of an aristocracy, from ancient Rome to modern Venice, that was not the universal tyrant and inquisitor of the species.'[64] Again there are hints of a personal sensitivity in this, and the possibility that his family background added a certain zest to his denunciation of aristocracy. According to Maria Edgeworth he found the minor misfortunes of the great peculiarly humorous and would have enjoyed nothing more than the sight of the daughter of a duchess falling from her horse and soiling her dress.[65] In *Sandford and Merton* he described rank as a regrettable necessity in popular societies and thought anyone who enjoyed it should 'plainly prove, by the courtesy and benevolence of his manners, that he laments the necessity of his own elevation; and instead of wishing to mount still higher, would willingly descend nearer to an equality with his fellow creatures'.[66] There is a story that he declined to attend one of the county meetings of 1780 on the grounds that it had been summoned in too high a style by a great magnate.[67] Certainly he seems to have been somewhat inhibited by the presence of such magnates. The two speeches which the Society of Constitutional Information published as his are distinctly dissimilar in tone. At Cambridge in March 1780, in the presence of many lords, including the current representative of the Montagus of Kimbolton, the fourth Duke of Manchester, he was noticeably less intemperate than at Essex in April where those present were commoners. As for the parliamentary Whigs, events seemed designed to confirm his revulsion against them. The detested coalition between Fox and North in 1783 was one of the main targets in the *Letters of Marius*, and the great exemplar Burke was now roundly denounced for his excessive attachment to hereditary principles and his absurd flights of fancy.[68] All this was a long way from the fawning dependence of the 'officier class' of early Hanoverian England, but in its main features it was not untypical of the revolt of enraged young Whigs against the political assumptions and conformity of their fathers.

Day's accusations against the inconstancy of previous generations of Whigs fitted well with the high importance which he attached to consistency of principle and purpose. In the guise of *Marius* he confessed to 'have a kind of antiquated prejudice in favour of consistency'.[69] In the sense that his views changed little over the years he was certainly entitled to make a claim of this kind. But in the sense that his views were internally coherent and consistent it is more doubtful. The fashionable creed which he adopted in the 1760s embraced many potential contradictions. A fair test of Day's standpoint in this respect and one on which he must be convicted, concerns his attitude towards women. The absurdity of female fashions was a favourite grievance of sentimental philosophers, for nothing, from a masculine point of view, seemed to embody so completely the artificiality and frivolity of contemporary society. Rousseau was only the most famous of those who identified their corrosive effect on human relationships. Modern marriage, it was commonly complained, was damned by its dependence on pin-money and jointures, and the consequent materialism which it induced. This view, emphasized heavily by Rousseau's English disciples, including, most notably, Henry Mackenzie in his influential *Man of Feeling*, was shared by Day.[70] In France he complained bitterly of the 'unnatural dominion' of French women with their obsession with fashion, in his essays he repeated the charge against English women and, of course, in *Sandford and Merton*, the opportunity was taken to inculcate contempt for such fripperies.[71] Like others he saw the root cause of this 'empire of fashion over the minds of women' in the vicious nature of contemporary education, and especially in the vogue for boarding schools, which seemed designed to turn out women fit only to be sold in the marriage market.[72] Education of this kind was inevitably at the expense of the sentimental virtues. 'A polite education may be considered as a species of inoculation, which effectually prevents the fair patient from feeling any subsequent attack of shame or tranquility during the rest of her life.'[73] If the diagnosis was a commonplace one, Day's own antidote would not have gained universal approval. His conception of female perfection was domestic, stressing above all the narrow circle of the wife and mother's proper duties, and her utter subjection to paternal authority. Even freedom of expression was frowned upon. The contemporary trend towards female authorship, perhaps one of the more liberating of mid-eighteenth century literary developments, he particularly disliked for its tendency to diminish a woman's essential quality of softness and to divert her from her proper duties.[74] This involved a high view of male prerogatives but Day certainly pursued it consistently. A principal objection which Honora Sneyd, one of the Lichfield sisters who successively rejected Day and married his friend Edgeworth, made to him as a suitor was his low opinion of women's rights; it was also apparently his ward Sabrina's incomplete submission to his will in a trivial matter which finally determined him against marrying her.[75] Long after his death Sabrina embarrassed Maria Edgeworth by alleging that Day had treated her like a slave.[76]

The marriage which he did eventually make, to Esther Milnes, daughter of a wealthy Derbyshire businessman, was contracted only after the most intensive process of scrutiny on this score. By all accounts the marriage itself was marked by the most thoroughgoing imposition of his views on his wife.[77] This patronizing view of the role of women hardly seems compatible with the urgent pleas made in the cause of equality for the entire human species. But if Day's views were characteristically extreme his basic inconsistency was not uncommon. It was one of Tucker's most effective arguments against the new Lockians that every argument which they used in favour of mass political rights applied equally to women.[78] Towers was reduced to admitting the claim but asserting that women's 'fibres' were not suitable for the hurry and bustle of parliamentary elections.[79] What Day would have said is not known, but when he attacked Burke for denying the electoral rights of seven million Britons, he was implicitly asserting the political claims of women.[80] It is difficult to believe that he meant this seriously. Certainly in his own rebuttal of Tucker's arguments he left the jibe unanswered.

Tensions of this kind derived partly from unresolved contradictions within sentimental politics and partly from the obvious difficulty of translating abstract principles into a precise formulation of objectives. This was not merely a matter of impractical approach. Day himself was plainly unsuited to the flexible tactical requirements of the party politician. But he did show some readiness to compromise in particular exigencies. He was certainly more adaptable than some of his friends in the metropolitan radical movement, and went out of his way to try and secure something from the wreck of the association movement after 1782. Though he had largely withdrawn from active participation as a county delegate he returned in May 1785 to the great meeting of reformers held in London shortly before the Younger Pitt put his celebrated motion for parliamentary reform before the House of Commons. Against friends like Jebb and Budgen who demanded the ideological purity of unwavering commitment to the Foxite programme, Day spoke strongly, and according to Christopher Wyvill 'with much force of eloquence' in favour of united support for any plausible proposal, whatever its source.[81] He showed some contempt for those, like his old friend John Jebb, who had unrealistic expectations of government: 'I am not myself such a child as either to expect or wish that all government should stand still in such a wonderfully complicated system of society as our own, in order that two or three reformers may try their skill in greasing the wheels.'[82] Nonetheless, there was a notable lack of definition in Day's own views in this respect. When attacking the absurdities of the existing system of parliamentary representation he spoke in terms which suggested the desirability of universal suffrage. At other times he thought that annual parliaments were more important.[83] Again he declared on one occasion that the most effective reform would be the adoption of single member constituencies of equal size with provision for a secret ballot, though as he admitted, 'this the Country Gentleman will never consent to'.[84] His own summary of his opinions is a candid one: 'Though I have always gone with those that asked the most, I have never formed any precise idea of what alteration would be best.'[85]

III

On America at least he seemed less uncertain, and in some respects the *Reflexions* which he published in October 1782 was his most plausible and effective piece of political writing. His first biographer, James Keir, thought it 'undoubtedly one of the best political productions in our language', a high claim but one which at least implies that he saw it as Day's best 'political production'.[86] But like his contributions to the debate on reform it was strongest when based on general grounds. His arguments were simple; independence after a disastrously unsuccessful war must be conceded, not merely because the war had been waged in an immoral cause, but because it was required to restore England's moral credibility in Europe, to divide her enemies, to sustain friendly trading relationships with America in future, and to make possible a reduction in the crushing burden of war debts. Of specific recommendations on the complex issues which beset the peace negotiations – mercantile debts, treatment of loyalists, and the question of future boundaries – there were none. Worse, the central strategy of the *Reflexions* was misconceived. Though Day believed that the Shelburne Ministry was preparing to continue the war, anyone with internal information or even diplomatic judgement would have grasped that the recognition of independence was inevitable. What was at issue in the tortuous negotiations of 1782 was the timing of such recognition, since on it depended much of the haggling with America's allies over British possessions in other parts of the world. The most generous explanation of Day's unsophisticated demand for outright recognition is that he sincerely supported independence and genuinely feared that a British government might be tempted by the unpopularity of peace into a last desperate endeavour to recover the colonies. A less charitable interpretation would be that he was duped by his American friends in London into attempting to increase public pressure on British negotiators. The point is a small one since not even they can have imagined that Day had very much influence on public opinion. It does, however, matter for an understanding of Day's position.

Certainly Day enjoyed a close relationship with some of the American community in London. He was present at tactical meetings held by Edward Bridgen, a prominent London merchant who acted as a forwarding agent for American correspondents and was himself active as Treasurer of the Society for Constitutional Information. These meetings were viewed with suspicion by at least one of Day's friends, who later advised him 'never to let these men have any further hold on his writings'.[87] In these complex manoeuvrings an important element was Day's relationship with Henry Laurens, whose mission as an authorized envoy for the United States had been interrupted by his capture at sea and imprisonment in the Tower of London. Day knew Laurens well through his friendship with Laurens' son, John. The latter's death in battle in 1782 deeply affected Day and doubtless drew him closer to the father. Through 1782 and 1783, while Laurens was being released on parole and then permitted to take his place among his country's negotiators, Day was in close touch with him. This does not make him a pawn of Laurens; the latter expressed some small reservations about what he called Day's 'little Tract', the *Reflexions*.[88] Even so there is no doubt that Day's line of argument was very close to that of Laurens, and that Laurens gave him much information concerning the negotiations in Paris. Laurens' own position at this time was a difficult one, and involved him in sometimes acrimonious exchanges with compatriots. But he himself believed that he had played an important part in convincing Englishmen of the need for an early peace.[89] Day can have had little real appreciation of the complexities in which he was concerning himself by his intrigues. Perhaps his very naivety assisted him: his *Reflexions* were unusual among such publications in appearing with his name on the title page. In any event it is scarcely surprising in retrospect that his new career as a controversialist proved less successful than he had planned. His belief in 'one great truth which is enough for a statesman to know' that 'moral honesty is the only support of public liberty' was hardly an adequate basis for a distinctive contribution to political analysis and debate.[90]

If imprecision and naivety were inherent tendencies in a sentimental politician, there was a further aspect of his attitudes which was even more damaging. This was the extreme pessimism which succeeded all too naturally to the high expectations of his youth. From 1782 Day's vision was an increasingly dark one. In Britain, though independence was duly conceded and a tolerable peace negotiated, though the hated Fox-North coalition was decisively defeated, he could discern no fundamental improvement: 'Our ministers as dishonest, our people as foolish, our parliament as venal and our burthens more heavy than ever.'[91] Pitt's early years in office seemed merely to add further to the growing mountain of debts and taxes. Across the Atlantic the infant republic in which so many Whiggish hopes had been invested was already causing disquiet. Even before the Peace was formally concluded Day thought he could see in the young Americans coming to London, 'more proper materials for making petit maitres than republicans', and confessed to long-standing doubts about American virtue.[92] To Richard Price he was equally disparaging about the 'Western genius' of American poets.[93] From his West Indian friend Walter Pollard, whom he had despatched to make his fortune in Virginia, came a stream of reports concerning the cynicism and corruption of public life in the new United States. Old friends, it seemed, were fast becoming enemies. Henry Laurens had taken back to America an epitaph for his son penned by Day, but thereafter their correspondence ceased. According to Day's widow this rift was felt deeply by her husband in his later years.[94] As for Day himself, his life was increasingly one of morose withdrawal. To Christopher Wyvill, leader of the Yorkshire Association and a tireless champion of reform even in the dog-days of the mid-1780s, he offered only such assistance as could be given without much mixing with others, and confessed 'my great aversion to all Public Dinners, Assizes, Elections, Justice-Meetings, and every other kind of Meeting by which Country Gentlemen in general eat and drink themselves into popularity'.[95] He plainly saw himself as a Cincinnatus, returned to a barren but not unfriendly soil where he could brood over the ingratitude of the society which he had so nobly served. 'To solitude indignant I retire, and leave the world to parasites and kings.'[96]

In such a state, asylum in the New World seemed an obvious possibility. 'I have several times felt the strongest impulse to join the American cause, while the American cause was doubtful: and I should have felt no remorse in fighting under the banners of such a cause. But what might have been noble then, may not be becoming now.'[97] The best that could be done was to cultivate lonely indifference: 'it was impossible for me to imitate the rest of the world, what mattered it whether the world imitated me'.[98] In the *Letter to Arthur Young*, his last attempt to influence public affairs, the rage was still there but only accentuated by the hopelessness and despair which went with it.

Neurotic though Day's disillusionment with the world may seem, it was arguably the inevitable destination of the sentimental voyage on which he had embarked as a young enthusiast for Rousseau 20 years before. Even in its most personal manifestation, his relationships with his friends, the extent to which extreme disappointment followed from extreme initial optimism is obvious. He was complaining about most of them by the 1780s. Not merely Laurens, but some of his oldest friends including William Jones, by then a distinguished judge in India, were accused of neglect. Unfortunately none of Day's friendships is adequately documented by surviving evidence, though Edgeworth's occasionally caustic recollections are suggestive. Only the letters of Walter Pollard provide anything like a continuous contemporary record, even if they are not made easier to interpret by Pollard's own failings.[99] Pollard was a young Barbadian whose family lost most of its property in the twin disasters of the American war and a Caribbean hurricane, and who took up the law to 'subsist by his industry and virtuous exertions'.[100] In fact he proved most successful at sponging on better-placed or more industrious friends; his benefactors included not only Day and William Jones (who probably introduced him to Day), but two young aristocrats, the future third Earl of Hardwicke and the future first Marquess of Abercorn. After Day's death he even drew on his widow.[101] His correspondence with Day is perhaps not least significant for the language of sentiment in which it was couched and in which these earnest young men had evidently learned to express themselves. His own torpor and feebleness he explained by reference to the overwhelming power of his feelings. 'I suffer from a sensibility of heart which perhaps is more than common ... I have given everything to sentiment and affection, within the bounds of honour'.[102] In return Day confided his growing despair of his friends. 'The behavior of almost all our fellow creatures is so unaccountable .... All the real, disinterested friendship in the world may be compressed into a surprisingly small compass.'[103] Privately Pollard may have had misgivings about such statements, for friendship with Day could be painful. He had himself been practically forced on board a boat for America in consequence of Day's desire to rescue him from a useless life of idleness and debt. 'The friend', he subsequently lamented, 'was benevolent, but the monitor was harsh. He could not brooke that a Man well educated should exist in such a place as London, without ostensible means of exertion; his austere system of life despised and suspected all such Characters.'[104] It was perhaps the rigour of Day's friendship as much as the ingratitude of his friends which led to eventual disillusionment; like the poor of Anningsley who were apparently insufficiently grateful for Day's benefactions,[105] they did not always fully appreciate his benevolence.

Gloom pervaded more than Day's friendships, however. For built into the sentimental vision of his youth was much underlying pessimism about the political prospects of mankind. The historical certainty of decay and decline was an article of faith for many believers in Enlightenment. 'Either all past experience is vain, or when the fruit is mellow it will not long want a hand to shake it from the bough', Day wrote shortly before his death.[106] Much depended, of course, on one's judgement as to the timing of this process. It was axiomatic that so far as western civilization was concerned the very process of commercial growth and sophistication which marked the emergence from barbarism was destined to corrupt and destroy its beneficiaries. Day's remarks on this point could have been drawn straight from Millar or Fergusson:

> When particularly favourable circumstances acting upon the savage tribes of the human species, force it to develop those faculties which produce arts, sciences, civilisation, commerce, and dominion, effeminacy, an inordinate love of sensuality, a dread of labour and danger, and an indifference to the public cause will necessarily follow with rapid steps; from this moment everything is upon the decline.[107]

In his *Letter to Arthur Young* Day commented on the inevitable advance of this historical process, likening it to a 'gentle river' which began by dispensing fertility, in due course became a 'salutary inundation' repaying the damage which it did, and eventually appeared as an 'impetuous torrent' bearing away 'liberty, public spirit, and every manly virtue'.[108] By the time that he was writing the *Letter to Arthur Young* Day was evidently convinced that the process was far advanced in England. Woollen manufacturers seeking to preserve their monopoly of English wool supplies were placed in the same category of wickedness as merchants in the slave trade; the Englishman's burden of debt, taxation and corruption clearly suggested that 'successful commerce and accumulated riches have long been spreading a secret corrosive poison, through every class of society; inflaming the wants, enervating the manners, and diminishing the public spirit of all'.[109] Day took this analysis of the ills of society seriously. His land purchases at Chertsey in 1779–80, which eventually led him to take up residence there in the house at Anningsley, were apparently made with funds withdrawn from investments in government stock and signified his belief that the vast edifice of national debt erected since the Revolution was at last about to come crashing down.[110] In one of his public speeches at this time he bitterly denounced the irresponsibility of a Parliament which had raised the burden of taxation far beyond what the nation could bear.[111] Though he firmly placed what little remaining faith he had in land and the rural economy he had nothing but contempt for the landed classes of his own day; he saw only clergy bent on 'decimat[ing] their agriculture, without performing in person a single duty of their office', and country squires concerned to 'preserve the breed of pointers by wholesale statutes, and defend their manors and their fishponds with all the artillery of penal laws'.[112] What remained beyond a last feeble attempt 'to retain a remnant of the liberties handed down by my ancestors, and to avoid being enslaved by croppers, combers, and pedlars?'[113] Such laments belonged, of course, to a long tradition of patriotic scepticism and conventional 'country' philosophy; but on this reading of recent history Day's brief political career had coincided with the decisive crisis of Anglo-Saxon civilization. He had first expressed his views on these matters at the start of the American war, itself the crucial evidence of England's descent into the abyss. There was certainly nothing original in his belief that over-extended empires were themselves the cause of decay nor in his conviction that Roman history offered clear hints as to the fate awaiting Britain. His poem *The Devoted Legions* (1776) did, however, make the connection particularly explicit. British troops were depicted as the natural successors of Crassus' ill-fated expedition against the Parthians, doomed to defend a corrupt empire and perish in the attempt. In Britain as in the Roman Republic in its last days, 'all reverence to the ancient discipline or institutions, seems to have been totally lost; all ranks of men rushed headlong into the most profligate luxury: the only contest between Patricians and Plebians, was, who should be the most corrupt; and the public Liberty, as might be expected, was abandoned to every invader'. The imperial threat to liberty remained strong in Day's mind; as late as 1783 he was arguing for the return of Gibraltar to Spain, on the grounds that the British were much too heavily committed in their endeavours to maintain a far-flung empire.[114]

## IV

How representative were such views? There were, of course, those who argued that after the successes of the Seven Years War Britain in the 1770s was on the brink of true greatness. Political economists such as John Campbell drew nothing but comfort from surveys of the economic strength of the mother country and its empire; a poet such as William Julian Mickle could offer in the *Lusiad* an extraordinary vision of the future growth and prosperity of the British Empire, not in conflict with liberty but sustained by it.[115] But among intellectuals such optimism was rare and among radical critics of contemporary politics and ethics Day's doctrines would have seemed curious only perhaps for the fervour with which they were expressed. For the inheritors of Rousseau's ideological bequest political commitment meant a perpetual but unequal struggle, corruption and decay being the inevitable victors. The cyclical view of history which this assumed may have owed much to Montesquieu, as they frequently claimed, but the moral pessimism was equally certainly Rousseau's. 'In a very few centuries', Day predicted, 'the whole civilized part of the species will have entirely lost the idea of a public cause'.[116] In the progress of luxury and commercialism which threatened virtue there was only the slender hope that the long decline might be arrested by a return to first principles. Day fiercely defended Rousseau for his apparently crude atavism, and for the alleged absurdity of his faith in nature. A perpetual political infancy was the logical programme of the rational politician: 'these observations may to thinking men perhaps apologize for Rousseau even in some of his greatest paradoxes as they are commonly called'.[117] What then was the role of such a politician in an increasingly corrupt society? Like the poet, it seems, he could only warn; but this was a sacred duty and one which Day saw as his true function. His statement on this point says much about the mentality of well-intentioned patriots in such an age:

If it is destined, by the inexplicable wisdom of Providence, that no climate shall be sacred from tyranny; if arts and civilisation, in their progress round the globe, have a natural tendency to debase the minds of the many, while they enlighten the understandings of the few, the term of political duration is at least no more fixed than the period of natural existence. Wisdom and courage may extend the date of freedom, as much as ignorance and pusillanimity may abridge it. But in order to defend our rights it is necessary that we understand their origin, and comprehend their extent. The first honour belongs indeed to the citizen whose successful valour opposes oppression in the field, and represses its encroachments; but neither is his merit small, who awakes his countrymen to the consideration of the most important questions, who exposes the artifices of sophistry, and defends from fraud and undermining the sacred fabric of human rights, and public liberty.[118]

What Day would have thought of that new and unexpected dawn for jaded radicals, the French Revolution, will never be known. He might have made an English Incorruptible, or he might have retreated into the dark pessimism which afflicted many of his generation after the Terror. He died in September 1789 before the Revolution was really under way. He was wrong about his death as about much else, for he had forecast a long life for himself, observing to Edgeworth in 1773 that he was 'destined, perhaps, to become very old, because I am very indifferent about the matter'.[119] His death was caused by a fall from a pony, and was said to have been brought about by a characteristically sentimental method of horse-breaking. Celebrated in bad verse by the Poet Laureate Henry James Pye, he left a reputation for invincible high-mindedness.[120] Edgeworth called him 'the man of the most perfect morality, whom I have ever known'; Wyvill thought that 'Rome in her best age could not have produced a Citizen more firm, more intrepid, more high-minded'.[121] In these respects he was doubtless exceptional. Yet his aspirations were those of his age and his failings those of contemporary intellectual fashion. If the prospects of reform in late eighteenth-century England depended on such a political *Man of Feeling*, they were remote indeed.

NOTES

\* I am grateful to Dr Marilyn Butler for reading and commenting on this piece.
1. The fullest biography is G. W. Gignilliat, *The Author of Sandford and Merton: A Life of Thomas Day, Esq.* (New York, 1932). Sir S. H. Scott's *The Exemplary Mr Day 1748–1789, Author of Sandford and Merton* (London, 1935), is essentially interpretative. More recent works which have added to our knowledge of Day are, most notably, R. E. Schofield, *The Lunar Society of Birmingham* (Oxford, 1963); M. Butler, *Maria Edgeworth: A Literary Biography* (Oxford, 1972); R. Lonsdale, 'Dr Burney, "Joel Collier", and Sabrina' in R. Wellek and A. Ribeiro (eds.), *Evidence in Literary Scholarship: Essays in Memory of James Marshall Osborn* (Oxford, 1979).
2. C. Colvin (ed.), *Maria Edgeworth: Letters from England 1813–1844* (Oxford, 1971) 121; National Library of Ireland, Edgeworth MSS, Sabrina Bicknell to Maria Edgeworth. 2 October. 1817.

3. *Memoirs of Richard Lovell Edgeworth, Esq.* (2nd edn., 2 vols., London, 1821) ii. 100.
4. It is also possible that some of the material published by the Society for Constitutional Information during these years should be credited to Day. The Society's *Second Address to the Public from the Society for Constitutional Information* (London, 1780) is one such candidate for inclusion among his works. See E.C. Black, *The Association: British Extra-parliamentary Political Organisation, 1769–1793* Cambridge, Mass., 1963) 185 and C. Benwick, *English Radicals and the American Revolution* (Chapel Hill, 1963) 320.
5. A. Seward, *Memoirs of the Life of Dr Darwin* (London, 1804) 19-20; *The Poetical Works of the late Mrs. Mary Robinson* (3 vols., London, 1806) i. 24.
6. R. Lonsdale, 'Dr Burney, "Joel Collier", and Sabrina' offers the most complete account by far of Day's collaboration with Bicknell, not merely in the composition of *The Dying Negro*, but also in revisions of Bicknell's satirical sally against Charles Burney, Joel Colliers' *Musical Travels Through England*, originally published in 1774.
7. *Edgeworth Memoirs*, i. 99.
8. William Gilmore Simms Collection of Laurens Papers, Kendal Whaling Museum, Sharon, Massachusetts (hereafter cited as Kendal Collection), 5 Jan. 1783.
9. *Letters of Anna Seward* (6 vols., Edinburgh, 1811), ii. 331.
10. *Edgeworth Memoirs*, ii. 76-7.
11. T. Fowler, *Corpus Christi* (London, 1898) Chap. X.
12. D.A. Winstanley, *The University of Cambridge in the Eighteenth Century* (Cambridge, 1922) 56ff.
13. *The Letters of Marius* (2nd edn., London, 1784) 19-20.
14. T. Lowndes, *Select Miscellaneous Productions of Mrs Day and Thomas Day, Esq.* (London, 1805) 107; cf. J. Disney, *The Works Theological, Medical, Political, and Miscellaneous of John Jebb, M.D., F.R.S.* (3 vols., London, 1787) i. 15.
15. See R.E. Schofield, *The Lunar Society of Birmingham*.
16. Ibid. 54.
17. *Edgeworth Memoirs*, i. 218.
18. B. Nicolson, *Joseph Wright of Derby, Painter of Light* 2 vols., London, 1968) i. 102, who suggests that Anna Seward was in fact describing an engraving. The association with the abolitionist cause is also postulated by Nicolson.
19. *Register of Admissions to the Honourable Society of the Middle Temple*, i. 363. He seems to have begun keeping his terms in 1768, though his residence must have been very spasmodic. After being called in 1779, he kept chambers, purely for convenience.
20. It will eventually be possible to follow their relationship through to its conclusion in the published *Papers of Henry Laurens*. The editors have kindly permitted me to consult transcripts of the MS correspondence between Day and Henry Laurens. I am grateful to them and in particular to Professor G.C. Rogers for providing me with this facility.
21. Kendal Collection, Day to Laurens, 29 June 1783.
22. p.24. See also *Select Miscellaneous Productions*, 91-101.
23. *The Desolation of America: A Poem* (London, 1777) 10, 19.
24. Prince Hoare, *Memoirs of Granville Sharp* (London, 1820) 191.
25. Gignilliat, 192; J. Keir, *An Account of the Life and Writings of Thomas Day, Esq.* (London, 1791) 122-3.
26. J. Keir, *An Account*, 63; T. Lowndes, *Tracts, Political and Miscellaneous, in Prose and Verse* (2 vols., London, 1825-7) ii. 324.
27. The Society published two of Day's speeches, at the Cambridgeshire and Essex meetings: *Two Speeches of Thomas Day* (London, 1780). Another of his Essex speeches was published with one of Fox's; see The Speech of the Honourable Charles James Fox; Delivered at Westminster, on Wednesday, February 2, 1780 (London [1780]).
28. The precise date of the move to Anningsley is not certain. Day was resident there from the spring of 1781 but he was also receiving letters at his Essex home, Stapleford Abbots, as late as September 1783. However, the Surrey land purchases, beginning in June 1779, can be followed in deeds among the Lowndes-Norton Papers at Surrey Record Office, 300/6, and also in British Library, eg. MS. 2651, f.212.
29. C. Wyvill, *Political Papers* (6 vols., York, 1794–1802) i. 384.
30. *The Notions of Mr Locke and his Followers ... considered* (Gloucester, 1778). The full dress version was published as *A Treatise concerning Civil Government* (London, 1781). It is partly reprinted in R.L. Schuyler, *Josiah Tucker: A Selection from His*

*Economic and Political Writings* (New York, 1931).
31. British Library, Add. MS. 29300, f.57: 29 Jan. 1779.
32. J. Towers, *A Vindication of the Political Principles of Mr Locke* (London, 1782).
33. *A Dialogue between a Justice of the Peace and a Farmer* (3rd edn., London, 1786) 93ff.
34. *Dialogue*, 108.
35. *Select Miscellaneous Productions*, 182-204.
36. J. Towers, *Vindication*, 95.
37. *Select Miscellaneous Productions*, 193. Day faithfully mirrored the attitude of the metropolitan radicals in this as in so much else. Towers not only published their 'official' reply to Tucker but also took Hume to task in print for the illiberal politics displayed in his *History of England*. See J. Towers, *Observations on Mr Hume's History of England* (London, 1778).
38. *Fragment*, 35.
39. *Select Miscellaneous Productions*, 183.
40. *Dialogue*, 78-9.
41. *A Letter to Arthur Young*, 32.
42. p.18; Day's contempt for protectionism in the shape of the Navigation Acts is suggested by *Reflections*, 26.
43. *Dialogue*, 110, 71.
44. *Edgeworth Memoirs*, i. 226.
45. *A Letter to Arthur Young*, 25.
46. *Select Miscellaneous Productions*, 85-86.
47. Ibid., 9, 5.
48. Ibid., 73-90.
49. Ibid., 204.
50. *Edgeworth Memoirs*, i. 193.
51. Ibid., i. 197.
52. R. Lonsdale, 'Dr Burney, "Joel Collier", and Sabrina', 297.
53. ii. 103-4, iii. 130.
54. *Select Miscellaneous Productions*, 192.
55. *Two Speeches of Thomas Day*, 13.
56. See J. Shebbeare, *A Fifth Letter to the People of England, On the Subversion of the Constitution: And, The Necessity of its being restored* (London, 1757).
57. According to Kimbolton register he was baptized 9 May 1693 (Cambridgeshire Record Office, Huntingdon, Bishops Transcript); his father, Nathaniel Day, was a substantial enough citizen to be named among a number of local worthies who were jointly granted property in Kimbolton for charitable purposes (Cambs. R.O., Huntingdon, 2774/23/I).
58. The complexity of his position as a trustee is revealed by the few of his letters which survive in the Manchester collection, as is his difficulty in dealing with the Dowager Duchess. (See Cambs. R.O., Huntingdon, Manchester Papers, M13/5, M22B/22, M49B/6, M71/1, M72/8, M72/13.)
59. The salary of the Deputy Collector in 1778 was stated at £200. Even allowing for additional fees and a childless first marriage, it seems unlikely that this can account for the quite considerable property and wealth described in his will (Cambs., R.O., Huntingdon, Manchester Papers, M49/11). His lands in Huntingdonshire had been his father's and came to him (bypassing an elder brother, it seems) on his mother's death in 1717. (See will of Mary Day in Cambs. R.O., Huntingdon.) But the rest he acquired with his own means. As agent and something like personal banker to the Manchesters he would have had ample opportunity to make out of his commission and also by speculating with the sums entrusted to his care. (See Cambs. R.O., Huntingdon, M49B/6.)
60. *Two Speeches of Thomas Day*, 13.
61. J. Disney, *Works of Jebb*, i. 109.
62. Pp.4-5.
63. Published minutes of the society, 1782, 24.
64. *Two Speeches of Thomas Day*, 16.
65. M. Butler, *Maria Edgeworth*, 74.
66. ii. 211-2.
67. J. Keir, *An Account*, 124.
68. *Letters of Marius*, 69.
69. Pp.74-5.

70. H. Mackenzie, *Man of Feeling*, ed. B. Vickers (London, 1967) 40.
71. *Edgeworth Memoirs*, i. 219; *Sandford and Merton*, iii. 302.
72. *Edgeworth Memoirs*, i. 212.
73. *Select Miscellaneous Productions*, 113. Female education was also the subject of some of Day's insertions in the third edition of Joel Collier's *Musical Travels in England* (London, 1775). See R. Lonsdale, 'Dr Burney, "Joel Collier", and Sabrina', 209–90.
74. Ibid., 111-3.
75. *Edgeworth Memoirs*, i. 245, 334-5.
76. *Maria Edgeworth: Letters from England*, 122.
77. *Edgeworth Memoirs*, i. 340-1.
78. J. Tucker, *A Treatise concerning Civil Government* (London, 1781) 26-7, 33.
79. J. Towers, *Vindication*, 72.
80. *Letters of Marius*, 80.
81. Wyvill, *Political Papers*, ii. 460; iv. 445.
82. J. Keir, *An Account*, 66.
83. *Two Speeches of Thomas Day*, 13.
84. Wyvill, *Political Papers*, iv. 444.
85. Ibid., iv. 443.
86. J. Keir, *An Account*, 54.
87. Add. MS. 35656, f.32.
88. Kendal Collection, Laurens to Day, 23 Oct. 1782.
89. D.D. Wallace, *The Life of Henry Laurens* (New York, 1915), 404.
90. Kendal Collection, Day to Laurens, 10 July 83.
91. South Carolina Historical Society, Charleston, South Carolina, Henry Laurens Papers, Day to Laurens, 24 Oct. 1784.
92. Kendal Collection, Day to Laurens, 5 Jan. 1783; Add. MS. 35655, f.253.
93. Bodleian Library, MS. Eng. misc. c.132, f.82.
94. Add. MS. 35656, f.82.
95. Wyvill, *Political Papers*, iv. 444.
96. R. Davenport (ed.), 'The Poems of Thomas Day' in *The British Poets*, Vol. 58 (Chiswick, 1822) 190.
97. Kendal Collection, Day to Laurens, 29 June 1783.
98. *Select Miscellaneous Productions*, 86.
99. These letters are in the British Library, Add. MS. 35655, 35656. They were the principal original sources used by Gignilliat.
100. Add. MS. 35655, f.99: William Jones to unknown, 27 Jan. 1781.
101. Add. MS. 35656, ff.66, 83.
102. Add. MS. 35655, ff.204, 208.
103. Ibid., f.279.
104. Ibid., f.318.
105. *Letters of Anna Seward*, ii. 330. On the other hand, when Maria Edgeworth visited Stapleford Abbot in Essex, in search of Day's house there, she found touching evidence of the respect in which Day had been held by his employees and by the poor of the district. See *Maria Edgeworth: Letters from England*, III.
106. *A Letter to Arthur Young*, 28.
107. Add. MS. 29300, ff.56-7.
108. p.3.
109. p.28.
110. See the deeds cited above, n.28.
111. *The Speech of the Honourable Charles James Fox; Delivered at Westminster, on Wednesday, February 2, 1780* (London, [1780]) 29-30.
112. *Reflexions*, 26; *Two Speeches of Thomas Day*, 15.
113. *A Letter to Arthur Young*, 5-6.
114. Kendal Collection, Day to Laurens, 5 Jan. 1783.
115. J. Campbell, *A Political Survey of Britain* (2 vols., London, 1774); W.J. Mickle, *The Lusiad* (Oxford, 1776) introduction.
116. Add. MS. 29300, f.55.
117. Ibid., f.56.
118. *Select Miscellaneous Productions*, 198.
119. *Edgeworth Memoirs*, i. 324.
120. J. Blackman, *A Memoir of the Life and Writings of Thomas Day* (London, 1862) 124.
121. *Edgeworth Memoirs*, i. 331; Wyvill, *Political Papers*, iv. 444.

# The March of Everyman: Mobility and the Imperial Census of 1901

by

## Colin Newbury

While the general content of imperial migration studies is still broadly divided into 'settler' and 'labour' migration, reflecting older typologies of colonization and recruitment, there is a recognition that state intervention at the metropolitan and colonial level was an important factor at periods when the development of imperial states was impeded by shortages of manpower.[1] On the whole, the role of the self-governing colonial states, in competition with the United States, is more evident than positive direction from the imperial metropolis for most of the nineteenth century. Colonial land sales policies and regulation of bounty and nomination schemes contrast with the unwillingness of successive British governments to do more than enforce the passenger acts and finance the Colonial Land and Emigration Board, between 1840 and 1878. Between the experiments inspired by Henry Goulburn and Wilmot Horton for Upper Canada and the Cape early in the century, and the drive for imperial migrant preference leading to the Empire Settlement Act of 1922, the initiative lay with colonial governments and a variety of local recruiters. The commissioners of the Emigration Board provided free and assisted passages from colonial land funds for 386,591 emigrants to Australia, New Zealand, the Cape, Natal and the Falkland Islands.[2] But measured against the great waves of the nineteenth-century and early twentieth-century exodus from Europe totalling some 51 million people between 1846 and 1939, this diversion of British stock to British colonies and self-governing states can hardly be said to have altered the predominant flow to the United States by very much. Only during the last phase of mass European emigration does the flow of British migrants, as well as British capital, show an increased preference for imperial destinations compared to the United States.[3] The empire as a whole took less than a third of British emigrants before 1900, and then increased its annual intake to 68 per cent in 1910 and 78 per cent in 1913. Thereafter, the American Quota Acts of 1921 and the Restriction Acts of 1924 played into the hands of imperial promoters of overseas settlement, though with indifferent results. By the 1930s the presumed 'complementarity of the *emigration* needs of European countries and the *immigration* needs of the New World had been broken'.[4] It was revived as part of the settlement of displaced persons after 1946, but under very different circumstances and patterns of international competition for manpower.

## I

For historians of empire who stress the linkages between the metropole and individual colonial states, the assertion of a demographic preference, like the belated moves towards economic preference, is an interesting but inconclusive phenomenon. The explanation for stocking up with settlers derives, for the most part, from attitudes and institutions in the United Kingdom. The diversion of emigrants to the empire, it has been argued, coincided with the lobbying of a variety of imperial enthusiasts, ranging from Lord Brabazon's National Association for Promoting State Directed Colonization, formed in 1882, to the voluntary philanthropic societies who viewed the exodus as a form of social relief. Officially, the Colonial Office Emigrants' Information service guided imperial recruits from 1886. Unofficially, the network of passage brokers and their agents operating for the shipping companies and the colonial agents, was instrumental in organizing the vast overseas labour market, in return for commissions. By the 1890s a political lobby of some 49 emigration societies had emerged under the Royal Colonial Institute; and by 1910 important figures such as Curzon and Milner had been won over to the cause of sponsored emigration. Imperial journals and the imperial conferences of 1907 and 1911 accepted migration as a factor in promoting imperial unity.[5]

The arguments for domestic social reform and imperial complementarity are easily analyzed from the propaganda; and it is clear that one of the principal effects of the First World War which tested to the full the willingness of the dominions to supply manpower to an imperial cause was to encourage further state planning. The Dominions Royal Commission reports were belatedly completed so as to include Canada in 1917, and Lord Tennyson's Empire Settlement Committee met the same year.[6]

Yet it was a curiously 'Dominions' Office' view of empire which paid little attention to the labour markets of the tropics in Asia, Africa and the Caribbean, part of the 'politics of race' which one historian has identified as an element of imperial thinking in the interwar period.[7] The case for 'social imperialism' as part of the ideology of dominions' consultation and direction is a strong one, at least for the period of Milner and Amery at the Colonial Office and Dominions Office. But before the movement for imperial settlement is equated with the anxieties of the metropolitan middle class, two other historical components have to be considered. One is the ambiguous reception of the notion of 'empire settlement' by the dominions in the context of their domestic patterns of economic growth and employment. The second is the increasing differentiation in imperial migration patterns between these developing economies and the predominantly subsistence and enclave economies of the imperial tropics, where mobilization of wage-earners had produced some export growth, but little *per capita* wealth. Some territories were labour markets reflecting both capital-intensive projects in mining and public works alongside agricultural sectors of pastoralists, subsistence farmers and the beginnings of capitalist agriculture, as in the colonies of South Africa, where there was a marked distrust of organized immigration to strengthen imperial ties.[8]

This differentiation is reflected in the reports of the Royal Commission, 1912–1913, which have been well quarried for evidence of 'social imperialism', but which are silent on most of the dependent empire. Even Canada was surveyed late in the day in spite of the diffidence of the Colonial Office to the whole exercise.[9] Of its two principal contributions to imperial thinking, the suggestion for a 'Central Emigration Authority' received a measured implementation in the Overseas Settlement Committee, but none of the statutory controls over brokers and their agents sought in the emigration bill of 1918 which was withdrawn in the face of opposition from shipping interests. The commission's suggestion for an 'imperial development board' was well received in 1919 and edged the Colonial Office towards a search for autarky. The commission also formulated a number of conclusions which were at variance with the notion of complementarity dear to the advocates of emigration and land settlement. First, the final report of 1917 recognized that the exodus of unemployed rural labour from the United Kingdom had passed its peak and was unlikely to provide a supply of labourers. Emigration meant recruitment of urban employed and unemployed – the class most vulnerable to the operations of passenger agents criticized by the commission. Second, the final report of 1917 confirmed other evidence from Australia and Canada on the marked trend towards rapid urbanization within those societies, where there was a demand for domestic labour, as dominion females entered factories and service industries. There was every possibility new immigrants would follow this pattern.[10] The commission also displayed a healthy scepticism about the reliability of passenger statistics as evidence of imperial or foreign emigration flows, as well as the passenger statistics kept by some of the dominions.[11] Despite this lack of reliable and comparable data, a good deal of importance was attached to evidence of inverse sex ratios between United Kingdom and dominions' populations which gave assurance to those seeking to redress the balance by the export of suitable females.[12] Finally, the commission anticipated the work of later historians of migration by citing the analysis of the statistician, E. C. Snow, who concluded that emigration was 'quite highly correlated' with volumes of exports from the United Kingdom in a three-phase cyclical series, 1879–1908, and argued that 'the periodic booms in trade in the civilised parts of the world require some distribution of labour, and this is brought about by migration'.[13]

But what kind of labour? And could the dominions absorb it anyway? By leaving these points in the air without examination of internal and regional labour markets overseas, except in South Africa, the commission left the way open for some of the unwarranted assumptions of Milner and Amery's Overseas Settlement Committee in 1919. True to precedent, the committee began its task by drawing a false distinction between 'settlement' within the empire and 'emigration' to foreign countries.[14] 'True settlement' meant reducing the 'excess of females' in the United

Kingdom and the 'surplus of men in the oversea Dominions' by subsidized fares, because the passenger rates had doubled since 1914. Both for females and ex-servicemen it was assumed that domestic service and land settlement would provide 'the only openings at present' and that immigration of industrial workers was likely to be 'vehemently opposed'.[15] The dominions, it was recognized, would have the last word on the reception of 'settlers' intended to relieve social pressures at home and develop resources for a balanced population abroad.

Dominions' attitudes to empire settlement have been sufficiently well documented and do not require reappraisal here.[16] What matters more than the mixture of race patriotism and national disillusionment which characterized Canadian and Australian experience of empire settlement schemes before the 1930s is the condition of the host societies after a century of immigration and population growth and their ability to reproduce the patterns of agricultural and industrial development which they adopted and adapted from Europe and the United States. It is of critical interest to histories of decolonization at other and later periods to identify the changing economic and occupational structures of the self-governing dominions, particularly when so much of the official ideology of empire emphasized the older complementarity thesis of social transfers to a rural environment and stated a preference for British nationals. As late as 1922 a former Canadian minister of the interior responsible for immigration still portrayed the idealized immigrant as 'a stalwart peasant in sheepskin coat, born on the soil, whose forefathers have been farmers for ten generations, with a stout wife and a half-dozen children'.[17] But Sir Clifford Sifton's stereotype which lingered on to haunt the apostles of settlement in the open spaces may not have been typical at all of the job-hunters who made up the last great waves of migrants to the dominions, though he has something in common with indentured labour recruited to the imperial tropics from India or China.

II

Some of the later qualifications levelled at advocates of imperial population selection, when overseas economies were depressed by the failure of commodity prices in the 1930s, might have been voiced earlier by careful reading of the imperial census of 1901. The document has barely been mentioned in the literature of imperial demography, possibly because it was incomplete and there are reservations to be made about the comparative techniques used by its compilers. Nevertheless, when used in conjunction with other materials, notably the Canadian and Indian census reports, it provides a remarkable synopsis of patterns of employment in the self-governing dominions and the dependent empire.

The origin of this detailed comparative survey lay with the Colonial Office, and its compilation helped shaped the official view of regional differences in migration and labour recruitment.[18] From 1861 the Office had provided summaries of colonial census returns, limited to territorial area and population, which were published along with the decennial census of the United Kingdom. But these contained little of value for the 'comparison of the social condition' of the dominions and dependencies which began to concern the Colonial Office at the end of the century and was one of the stated aims of the 1901 survey.[19] The final report which accompanied the census, moreover, was addressed to John Burns MP, President of the Local Government Board, who had defended the Liberals' neutrality on sponsored emigration by arguing that the different requirements of the dominions made it impossible for the British Government to favour any particular scheme, lobby, or colony, despite the demands of the imperial enthusiasts.[20] He, too, had certainly read the 1901 census and probably reflected on some of its more sobering indications of regional and differential development in the empire.

These measures of imperial trends in population and employment were contained in sets of comparative tables based on the general format of the United Kingdom census which was not universally adopted in the dominions and dependencies. Such comparative re-tabulation had entailed a good deal of 'construction' in the General Register Office, using the materials supplied by overseas registrars and setting the data out in the United Kingdom's model tables. The tables concentrated on territorial areas, housing, basic population data, religions, education, occupations and 'infirmities'. There were inevitable gaps, because of shortage of local enumerators, fear of taxes in some societies, and lack of finance in some smaller territories. Some returns were late, most notably the important Canadian census and the politicaly sensitive census of 1904 for the Transvaal. Altogether it was an heroic effort to cover nearly 400 million people of the end-of-century empire by re-compiling reports ranging from ten pages for the Falkland Islands to the 60 volumes on the demography of 295 million Indians. It was also the last time the Colonial Office attempted the exercise through the General Register Office in such detail which accounts, perhaps, for the lack of interest in the results by imperial historians thrown back on the census materials for individual territories, or making do with the inadequate migration tables in the *Board of Trade Journal* and the *Annual Abstracts*.

Almost all of the 45 states covered in the census completed population returns by age groups, though only about half included marriage data.[21] The overseas empire shared the problem of United Kingdom census returns in recording 'errors due to wilful mis-statement and the tendency ... to return the age as an exact multiple of ten', and because, both at home and abroad, 'a large proportion of persons do not know their precise age'.[22] There was also a very imperfect record of literacy ratios with percentages ranging from 78.8 per cent of total population (Australian Commonwealth) to 5.3 per cent (Indian Empire) among the 13 states providing returns. The mean literacy rate for the states as a whole, including Ireland, was only 43.4 per cent of population.[23] The data on birth and mortality rates are also deficient, because of emphasis in the tabulation on what the registrar's report terms 'sex constitution', or male/female ratios, rather than reproduction rates.[24] Attention was drawn not to natural increase, but to those parts of the empire where there was a perceived 'excess' of males over females – in some 23 colonies and territories. This phenomenon was attributed to 'excess of immigration' by males, especially in Western Australia, Straits Settlements, Federated Malay States and Hong Kong and by Indian emigration to Ceylon. More pointedly, England, Wales, Scotland and Ireland were found to have an 'excess' of females, a point taken up later by the Dominions Royal Commission. No similar remedy was offered to the large number of British West Indian Islands, Natal, Southern Rhodesia and the Gold Coast which were also singled out for the high proportion of females in their populations.

No very clear statistics emerged for gross and net reproduction rates, though these can be worked out from some of the more sophisticated returns. The registrar's office discerned a 'general decline' in natural increase in the empire, 1881–1901, which was a very bold conclusion in the face of acquisitions in Africa which confused the imperial census with gross additions of population. Where the statistics were reasonably good, the report concluded there was still a relative decline in the rate of natural increase in the dominions, the Straits Settlements and (more surprisingly) Mauritius and India, but an increase in Natal, the West Indies and Ceylon for the decennial period 1891–1901.

One consequence of this pessimism about local ability to fill the empty spaces in North America and Australia or New Zealand was to concentrate attention in the report on the more easily measurable additions to population by immigration and the proportions of 'foreigners' and 'British born', as revealed by birthplace statistics. Coupled with this was an anxiety in the report that imperial colonies of high immigration were also among the most rapidly urbanizing societies which 'presents among the older communities one of the most important social difficulties of the day'.[25]

Measured against the United Kingdom 'urbanization' standard for towns, cities and boroughs over 5,000 people which produced 77 per cent for England and Wales, 70 per cent for Scotland and 31 per cent for Ireland, the Australian states and New Zealand were clearly well along the same rural-urban road with an urbanization percentage of 68 per cent for New South Wales and a general mean of 46.7 per cent for the seven southern colonies. The Fourth Census of Canada, 1901, yielded a population percentage of 24.6 per cent for towns over 5,000 persons which was lower than the other dominions. But there was a steady increase in urban population since 1871 by an aggregate of 30 per cent.[26] Unfortunately the main body of the report used a different urban population as the standard for a 'town', compared with the tables, so that none of the detailed evidence served to illuminate the general discussion of empire urbanization.[27] Despite the muddle, it is clear enough that Cape Colony, Orange River Colony, the Transvaal and Natal were still comparatively unurbanized, though the phenomenal growth of Johannesburg (51.5 per cent in the period 1896–1904) was commented on together with the rapid growth of 14 other imperial cities. It is also clear that the vast proportion of the empire's population consisted of rural vllagers in countries with an urbanization rate of under 10 per cent.

Statistics of birthplace were more important for the advocates of empire settlement, because these attested the relative contribution of British and foreign elements in colonial populations and, in a number of cases, the rates of internal migration between states and provinces.

If the tabulated birthplace statistics are arranged in order of increasing percentages of locally-born within the total population, then 12 of the imperial territories appear with high proportions of their inhabitants born outside the territorial boundaries (Table 1). These include the six Australian colonies at federation and New Zealand considered as part of the Australian group. Hong Kong was something of an exceptional case and by far the most recent and rapid example of immigration. Some of the West Indian islands and British Honduras also contained substantial immigrant elements from India and other Caribbean islands. Imperial territories in which the native born were less than 80 per cent of population in 1901 numbered 14 out of the 40 census returns with this information. The most surprising exception was Canada, where 87.2 per cent of the total population were born in the dominion. There were also a million or so persons of Canadian birth enumerated in the United States census for 1900, a net out-migration that had been repeated in every Canadian and United States census since 1880.[28] Conversely, the low rank order of India as a country of immigration tends to disguise the fact that there were nearly 600,000 foreigners from Nepal, Afghanistan and China enumerate in the census. Indians in Ceylon had increased to 436,622 – some 65 per cent more than their total in the census of 1891.

More worrying for those who advocated imperial preference in migration was the inter-censal decline in the absolute numbers of British emigrants enumerated in British colonies, 1881–1900, compared with the decennial increase of Europeans and other foreigners enumerated within the empire in 1891 and 1901.[29] In fact a good half of these immigrants from Europe (especially from Germany and Russia) were settled in the United Kingdom, one of the principal employers of foreign-born labour by the 1890s. Overseas, the Cape, Natal, Canada and even New Zealand, though not Australia, showed very small increases in foreign European settlers. The balance of immigrants was still in favour of United Kingdom origins and other parts of the empire which supplied 46 per cent and 24.4 per cent respectively of the 'migratory six millions' recorded in the birthplace statistics, while all foreign countries supplied only 29 per cent, more particularly to Hong Kong, India, British Honduras and Canada.

The most original feature of the census was to draw attention to internal migration between contiguous states and provinces. To some extent this was fortuitous, because the returns for the Australian Commonwealth were furnished by state governments with common boundaries. But it made sense to group together these and other developing

TABLE 1
ENUMERATION BY BIRTHPLACE

| Rank | Country or Colony | Born where Enumerated | British Empire UK | British Empire Elsewhere | Foreign Countries Europe | Foreign Countries Elsewhere |
|---|---|---|---|---|---|---|
| | | % | % | % | % | % |
| 1 | Hong Kong | 1.7 | 0.82 | 0.16 | 0.02 | 97.3 |
| 2 | W. Australia | 30.57 | 21.97 | 41.71 | 3.2 | 2.55 |
| 3 | Gibraltar | 53.82 | 28.03 | 3.67 | 10.32 | 4.16 |
| 4 | Queensland | 59.19 | 24.13 | 8.29 | 4.11 | 4.28 |
| 5 | Trinidad and Tobago | 63.31 | 0.51 | 32.95 | 0.55 | 2.68 |
| 6 | Orange R. Col. | 65.21 | 4.78 | 28.07 | 0.70 | 1.24 |
| 7 | New Zealand | 68.59 | 25.15 | 3.84 | 1.68 | 0.74 |
| 8 | New South Wales | 72.29 | 16.23 | 8.73 | 1.53 | 1.22 |
| 9 | Victoria | 73.23 | 17.92 | 6.58 | 1.41 | 0.86 |
| 10 | Bermuda | 73.49 | 21.02 | | 2.34 | 3.15 |
| 11 | South Australia | 76.7 | 14.6 | 5.09 | 2.39 | 1.22 |
| 12 | Br. Honduras | 76.7 | 0.47 | 4.28 | 0.15 | 19.0 |
| 13 | Isle of Man, Channel Islands | 78.58 | 14.65 | 0.84 | 5.68 | 0.25 |
| 14 | Tasmania | 79.44 | 11.52 | 7.64 | 0.84 | 0.56 |
| 15 | Mauritius | 82.42 | 0.11 | 15.95 | 0.12 | 1.4 |
| 16 | St Lucia | 83.76 | 0.95 | 13.45 | 0.18 | 1.66 |
| 17 | Seychelles | 85.93 | 0.28 | 5.11 | 0.58 | 8.1 |
| 18 | Canada | 87.22 | 7.28 | 0.3 | 2.37 | 2.38 |
| 19 | Ceylon | 87.48 | 0.16 | 12.33 | 0.01 | 0.22 |
| 20 | Natal | 87.79 | 3.32 | 8.28 | 0.52 | 0.09 |
| 21 | Grenada | 91.26 | 0.22 | 7.53 | 0.11 | 0.88 |
| 22 | Scotland | 91.35 | 7.61 | 0.36 | 0.46 | 0.22 |
| 23 | Cape Colony | 91.54 | 3.66 | 3.18 | 1.27 | 0.35 |
| 24 | England and Wales | 96.13 | 2.40 | 0.42 | 0.87 | 0.18 |
| 25 | Malta | 96.35 | 1.02 | 0.16 | 1.52 | 0.95 |
| 26 | Ireland | 97.04 | 2.4 | 0.18 | 0.14 | 0.24 |
| 27 | Bahamas | 97.13 | 0.3 | 1.22 | 0.07 | 1.28 |
| 28 | Newfoundland, Labrador | 97.78 | 0.89 | 0.96 | — | 0.37 |
| 29 | Cyprus | 98.94 | 0.06 | 0.03 | 0.85 | 0.12 |
| 30 | India | 99.76 | 0.03 | 0.01 | 0.00 | 0.2 |

Source: Census of the British Empire, 1901 (London, 1906), Cd. 2660, xl.

territories into regional clusters with common labour markets which operated across separate political administrations. The Caribbean colonies had strong demographic links with central America; the Canadian provinces and the northern United States, Australia and New Zealand (and some Pacific islands), the South African colonies, India, Ceylon and Burma, contained societies which were engaged in internal colonization from their own resources and had become part of circulatory migration flows to centres of industrial, mercantile and agricultural investment. In time Western Africa and East Africa followed this pattern of intra-regional migration, while elsewhere political boundaries were drawn to lessen ethnic exchanges. The 1901 census missed some of the fine detail of these population movements, failing to record, for example, the geographical origins of African immigrants into Natal, or Indians and 'Polynesians' in Fiji.[30] But there was enough material in the statistics of birthplace to demonstrate that 'overseas' or 'international' migration between states was only one aspect of important population mobility in the regions of Europe's overseas government and investment.

In the case of New Zealand and the Australian states there were very high internal migration rates, measured as the ratio of birthplace to place of enumeration (Table 2). Within the inter-censal period, 1891–1901, there had been considerable population movement from Tasmania, South Australia and Victoria to Western Australia, New South Wales and Queensland, while flows between Australian states and New Zealand tended to balance out with little net gain or loss either way. How much of these movements within a common culture is accounted for by marriage is not discernible in the statistics; nor is it possible to show how many internal migrants were first-born Australians or New Zealanders, compared with immigrants enumerated for the first time.

TABLE 2
AUSTRALIA AND NEW ZEALAND: ENUMERATION BY BIRTHPLACE

| Colony of Birth | Enumerated in: | | | | | | | Total |
| --- | --- | --- | --- | --- | --- | --- | --- | --- |
| | New South Wales | Victoria | Queensland | South Australia | Western Australia | Tasmania | New Zealand | |
| New South Wales | — | 22,417 | 24,860 | 4,128 | 14,124 | 2,075 | 6,430 | 74,034 |
| Victoria | 56,019 | — | 10,272 | 10,324 | 39,491 | 7,949 | 12,583 | 136,638 |
| Queensland | 14,968 | 3,032 | — | 606 | 2,619 | 288 | 1,271 | 22,784 |
| South Australia | 22,059 | 21,929 | 2,384 | — | 16,327 | 887 | 1,575 | 65,161 |
| Western Australia | 887 | 1,468 | 199 | 956 | — | 96 | 190 | 3,796 |
| Tasmania | 7,577 | 15,363 | 1,308 | 819 | 1,750 | — | 3,720 | 30,537 |
| New Zealand | 10,589 | 9,020 | 1,571 | 711 | 2,704 | 1,193 | — | 25,788 |
| Total | 112,099 | 73,229 | 40,594 | 17,544 | 77,015 | 12,488 | 25,769 | 358,738 |

Source: Census of the British Empire, 1901 (London, 1906), Cd. 2660, xliv.

More important was the omission from the imperial census of data on 'inter-migration' (as the registrar termed it) for Canada, because the returns from the dominion's fourth census of 1901 did not come to hand in time.[31] These returns would have shown that between Canadian provinces there was a re-distribution of Canadian-born to British Columbia, the North West, Manitoba and the Unorganized Territories (Alberta) (Table 3). The internal migration coefficient for Canada, 5.85 per cent of total population, is slightly lower than the 7.7 per cent for Australia and New Zealand. Both are much lower than the internal migration rates of 22.8 per cent for Natal and 31.8 per cent for Orange River Colony.

There were special problems about measuring internal migration from birthplace statistics (or inter-migrants) for South Africa which were recognized, but not accounted for, in the registrar's report.[32] Bechuanaland, Rhodesia and, of course, the Transvaal, were all part of the regional cluster, but did not provide the birthplace and immigration statistics required to complete the South African regional table (see Table 4). The geographical origins of large numbers of immigrants into Orange River Colony are not specified and it would be safe to assume much of this was periodic migrant labour rather than migration for land settlement. Similarly the largest contribution to Natal's share of inter-regional migration came from Zululand, while the Cape as the largest state in the region supplied migrants to other centres of development and drew on Basutoland, the Transvaal, Orange River Colony, Bechuanaland and Rhodesia. The apparently low percentage of migrants from these internal sources (3.0 per cent of the Cape's population) is to some extent because of the size of the territorial unit, especially after the annexation of British Bechuanaland and Pondoland in 1904.

TABLE 3
ENUMERATED IMMIGRANTS AS PERCENTAGES OF PROVINCIAL POPULATIONS

|  |  | Foreign Born | British Isles and British Territories |
|---|---|---|---|
|  |  | % | % |
| North West Territory | 48,981 | 30.8 | 11.1 |
| British Columbia | 46,110 | 22.8 | 18.2 |
| Unorganized Territories | 10,007 | 19.1 | 5.2 |
| Manitoba | 40,201 | 15.8 | 13.1 |
| Ontario | 76,913 | 3.5 | 11.1 |
| Quebec | 42,273 | 2.6 | 2.7 |
| New Brunswick | 6,757 | 2.0 | 3.3 |
| Nova Scotia | 6,277 | 1.4 | 3.8 |
| Prince Edward Island | 860 | 0.8 | 3.2 |

Source: *Fourth Census*, Vol. 1.

It is likely that the general coefficient of internal migration in the South African territories would have been much higher if the Transvaal census of 1904 had contained birthplace statistics. Such information was deliberately excluded by Milner's administration from the local registrar's tabulations to avoid exacerbating Anglo-Boer relations in the negotiations on franchise and constituencies in the period prior to responsible government.[33] Because of this considerable omission it was not possible to compare British, Afrikaner and foreign elements in the population, though naturalization statistics were produced and published.

The 1901 census also said little about internal migration in India and accepted the opinion of the compilers of the local census that there was a very low incidence of movement between states and provinces – some 2.4 per cent of total Indian-born population.[34] This was attributed to the habits of an 'intensely home-loving people', rather than lack of regional development.[35] If the ratios of birthplace statistics to provincial and state populations are examined in detail, however, it is clear that there were provinces such as Assam, Ajmer-Merwara, Berar and Coorg which contained internal migrant populations as high as 15 per cent and 30 per cent of local populations. This was a pattern of migration consistent with the results of the 1891 census. It does not dispose of the problem of quantifying movements between territorial and demographic units of enormous variation, but it does suggest that the India-wide census obscured intra-regional movements beneath a general appearance of demographic passivity.

The Colonial Office and the British census compilers were more interested, however, in the fate of British-born in Canada than settlers from Madras in Burma. And in the Canadian census it was possible to compare foreign and British immigrant percentages in each province (Table 4). This suggests some immigrant foreigners were being pushed out into the North-West and those Unorganized Territories, soon to be constituted as Saskatchewan and Alberta, while both sets of migrants pioneered Manitoba and British Columbia in roughly equal proportions. Ontario was favoured by migrants of British origins, and there was relatively little internal migration to or from New Brunswick, Nova Scotia, Prince Edward Island or Quebec.

TABLE 4

INTERNAL MIGRATION OF CANADIAN, AUSTRALIAN, NEW ZEALAND AND SOUTH AFRICAN BORN, AS PERCENTAGE OF PROVINCE OR COLONY POPULATION

| Canada | | Australia | | South Africa | |
|---|---|---|---|---|---|
| Provinces and Territories | % | Colonies | % | Colonies | % |
| 1 Unorganized Territories | 50.3 | 1 W. Australia | 42.7 | 1 Orange River Colony | 31.8 |
| 2 Manitoba | 36.0 | 2 Tasmania | 24.9 | 2 Natal | 22.8 |
| 3 New Territories | 35.5 | 3 S. Australia | 21.2 | 3 Cape of Good Hope | 3.0 |
| 4 British Columbia | 22.9 | 4 Victoria | 17.5 | | |
| 5 Prince Edward Is. | 11.2 | 5 New South Wales | 13.7 | | |
| 6 Ontario | 9.96 | 6 Queensland | 12.1 | | |
| 7 New Brunswick | 9.9 | 7 New Zealand | 6.3 | | |
| 8 Quebec | 6.7 | | | | |
| 9 Nova Scotia | 6.6 | | | | |

Source: *Census of the British Empire,* 1901 (London, 1906), Cd. 2660; *Fourth Census of Canada,* 1901 (Ottawa, 1902), Vol. 1, 482.

Ideally, it should have been possible to carry this investigation of the geographical dispersal of immigrants in colonies of high immigration into the occupation structure of colonial societies. Only the Canadian census went some way towards this sophisticated analysis of employment by use of 'mechanical tabulation' and supplied a retrospective analysis of immigrant and non-immigrant occupational status in the fifth census of 1911.

For the rest of the empire the compilers of the 1901 census were faced with the mammoth task of reconciling the different denotations of 'occupation' in the metropolitan and overseas territories. The difficulty was not merely semantic or a failure to apply the United Kingdom occupational headings used in the final tabulation. Rather, the export of occupations along with industrial technology in the nineteenth century, as the registrar noted, had accelerated by the 1880s, 'as the number of distinct manufactures and industries in all civilised Countries has greatly increased, and moreover most of these manufactures and industries are continually tending towards greater subdivision'.[36] Imperial job-hunting reflected the diversification of Europe's industrial revolution overseas. This was a point not generally considered by imperial enthusiasts who looked on empire in terms of economic complementarity, and it is a point that requires testing in the occupational data available. But it is clear from the exercise that emigration and development overseas resulted not in a simple division of labour between industrial metropole and agricultural periphery, but in localized divisions within colonial states and regional economies.

But before comparisons are made there is an initial difficulty to be noted about the notion of 'United Kingdom' occupational groups which displayed considerable regional differences when broken down into populations for England and Wales, Scotland and Ireland. The Irish statistics, as percentages of total population, have more in common with some of the underdeveloped overseas territories, especially for agricultural employment (19.18 per cent) and the low percentage of occupations classified under manufactures (0.9 per cent) which is well below the mean for the dominions, though higher than the South African and Asian colonies. For brevity, a general United Kingdom set of occupational percentages is given in Table 5, as the demographic weight of the Irish component does not greatly influence the result except in the case of agricultural employment.

A second difficulty arises over the assumption of totally occupied categories in societies engaged mainly in subsistence farming and employing dependents. There were wide variations in the totals of occupied males and females, as percentages of population, especially under domestic service and agriculture, with a tendency to overstate ratios, where there was little wage employment for males. For this reason Table 5 includes the total percentage of all census occupations for listed colonies, as well as the total of the ten selected occupations listed. The total of occupations for Canada is low as a percentage of total population, because of the Canadian definition of 'occupation' for 'gainful workers' over ten years of age; and the percentage of all occupations is high for Orange River Colony and the Malay States, where no such definition was made. General totals were also affected by comparisons based on total male and female populations, rather than populations aged ten and

TABLE 5
SELECTED OCCUPATIONS AS PERCENTAGE OF TOTAL POPULATIONS

| Census Orders | United Kingdom | Canada | New S. Wales | Victoria | Queensland | South Australia | Western Australia | Tasmania | New Zealand | Cape | Orange River Colony | India | Ceylon | Fed. Malay States |
|---|---|---|---|---|---|---|---|---|---|---|---|---|---|---|
| I General or Local Government | 0.612 | 0.325 | 0.689 | 0.613 | 0.514 | 0.575 | 1.328 | 0.708 | 0.536 | 0.508 | 0.588 | 0.631 | 0.564 | 0.87 |
| III Professions[1] | 1.766 | 1.565 | 2.128 | 2.245 | 1.816 | 1.649 | 2.392 | 2.098 | 2.164 | 0.755 | 0.724 | 0.707 | 0.913 | 0.426 |
| IV Domestic Service | 5.8 | 3.1 | 3.6 | 3.7 | 3.5 | 3.9 | 3.2 | 3.7 | 2.9 | 4.1 | 15.7[2] | 1.3 | 2.3 | 1.3 |
| V Commerce[3] | 1.719 | 2.986[3] [1.347] | 1.155 | 1.403 | 1.174 | 1.104 | 1.339 | 0.976 | 1.294 | 0.894 | 1.065 | 0.072 | 0.229 | n.a. |
| VI Transport:[4] Rail: | 0.984 | 0.535 | 0.716 | 0.799 | 1.096 | 0.822 | 2.211 | 0.692 | 0.619 | 0.333 | 1.008 | 0.072[4] | 0.229 | |
| Road: | 1.224 | 0.999 | 1.182 | 1.081 | 1.377 | 0.864 | 1.388 | 0.699 | 0.879 | 0.584 | 0.547 | 0.235 | 0.523 | |
| Total | 2.209 | 1.533 | 1.898 | 1.881 | 2.473 | 1.687 | 3.599 | 1.361 | 1.498 | 0.916 | 1.555 | 0.307 | 0.752 | 1.514 |
| VIII Agriculture[5] | 5.291 | 13.478 | 9.577 | 10.9 | 12.607 | 10.618 | 8.311 | 12.665 | 11.293 | 41.7 | 39.5 | 30.9 | 29.8 | 24.7 |
| IX Mines and Quarries | 2.277 | 0.539 | 2.884 | 2.688 | 3.369 | 1.656 | 10.506 | 3.2 | 2.296 | 1.095 | 1.556 | 0.069 | 0.616 | 23.56 |
| X 'Metals, Machines'[6] | 3.58 | 2.074 | 1.774 | 1.755 | 1.595 | 2.151 | 2.394 | 1.622 | 1.771 | 0.381 | 0.191 | 0.322 | 0.199 | 0.37 |
| XII Building, Construction[7] | 2.994 | 4.01 | 2.645 | 2.268 | 1.936 | 2.2 | 3.001 | 2.266 | 2.758 | 2.443 | 1.435 | 0.187 | 1.291 | 1.14 |
| XVIII Textiles[8] | 3.526 | 0.277 | 0.711 | 1.183 | 1.566 | 0.633 | 0.664 | 0.583 | 0.966 | 0.109 | — | 1.943 | 1.41 | — |

| | | | | | | | | | | |
|---|---|---|---|---|---|---|---|---|---|---|
| Selected Orders as Percentage of Population | 29.81 | 29.9 | 27.06 | 28.6 | 30.55 | 26.2 | 36.7 | 29.2 | 27.5 | 52.9 | 62.3 | 39.9 | 38.3 | 54.9 |
| All Census Orders as Percentage of Population | 57.5 | 33.5 | 40.6 | 43.3 | 43.5 | 38.3 | 53.7 | 41.4 | 40.6 | 57.9 | 70.1 | 46.1 | 45.9 | 69.6 |

NOTES TO TABLE 5

1. Including clerical, legal, medical, teaching, literary, engineers, art, music, drama.
2. No explanation is offered for the inclusion of 53,803 females in the 'domestic indoor service' category in the Orange River Colony census. It may include 'farm servants' listed under agriculture in other returns.
3. Merchants, agents, accountants, business clerks, dealers in money, insurance. The Canada census includes general shopkeepers and hawkers excluded from the British Empire tabulation. If these are omitted, the percentage is reduced to 1.347.
4. The Indian census excludes railway labourers, whereas these are included with other occupational categories under transportation for the Canadian and Australian returns.
5. 'On farms, woods and gardens'.
6. Tool making, construction of ships, boats, vehicles and dealers in metals, machines, tools, conveyances.
7. Includes railway labour for India and thatch-makers, road labour for Ceylon, Australian states and New Zealand.
8. Cotton and flax, wool and worsted, silk, hemp, processing and dealers in textiles.

Source: *Census of the British Empire*, 1901, Table 7; *Fifth Census of Canada*, 1911, Vol. vi (1915)

upwards, as was usual in the British and Canadian census returns. The imperial census of 1901, however, was obliged to use total population and ignore age demarcations in employment, and this has been followed in Table 5.

## III

How, then, did the empire labour? The general report noted the nearly standard percentages of populations employed in national and local government, especially if the male employees are considered for each territory (0.9 to 1.4 per cent of male populations). The percentage is diluted but still constant with the inclusion of female workers. The high percentage for Western Australia resulted from an unusually large number of clerks and police in a colony with a low population density and a boom in mining. It approximates to the relatively high percentages of government employees in all of the smaller territories with limited opportunities for skilled employment (Cyprus, Gibraltar, Malta). Canada would appear to have been undergoverned in 1901 with only 17,306 civil and municipal government employees (0.325 per cent of population), but the percentage rose rapidly to 1.07 per cent by 1911 and included a large immigrant component.

The notion of 'professions' produced some understandable anomalies across the empire. For example, India was credited with a larger percentage of clerical occupations (0.65) than any other territory, and a paucity of lawyers, doctors and teachers. Religious mendicants and half a million priests and ministers also swelled the numbers of males included in the Indian professional class. The relatively high percentages for the Australian states and New Zealand are accounted for by females in the teaching and medical professions, including nursing, and were higher than percentages for Scotland, England and Wales. The female component in the domestic service category was also especially high in the United Kingdom and the dominions (and would be higher for Australia, if hotel and boarding house employees were included). For much of the empire, however, male domestics exceeded females in India, Ceylon, Malay States, Cyprus, Mauritius and Natal. The very high percentages for Orange River Colony domestics passed without comment in the report. The 53,803 females listed as domestics represented 30.4 per cent of the total female population and included a large proportion of unmarried females over 15 years (33,873) enumerated in the 1904 census for the colony.[37]

Commerce also passed without comment in the registrar's report, though as a category it contained a rich and variegated assortment of sub-categories. Canada returned a disproportionately high percentage which is reduced to comparability at 1.347 per cent of population by subtracting the general shopkeepers and hawkers listed under other orders elsewhere in the empire. In general, the empire percentages were little below the United Kingdom average for this category which befitted a nation of exportable business occupations.

Transport in Table 5 includes only road and rail abstracted from a more inclusive category of 'conveyance of men, goods and messages', and is more compatible with Canadian census usage, though it omits employment at sea ports, rivers and canals important to a number of colonial economies. There is a fair uniformity about percentages employed on road transport. Some of the smaller colonial populations such as those in Western Australia and Queensland were still funding a transport investment programme which employed a large proportion of the male labour force. Considering there were more miles of line open for traffic in British India (27,600 miles) than in the United Kingdom by 1904, the Indian male work-force of 207,815 appears small and excludes general labourers who were included in the total of males employed on 'works of construction and roads'.[38] For this reason it is difficult to be certain about the skilled component in the imperial railway networks, though it was certainly not large, perhaps less than one per cent of population, and certainly smaller than equivalent percentages for mining, the machine tool and construction industries. Possibly our historical view of the importance of transport technology for colonies requires modification by examination of manufacturing. The outstanding industrial percentage for an underdeveloped country in the mining category of employment resulted from the 157,000 males, mostly Chinese, engaged in Malayan tin mining. The gold mines of the Australian Commonwealth and the diamond mines of the north Cape also accounted for large employment percentages, especially in Western Australia and Queensland, and so would the Transvaal for this period, if the 1904 census had listed occupations.

The occupations under 'Metals, Machines' included all forms of metal working, ship building and similar engineering activities, and are an indication of the relative size of imperial work-forces in an expanding industrial sector overseas. None of the colonies, of course, approached the percentages of the industrial male work-force in England and Wales, or Scotland (7.5 and 9.3 per cent), though many were more industrialized than Ireland. Canada and the Australian states already employed considerable engineering skills in their general work-force. The Cape, India and the Malay States contained small industrial sectors, particularly for vehicles and dealers in machinery. The same territories also employed small but significant numbers of workers in gas, water and electricity supply, though about half of the 40 listed territories had no workers in this form of power generation. Building construction is also an indicator of industrial growth with a large component of carpenters, joiners and skilled trades in the census classification. It was a major industry in Canada, the Australian states and the Cape, all of which approached or exceeded the United Kingdom general percentage in 1901; and construction was important for Ceylon and the Malay States, though surprisingly unimportant for India as a percentage of population or of the listed occupied work-force. Finally, textiles, which held a prime place in United Kingdom manufactures, had not discouraged empire production entirely, judging by the small but widespread percentages of males and females engaged in cotton, wool, flax, jute and hemp processing and dealing, notably in India and two of the Australian states. By comparison, Canada and South Africa, the Malay States and most of the rest of Africa and the Caribbean had little to compete with British textile imports.

Taken together the five industrial or semi-industrial orders of employment under railways, mines, metal-working, building and textiles, provide a rough indication of the extent to which Europe's technology, combined with local crafts, created local divisions of labour within the imperial work force. All of the Australian states, Canada and New Zealand had employed percentages of population over 7.4 in these categories, compared with the United Kingdom percentage of 13.36 of population. Western Australia and the Malay States had unusual mining enclaves which raised their proportion of workers in these five categories to 18.8 per cent and 25.0 per cent of total population. South Africa, India and Ceylon showed less than 4.5 per cent in these industrial orders, and other overseas territories in Africa or the Caribbean had hardly any industrial employment at all.

## IV

Clearly the economic differentiation within the empire precluded a simple distinction between 'industrialized metropolis' and 'agricultural colonies', particularly as some of the states with skilled industrial sectors were also major food producers. It is nevertheless evident from the occupational returns that by far the greatest proportion of the empire's population lived on the land and not in towns. Again, the statistics of males and females employed in agriculture, while demonstrating the decline of the rural work-force in Scotland, England and Wales to less than eight per cent of population, indicate that similar reductions had already begun in other parts of the empire. Canada, New Zealand and the Australian states, as exporters of primary produce (rather than unprocessed raw materials) had no more than 10 or 12 per cent of their populations engaged in the agricultural sector, though there were a number of important service industries dependent on agricultural production. Thereafter, there is a major increase in the percentages for Asian and African colonies, where a good third of populations were listed as employed directly on the land. Of the 90 million so employed in India, a further 104 million were dependents. The paradox of imperial primary production which the enthusiasts of overseas 'settlement' had yet to learn was that exportable surpluses came from the lands of small farmers, company plantations and the pastoralists of the temperate grasslands, as well as from regions of high population density and internal consumption of subsistence crops. Export values were out of proportion to the numbers employed in agriculture or in mining.

In any case, were immigrants going onto the land? The returns of the imperial census were not sophisticated enough to record occupations with birthplace data, and the general report did not draw attention to this aspect of the occupational destinations of British or foreign immigrants. Other investigators have used the passenger statistics as a guide to male occupations among emigrants from the United Kingdom to the United States and the empire, notably Brinley Thomas in his study of migration and economic growth.[39] The study drew attention to the relative distribution of skilled and unskilled grades of labour, as influenced by rates of economic growth and by slower, secular changes in economic structures in the host societies and countries of origin: 'indeed the story of oversea settlement over the last century may be said to be a commentary on their interaction'.[40] In the case of the United States, Thomas detected a change between the late 1870s and 1890s as British skilled manpower displaced unskilled immigrants. He found little change in the occupational structure of Canada's British immigrants, except a rise in the proportion of farmers. Emigrants to Australia and New Zealand displayed a rise in the proportion of professional men and merchants and a decline in agricultural labourers, while the empire as a whole drew from the United Kingdom an increased proportion of skilled manpower towards the end of the century.[41] The change in the classification of occupations introduced by the Board of Trade into the passenger statistics in 1903 interrupted the analysis by quinquennial series, but Thomas was able to suggest that in the great imperial upswing in migration flows prior to 1914 Canada took the greatest share of British emigrants, especially labourers, agriculturalists and skilled workers, while the United States' share of skilled emigrants declined.

Unfortunately Thomas did not refer to Canadian census materials to confirm this presentation, though he did use United States Bureau of Statistics returns to show the distribution of British immigrants by occupation over a long-time series, 1875–1930, in which the percentages of skilled categories rose, between 1903 and 1914, which was at variance with the argument from United Kingdom returns.[42] The Canadian census of 1911 contained a valuable juxtaposition of birthplace and occupational data without, however, distinguishing between British and foreign immigrants in such data. But the tabulations do demonstrate the predominance of British immigrants generally by place of birth which had been a feature of every census since 1881.[43] The question for Canadian development by 1911 was not so much the origins of immigrants but whether all immigrants were disproportionately represented in specific occupations. Table 14 of the 1911 census was the first evidence produced on this point. It showed that out of the 11 main occupational categories the foreign-born – whether British or not – held 31.9 per cent of jobs. Of these categories agriculture was ranged eighth in order of foreign-born percentages, demonstrating a low preference for moving out onto the land within the generation of recent arrivals. The one category in which the foreign-born predominated was mining, where they held 51.9 per cent of jobs. Other occupations in which they were represented at rates higher than their general occupational percentage (31.9 per cent) included civil and municipal government (47.7 per cent), transport (44.5 per cent), domestic services (39.5 per cent), while in building (38.3 per cent) and manufacturing (31.8 per cent) they fell slightly below their general percentage. Only in agriculture, forestry, fishing and hunting, the professions, trading and merchandising, were there dominant Canadian-born work-forces of over seventy per cent. The general conclusion might be that immigrants were highly differentiated in skills by the end of the century and tended to move into urban and industrial jobs in Canada and that this pattern is consistent with United States patterns of immigrant employment from 1903. It may also be further confirmation that the passenger statistics are very unsafe guides to migrant occupation within a host economy.

The Canadian example is also supported by the distribution of Canadian-born and all immigrants in the 26 Canadian cities and towns with populations over 15,000. The percentage of urban male immigrants in 1911 was 43.7 per cent of males which is higher than the dominion percentage of males in occupations (33.2 per cent). Employed immigrant males predominated moreover in eight cities and towns: Fort William, Edmonton, Brantford, Regina, Victoria, Calgary, Vancouver, Winnipeg and Toronto. Sifton's 'stalwart peasant' may still have been entered on the passenger lists, but he had long since begun to turn in his sheepskin coat for overalls and a suit and send his six children to urban schools.

Unfortunately none of the other dominions' census reports displayed a similar degree of sophistication by tabulating birthplace with occupations, though it is possible the raw materials for such cross-references still exist within registry archives.[44] Nevertheless, the indications of widespread urbanization through incorporation of British and foreign immigrants in the dominions was sufficiently well documented to give pause to those who still entertained a rural concept of overseas empire. The high degree of internal migration, moreover, suggests that ocean passages are only one form of mobility, and that such labour transfers were for many only the beginning of a longer process of geographical displacement and settlement, just as for many internal migration within Europe and the United Kingdom served as a preliminary phase to participation in the more visible 'great migration'.

There were indications, too, in the imperial census of local patterns of labour recruitment and migration within the clusters of imperial and foreign states making up regional economies. The dominions' royal commission volume for South Africa repeated some of the 1904 census material, noting that the very high share of trade with the United Kingdom (76.5 per cent of South Africa's total trade) in 1913 did not depend on British immigration, but rather on immigrant labour from internal and foreign reserves which were the 'indispensable condition' for development.[45] The commissioners concentrated on reform of the conditions of recruitment, rather than on recommendations for imperial migrant preference. New locations and stabilization of African families contrasted with the usual argument for more white settlers in other reports on the dominions.[46]

The relationship between industrial growth and internal migration was also a feature of the Indian census of 1901 which hailed the growth in the numbers of mills and factories and joint stock companies, 1891–1901, as the mark of 'an era of great industrial development' requiring mobilization of labour supplies to Calcultta and other centres by state labour agencies.[47]

In longer perspective some of this optimism looks like recognition of enclaves in a predominantly agricultural and low income society which the 1901 imperial census tabulations reveal were also hampered by lack of skilled manpower.

The royal commission did not visit any tropical dependencies. Had it done so commissioners might have noted, as the imperial census had done, an increasing amount of migration between islands of the West Indies, recruitment of labour for the Panama Canal from Barbados and Grenada, local movements to the plantations of Cuba and the oilfields of Curacao, Aruba and Venezuela. Circulatory migration after emancipation had a long history in the West Indies which prepared the way for recruitment from Jamaica to the United States and to Great Britain during the Second World War.[48] The pattern of Chinese and Indian regional migration to Burma, Ceylon, Straits Settlements and the Malay States is also discernible in the imperial census, though little of the savannah-coastal migrations in Africa which became a feature of the later colonial period and the first decades of independence.[49]

A study of the 1901 Imperial Census, therefore, indicates the distorted view of contemporary demographic and occupational change held by the 'empire settlement' school. Amery was wrong in his view that 'Empire development is only social reform writ large'.[50] Such development as there was entailed recruitment of a highly differentiated and skilled population from Europe for the dominions and considerable intraregional mobility to service investment in the tropical enclaves. As the dry statistics of the 1901 census indicated, the growth of trade and population in the empire was wider than the sum of its political parts.

NOTES

1. For an overview of the main themes, see Shula Marks and Peter Richardson (eds.), *Historical Studies in International Labour Migrations* (forthcoming) based on the valuable seminar series on 'Labour Migration within the Empire-Commonwealth since 1780' conducted over a number of years by the Institute of Commonwealth Studies, University of London.
2. G. F. Plant, *Oversea Settlement. Migration from the United Kingdom to the Dominions* (London, 1951) 91; and for assisted emigration 1922–1931, W. A. Carrothers, *Emigration from the British Isles; with Special Reference to the Development of the Overseas Dominions* (London, 1929) 310-11; Ian Drummond, *British Economic Policy and the Empire* (London, 1972) 17-36; *Imperial Economic Policy* (London, 1974) 43-145.
3. Brinley Thomas, *Migration and Economic Growth: A Study of Great Britain and the Atlantic Economy* (Cambridge, 1954); 'Migration' II, 'Economic Aspects', *International Encyclopedia of the Social Sciences* (ed. D.L. Sills), 10 (1971), 292-99.

4. W. D. Borrie, *The Growth and Control of World Population* (London, 1970) 92, and Chap. 5 'The Great Migrations', 85-127.
5. Plant, 48-60; Keith Williams, 'Labour Migration as Social Imperialism: The Ideology of Empire Settlement, 1880–1922', Institute of Commonwealth Studies Seminar (1980) 8; Trevor Reese, *The History of the Royal Commonwealth Society 1868–1968* (London, 1968) 161-66.
6. A. Marwick, *The Deluge* (London, 1965) 31; Plant, Chap. 3.
7. R. F. Holland, *Britain and the Commonwealth Alliance 1918–1939* (London, 1981) 32.
8. See Richard Solomon to Smuts, 28 April 1910 in W. K. Hancock and Jean van der Poel (eds.), *Selections from the Smuts Papers* 4 vols. (Cambridge, 1966) Vol. 2, No. 473.
9. *Dominions Royal Commission. Fifth Interim Report* (London, 1917), Cd. 8457; *Final Report* (London, 1917), Cd. 8462; Suzann Buckley, 'The Colonial Office and the Establishment of an Imperial Development Board: The Impact of World War I', *The Journal of Imperial and Commonwealth History*, 2, 3 (1974), 308-17.
10. *Dominions Royal Commission. Second Interim Report* (London, 1912), Cd. 7210, 10ff.
11. Ibid., *Final Report* (London, 1917), Cd. 8462, 84.
12. Ibid. (London, 1914), Cd. 7173; A. J. Hammerton, *Emigrant Gentlewomen* (London, 1979).
13. Ibid. (London, 1914), Cd. 7173, 61-63.
14. Oversea Settlement Committee, *Report*, 1919, Cmd. 573.
15. Ibid., section 15.
16. See, especially, Sidney Wertimer, *Migration from the United Kingdom to the Dominions in the Interwar Period*, Ph.D. thesis, University of London, 1952; J. A. Schultz, 'Canadian Attitudes Toward Empire Settlement, 1919–30', *The Journal of Imperial and Commonwealth History*, 1, 2 (1973), 237-52; R. T. Appleyard, *A Study of Population Movements Between Great Britain and Australia, 1918–1938*, M.A. thesis, Duke University, 1957; A. Geoffrey Searle, *Social and Political Aspects of Migration from Great Britain to Australia, 1919–1938* (typescript), Royal Commonwealth Society Library, 1948; Borrie, 1970, Chap. 5.
17. Sifton was Minister of the Interior, 1896–1905; his often-quoted remarks to the Toronto Board of Trade were made in 1922: *Maclean's Magazine*, 1 April 1922.
18. *Census of the British Empire*, 1901 (London, 1905), Cd. 2660. The general report was signed by W. C. Dunbar, the Registrar General, December 1905. It is listed in R. R. Kuczynski's *Demographic Survey of the British Colonial Empire*, Vol. III, *West Indian and American Territories* (London, 1953).
19. Ibid., Dunbar to President of the Local Government Board, xv.
20. Williams, 'Labour Migration', 8.
21. *Census*, 1901, report, section v.
22. *Census*, 1901, xxvii.
23. *Census*, 1901, liii.
24. *Census*, 1901, xxv-xxvi.
25. *Census*, 1901, xxii.
26. *Fourth Census of Canada*, 1901, 4 Vols. (Ottawa, 1902), 1 *Population*, 22.
27. *Census*, 1901, xxii-xxiii, and Table 4, 189.
28. *Census*, 1901, xlv; see, too, Marcus Lee Hansen, *The Mingling of the Canadian and American Peoples* (Toronto, 1940); Leon L. Truesdell, *The Canadian-Born in the United States* (New Haven, 1943).
29. *Census*, 1901, xlvi.
30. Birthplace and occupational data were given only for whites in Natal and Fiji, though the Fijian returns listed 17,105 Indian and 1,950 Pacific islands' immigrant workers.
31. See above, Note 26. Some Canadian returns were, however, included.
32. *Census*, 1901, xliii.
33. Milner to Lyttelton, 5 Dec. 1904, Colonial Office Confidential Print (Africa South), No. 747 (Secret), p. 76.
34. *Census of India*, 1901, 2 vols. (Calcutta, 1903), Part 2, Table 11.
35. Ibid., Part 1, 88.
36. *Census*, 1901, xxix.

37. *Census Report of the Orange River Colony, 17 April 1904* (Bloemfontein, 1904), xxxv.
38. *Census*, 1901, xxxiii.
39. Thomas, Chap. 5, Table 10; Appendix, Table 82.
40. Thomas, 59.
41. Thomas, 59-62.
42. Thomas, Tables 12, 80.
43. Though a declining percentage: 1881 (78 per cent), 1891 (75.7 per cent), 1901 (59.3 per cent). Cf. Donald Avery, *Dangerous Foreigners* (Toronto, 1979) which fails to distinguish the British component from general immigration from Europe or the United States.
44. See, for example, *Results of the Census of the Colony of New Zealand 29 April 1906* (Wellington, 1907) which supplies birthplace data by nationality and provinces, but does not cross index these data with occupations (except for Chinese).
45. *Dominions Royal Commission, Third Interim Report* (London, 1914), Cd. 7505, 13-25.
46. Ibid., see Appendix, Part II, 116-7.
47. *Census of India*, 1901, Part 1, 85, 94.
48. Elizabeth M. Thomas-Hope, 'The Establishment of a Migration Tradition. British West Indian Movements to the Hispanic Caribbean in the Century after Emancipation', in C.G. Clarke (ed.), *West Indian Social Relations*, Centre for Latin American Studies, Liverpool (1978) 66-81.
49. K.C. Zachariah and Julien Condé, *Migration in West Africa Demographic Aspects*, World Bank, Development Economics Department (Washington, 1979).
50. *Imperial Economic Conference 1923, Report of Proceedings* (London, 1924), Cmd. 2009, 114. See, too, for an approach to the colonial frontier from urban growth, Eric Pawson, Neil C. Quigley, 'The Communication of Information and Frontier Development: Canterbury 1850–1890', *New Zealand Geographer*, 38, 2 (1982), 65-76.

# British Foreign Policy and the Influence of Empire, 1870–1920

by

Paul Hayes

To write on imperial issues is immediately to enter a world of controversy. Conflicting views on the nature and purpose of the Empire have coloured all aspects of history which touch upon matters imperial. At the height of imperialist fervour the rival schools of thought were represented by propagandists of great ability and resource. If Joseph Chamberlain believed that 'The days are for great Empires and not for little States',[1] his contemporary, Keir Hardie, argued that the Empire was an obstacle to internationalism and a prop to the capitalist system. The state of affairs which the two politicians described was the same, even if interpretations, explanations and expectations differed. From the turn of the century to the dissolution of the remains of the Empire in the 1960s the rival claims of these opposed schools of thought were maintained and refined as, indeed, were many other less uncompromising views of the Empire and the imperial process.

I

The debate concerning the relationship between British foreign policy and the Empire is necessarily part of a wider disagreement about imperialism itself. Yet at the same time it is atypical of that wider discussion, for even enthusiasts for Empire disagreed profoundly about the precise relationships which could, should and did exist between the constituent parts of the Empire and the mother country. During the whole of Queen Victoria's reign hardly a year passed without some important constitutional or economic question involving the relationship between Britain and one of her possessions demanding urgent attention. What was true of economic and constitutional issues applied also to defence and foreign policy questions. As the Empire grew governments were faced with demands for an increased allocation of resources at a time when domestic expenditure was rising and politicians of all parties were rather hostile to proposals for increased taxation. The anti-imperialists tended to view this as a problem to be solved by a process of imperial withdrawal. The enthusiasts for Empire were united in their opposition to that solution, but unable to agree upon an order of priorities – not least because of repercussions on British defence and foreign policies.

The renewal of imperial expansion in the second half of the nineteenth century thus created new problems for British governments. It was hardly possible to divorce imperial expansion from demands for increased expenditure upon the armed forces; as the distances from Britain (or a secure and well-established base) increased so too did costs of military and naval actions and establishments multiply. Nor did any relaxation of the pressures on Britain seem at all probable. Successive governments were driven onward by the pressures of rivalry with major powers, by importunate dominions, by trade lobbies such as the China Association and often by the demands of the armed forces in difficult local situations which might involve punitive expeditions, the establishment of forward posts, the securing of lines of communication by naval bases or a wide variety of different possibilities which shared but one common feature, that of costing money. By 1892 an exasperated Salisbury, admittedly never an enthusiast for action when inaction was a plausible alternative, wrote to Sir Evelyn Baring in the following terms: 'I would not be too much impressed by what the soldiers tell you about the strategic importance of these places. It is their way. If they were allowed full scope, they would insist on the importance of garrisoning the moon in order to protect us from Mars.'[2]

Salisbury's observation indicated the existence of a difficult problem. A successful foreign policy could not be conducted in the absence of a consistent and balanced defence policy. Any sensible defence policy necessitated an integration of Britain's home and overseas defence requirements. Far-flung imperial possessions made centralized control impractical, yet no government could accept that questions of foreign policy (involving perhaps several major powers) might be decided by the actions of low-ranking officers in distant lands. In another letter to Baring Salisbury had put it thus: 'It is always open to the military authorities to discover ... some danger against which it is absolutely necessary to guard .... You have no means of arguing against them. They are upon their own territory, and can set down your opposition to civilian ignorance.'[3] The dangers inherent in this situation were well-illustrated by events in West Africa in 1898 when Chamberlain's forward policy contributed to a confrontation between British and French forces. Chamberlain's biographer thus described the situation:

> In the area of dispute ... the Union Jack and the tricolour now flew in sight of each other. The rank and file on both sides were native levies eager to prove their mettle. The existence of the officers was feverish .... They were severed from ordinary communication with their Governments. We may well marvel again that the guns did not go off of themselves.[4]

Such situations were grist to the anti-imperialist mill.

Events in both the nineteenth and twentieth centuries have shown the impossibility of creating a system which would guarantee that local disputes could not upset a broader balance of power. Much depended upon the quality of judgment of those in local situations, even in a period of rapid communications. At the same time those occupying local positions of responsibility were unlikely to have enough time or knowledge to estimate accurately the scope of international repercussions resulting from their actions. In a largely peaceful world such problems probably mattered little. In a world of fierce nationalisms and power competition imperial expansion inevitably encouraged this element in the process of political destabilization. By the late nineteenth century statesmen were already familiar with the problem and it exercised them greatly. They were prudent enough to understand that the problem could not be evaded by political legerdemain and wise enough to realize that it could be limited but not solved.

Though this problem existed for all of the imperial states it was exceptionally serious for Britain. In the first place, British imperial possessions were larger and more numerous than those of other states. Secondly, Britain did not possess a large army and in some situations (for example, the Boer War) control of the seas – which was in any case tenuous from the 1890s onwards – might prove insufficient to resolve a dispute successfully. Furthermore, the established political tradition of the devolution of power within Britain inclined the English-speaking peoples, at home and overseas, against centralized foreign and defence policies. It was not uncommon in the imperial age for adventurers such as Gordon to be idolized. When their idiosyncratic behaviour contributed to a mishap the general public was nevertheless still inclined to turn on the government of the day, even though popular attitudes had denied government the capacity to exercise real control. Governments were thus confronted with a quite impossible task. The popular image of an immensely powerful Empire, a testimony to British enterprise and resolution, suggested no hint of frailty or uncertainty in foreign affairs. Those who conducted foreign policy were expected to be able to resolve almost without effort the most difficult of problems. The support of Germany in Egypt, for example, was to be secured without conceding interests in Africa or the Pacific. Diplomats and politicians knew, however, that the task of maintaining a balance of power favourable to British interests was made more complex by imperial considerations, no matter what the most belligerent imperialists thought or said.

This knowledge did not make policy-makers 'anti-Empire' but rather encouraged a cautious, and often pessimistic, frame of mind. It was this caution and pessimism – of which Salisbury was perhaps the supreme exponent – which contributed greatly to the failure to try to resolve problems by means of a sweeping solution. Until the 1890s difficulties were attacked piecemeal rather than comprehensively. Three aspects of the problem received the most attention:

(a) the condition of the Army;
(b) the limitation of formal commitments overseas; and
(c) the devolution of responsibilities to overseas assemblies.

There was no master-plan but a recognition that the problem was amenable to treatment in different ways.

Reform of the Army was undertaken in Gladstone's ministry of 1868–74. Events in Europe had forced Army reform to the forefront of the political stage, though a series of disasters overseas (Kabul, the Crimea, the Indian Mutiny) had played some part in influencing public opinion. It was, of course, in those places where the Army was most regularly on active service that the benefits of improved pay, organization and officer-training were strongly felt. The possibility of disaster overseas was not eliminated, as events at Isandhlwana in 1879 showed, but more efficient education and organization and the adoption of a more professional attitude certainly had some effect.

The limitation of overseas commitments was a more difficult nettle to grasp, but in 1870 British garrisons were withdrawn from New Zealand and Australia, and in the next year from Canada. Many in the dominions were displeased and a number of bodies, for example, the Royal Colonial Institute, acted as pressure groups with the intention of trying to persuade Britain to reverse the policy of retrenchment. But even Disraeli's government was unsympathetic on this issue. Indeed, from 1880 to 1882 Carnarvon presided over a Royal Commission to examine the defence of the Empire and even the appearance of delegates from several colonies failed to persuade the government to alter course. As it turned out, it was the scramble for Africa and the Egyptian crises which forced a change in policy, and increased commitments in those areas diminished the prospects of a reversion to the pre-1870 situation.

It proved equally impossible to persuade the largely self-governing territories of Australia, Canada and New Zealand to take up the burden of defending themselves. Enthusiasts for Empire apparently saw nothing inconsistent in demands for autonomy and a sizeable imperial garrison. In Canada the policy was accepted more readily than in the other two countries, perhaps because the proximity of the United States made any intervention by a European power unlikely. In New Zealand and Australia the populations wanted the best of both worlds. If in fact a serious external threat had existed in the 1870s (as distinct from supposed dangers) it seems likely not only that these territories would have been willing to spend significant sums on defence but also that Britain would have responded similarly.

The fact remained that there was no shared perspective on foreign affairs between Britain and the dominions. It was believed in some quarters in the dominions that they might be dragged into war as a result of Britain's policies elsewhere. The future premier of Victoria, Charles Duffy, expounded this view in a famous debate in 1869, arguing that an arrangement should be made by which in time of war the colonies might be regarded as neutral. It followed logically from this that the colonies should be completely independent and have the power to make treaties themselves. This opinion was not that of a majority but it was not uncommon either. In Britain it was similarly feared lest the mother country be embroiled in disputes in which she not only did not share the objectives of the dominion but actually wanted to avoid an involvement which might complicate relations with another European power to the detriment of British interests. The party which considered colonial connections a risky venture was not uninfluential in British political life; at one time or another, Derby, Gladstone and Salisbury all expressed apprehension.

It was unfortunate that the behaviour of the dominions lent colour to these fears. Australia and New Zealand argued that imperial expansion in the Pacific could win Britain a huge Empire. What use such territory would be in economic terms was obscure and in this period any strategic value seemed negligible, though the issue continued to be pressed. In 1883 Derby was visited by some Australian representatives who wanted him to annex Samoa, New Guinea and the islands to its north, and the New Hebrides. Writing to Sir Henry Ponsonby he lamented:

> I asked them whether they did not want another planet all to themselves? and they seemed to think it would be a desirable arrangement, if only feasible. The magnitude of their ideas is appalling to the English mind .... It is hardly too much to say that they consider the whole Southern Pacific theirs de jure; the French possession of New Caledonia they regard as an act of robbery committed on them. It certainly is hard for four millions of English settlers to have only a country as big as Europe to fill up.[5]

Despite the lack of official enthusiasm for a strengthening of the bonds of Empire, the early 1880s witnessed a good deal of unofficial activity. In 1884 the Imperial Federation League was founded, surviving until 1893, and its arguments gradually came to be deployed in favour of regular conferences to discuss important problems, of which the most pressing were economic and defence issues. For a variety of reasons Salisbury's government was willing to accept this suggestion and in 1887 the first Colonial Conference was held in London. The Prime Minister did not have great hopes of any positive outcome regarding the issues which troubled relations with the dominions, telling the Secretary for the Colonies, 'I will do my best to keep my temper, but the *outrecuidance* of your Greater Britain is sometimes trying.'[6] A few days later Salisbury had clearly found Australian demands for action in the New Hebrides intolerable:

> They are the most unreasonable people I ever heard or dreamed of. They want us to incur all the bloodshed, the dangers and the stupendous cost of a war with France, of which almost the exclusive burden will fall upon us, for a group of islands which to us are as valueless as the South Pole, and to which they are only attached by a debating club sentiment.[7]

In these circumstances it is hardly surprising that no real progress on defence and foreign policy issues was made.

Although formal achievements were minimal at both the 1887 conference and the subsidiary colonial conference held at Ottawa in 1894, the meetings were not entirely profitless. Salisbury's request in 1887 for the colonies to make general contributions to defence was rejected, though both in 1887 and 1894 Jan Hofmeyr agreed in favour of a surcharge of two per cent on existing duties on foreign imports throughout the Empire and the allocation of this revenue to the Royal Navy. Furthermore, it is evident that as a result of the conferences all parties understood more clearly the nature of the foreign policy problem. If agreement on a solution was not reached, at least all recognized the fact that it was difficult for Britain to pursue a consistent foreign policy which incorporated the potentially conflicting claims of Empire and Europe.

Those favouring closer ties soon appreciated that deeds rather than words were the most effective weapons. Duffy's views of 1869 were rejected by the Australian delegations of 1887 and 1894. The idea of independent treaties between colonies and foreign powers was derided as detrimental to imperial unity. When Britain found herself in difficulties in South Africa and Egypt in the 1880s volunteer forces appeared from Australasia. Even the vexed question of protectionist policies faded into the background for a few years. An atmosphere of goodwill towards an implied goal of imperial co-operation was thus created and with a change in international circumstances in the mid-1890s this more pleasant atmosphere was to be of some importance.

## II

In 1895 a change of government in Britain brought Chamberlain to the Colonial Office. His concern for the British economy and for the preservation of British influence was soon to lead to a sharp change of course. After only a few months in office, in November 1895, he declared: 'I am told on every hand that Imperial federation is a vain and empty dream.... Dreams of that kind which have so powerful an influence upon the imagination of men, have somehow or other an unaccountable way of being realized in their own time.'[8] Chamberlain threw himself into the task of re-organizing and strengthening imperial relationships, a process described by Garvin as 'moving in its own way not at all towards rigid centralization of any sort, but towards some elastic kind of Zollverein and Kriegsverein'.[9] The Jameson Raid and attendant political controversy were to delay but not deflect Chamberlain from his course, but by the beginning of 1897 he was 'hurrying to prepare a British empire to survive in a world of continental super-states'.[10]

Early in 1897 Chamberlain realized that the celebration of the Diamond Jubilee later that year would provide a suitable occasion to attempt to strengthen imperial connections. Accordingly, invitations were sent to the premiers of the self-governing colonies (Canada, New Zealand, Newfoundland, the Cape, Natal and the six Australian states) to attend another colonial conference, to be held from 24 June to 8 July.

On their arrival all 11 premiers were named as Privy Councillors, some indication of the importance attached to the meeting. At the opening of the conference Chamberlain spoke in general terms of a closer political connection, including the possibility of a Federal Council, but laid greater emphasis upon the more urgent tasks of promoting co-operation in the fields of trade and defence.

Yet despite all the goodwill shown by the premiers the conference achieved very little. The strongest support for the notion of an imperial council came from Seddon, thus accurately reflecting Trollope's opinion that the New Zealanders were more English than any Englishmen at home. The Canadian, Laurier, believed that existing political relationships were satisfactory but recognized that the situation could not endure; the link would invariably either become much stronger or much weaker. The premier of New South Wales, Reid, was reluctant to adhere to a more precise formulation of closer ties but his general view of the imperial relationship was unusually prescient: 'The great test of our relations ... will be the next war in which England is engaged ... our money would come; our men would come.'[11] In the end the principal achievement was the decision of 5 July that regular conferences should be held, preferably every three years. If Chamberlain had hoped for more, he was, nevertheless, not displeased by the outcome – which he saw as 'the beginning of it – the beginning of a Federal Conference'.[12]

The outbreak of the Boer War in October 1899 demonstrated the strength of pro-British sentiment in Australia, Canada and New Zealand. Large numbers of volunteer troops came from all three countries and distinguished themselves in difficult conditions. The goodwill of the self-governing colonies stood in marked contrast to the anti-British sentiments prevalent in Europe, even in those countries with which Chamberlain had been trying to develop closer links in 1898–99. It is hardly surprising, then, that the attractiveness of the arguments used by those who wanted the imperial connection to be given first (and dominant) priority in the determination of foreign policy was strongly reinforced.

At this moment of apparent imperial amity, made all the more conspicuous by the malevolence shown elsewhere in the world, there were still indications that the establishment of a closer relationship might pose problems. In July 1899 Laurier had argued that Canada should show sympathy towards British problems with the Boers but insisted that Canada was not bound to take part in any conflict. His decision in October that year to send volunteers to South Africa produced violent protests from Bourassa and his followers among the French-speaking Canadians. By November 1899 negotiations over Samoa between Britain, Germany and the USA were completed, but the agreement between the major powers left opinion in New Zealand distinctly disgruntled. Australia, responding to similar domestic feelings, used the opportunity provided by the Boer War to assert the right to influence foreign affairs within her geographical region. Important diversities of attitude resulting mainly from differences of geographical location surfaced even at this time of a strong tide of pro-British feeling. In Britain, too, not all of those who were dismayed by European attitudes drew the conclusion that the answer lay in a consolidation of imperial connections. In April 1901 Hamilton asserted openly that

> we must alter our foreign policy, and throw our lot in for good or bad, with some other Power.... As we now stand, we are an object of envy and of greed to all the other Powers.... Our interests being so extended makes it almost impossible for us to concentrate sufficiently, in any one direction, the pressure and power of the Empire so as to deter foreign nations from trying to encroach upon our interests in that particular quarter.[13]

In an attempt, perhaps, to avoid any final decision between the rival schools of thought in the next few years Britain seems to have tried simultaneously to strengthen imperial ties and to diminish tensions with other powers. Agreements with Japan (1902), France (1904), and Russia (1907) were reached, but they were not received without criticism from fairly predictable quarters in both Britain and the dominions. The Anglo-Japanese treaty was especially disliked in Australia and New Zealand where racial antipathy towards Asiatics was already strong. Indeed, in Australia the issue helped promote the cause of compulsory military training and also contributed to the beginnings of the Australian navy in 1909. The other agreements attracted less unfavourable comment in the dominions, though in 1907 signature of an Anglo-French convention regulating the New Hebrides excited antipodean feelings.

Meanwhile the system of colonial conferences was continued with further meetings in 1902 and 1907. The 1902 conference resolved some outstanding problems involving subsidies for British naval protection but otherwise demonstrated a lack of imperial cohesion. Seddon proposed the creation of an imperial militia in each of the countries which would be equipped for overseas service in the general imperial interest; strongly backed by Brodrick, the Secretary for War, the scheme was abandoned because of strong opposition from Canada and Australia. More generally, Chamberlain opined that 'the political federation of the Empire is within the limits of possibility'.[14] His view was not only opposed by some premiers but also by his own Prime Minister who very wisely observed: 'an attempt to force the various parts of the Empire into a mutual arrangement and subordination for which they are not ready ... may only produce a reaction'.[15] Nor were negotiations on commercial questions any more successful than those on other issues. Chamberlain and Brodrick were very disappointed, not least because both of them believed that the opinions which had prevailed were not based upon realistic strategic analysis.

The disappointments of the 1902 conference were to a certain extent offset by the emergence of the Committee of Imperial Defence. Its origins can be traced back to 1895 but it was during the period from December 1902 to May 1904 that the committee was reshaped; on 4 May

1904 a permanent secretariat to service the CID was created. Most of the credit for this creation should be given to Balfour, following an initial prompting by Brodrick and Selborne, the First Lord of the Admiralty. It was Balfour, too, who realized most clearly the necessity of flexibility within the committee – both in terms of membership and competence. Curiously, this made the CID appear more attractive to both enthusiasts for, and sceptics of, imperial federation. During the transitional stage of the formation of the CID 'in order to bring imperial matters more into focus, Balfour invited the Canadian War Minister, Robert Borden, to attend meetings as a member. Balfour told the King that the Committee had the potentiality to become an Imperial Council.'[16] Whether or not dominion representatives participated, the CID was to perform a function vital to the adjustment of defence and foreign policy requirements. Such a review body had long been needed; it was ironic that it was born in the aftermath of the failure of the imperial federalists in 1902 and the departure of Chamberlain from the Colonial Office in September 1903.

The trend towards a full-scale review of British commitments continued in the next few years. Garrisons were sharply reduced in a number of areas, including South Africa, and withdrawn entirely from the Caribbean. Despite this adjustment of commitments pressure grew in Britain for conscription, leading to the foundation of the National Service League in 1905. The importance of the CID grew as British governments became increasingly alarmed by the extent of their obligations and the paucity of their resources. In these circumstances (despite the rebuffs on all fronts, political, military and economic, in the 1902 conference) pressure for the pooling of the resources of Empire was maintained. Chamberlain's successor, Lyttelton, advocated re-naming the conference the Imperial Council and, after the change of government in December 1905, his successor, Elgin, took up the idea. The changes in international circumstances, coupled with changes in personnel, produced a rather different atmosphere at the 1907 conference. The premiers of Australia and New Zealand, Deakin and Ward, put forward a plan for an Imperial Council staffed by a permanent secretariat. This seemed to complement the continuing campaigns within the Conservative party for tariff reform and imperial preference. Shortly before the 1907 conference, held in April and May, the economist Hewins told Balfour that the purpose of tariff reform was 'the deliberate adoption of the Empire as distinguished from the United Kingdom as the basis of public policy' which would in turn lead to 'the greater political or social stability, or greater defensive power, of the Empire'.[17]

If circumstances had seemed to favour the protagonists of integrated imperial policy, the 1907 conference, nevertheless, enjoyed only the limited success of agreeing to create an Imperial General Staff. Opposition from Laurier, whose nationalism contained a certain element of isolationism, prevented the establishment of an Imperial Council. Laurier in fact took rather a gloomy view of international developments, having remarked on 27 March 1907 that 'I must adhere to the view I expressed five years ago that for no consideration would Canada be induced to be drawn into the vortex of European militarism'.[18] Other leaders were not as critical or as pessimistic as Laurier but the records of the 1907 conference show that the opinion was gaining ground that the countries were autonomous nations within the Empire. If an Imperial Council or an Imperial General Staff were to be created then it would only be on a basis of constitutional equality rather than disguised subservience to British foreign policy requirements. The implication that British and imperial interests in defence and foreign policy might diverge was clear. On balance, then, the 1907 conference witnessed a further rejection of federalist dreams; a rather important concession to the federalists was that future meetings would be Imperial rather than Colonial conferences.

By the end of 1907 the process of promoting rational re-examination of defence requirements within the framework of national foreign policies had been advanced in both Britain and several dominions. The integration of defence and foreign policy on an imperial basis had not only not been achieved but looked distinctly improbable. Although some enthusiasts had hoped to make Britain independent of European politics, events in Europe and overseas had worked against this vision. It was becoming evident that it was both possible and legitimate for Britain and the dominions to hold markedly different views on important foreign policy issues.

Relations with Japan provided perhaps the best illustration of this state of affairs, as they had threatened so to do ever since 1902. In the long run British and Japanese interests in East Asia were probably incompatible, but this was certainly not recognized by Grey, who declared in 1911 that 'The Japanese Government have been good allies; they have never strained that alliance'.[19] The Foreign Secretary pointed out later in the meeting that none of the British arrangements with Japan, either existing or envisaged, would affect the rights of the dominions to treat the question of immigration in whatever fashion they wished. The official Foreign Office view similarly provides an interesting insight into the divergence of interests: 'the maintenance of the Alliance is of such vital Imperial interest that its prolongation or otherwise should not be dependent on the view of the Dominions'.[20] In strong contrast, Australian statesmen throughout the period argued that the expansionist aims of the Japanese were bound to threaten the security of other powers in the Pacific. In addition there was trenchant criticism of the 1907 and 1910 agreements on Manchuria made between Japan and Russia; it was argued that these agreements would not only directly threaten British interests in China but would in the long run leave Japan more of a free hand to be active in the Pacific. These protestations were ignored in Britain as it was felt that opposition to Japan would create insuperable strategic problems for already over-stretched naval and military resources.

In July 1909 a special imperial conference on defence was held, but served only to show how far apart views were. The Admiralty, quite understandably, wanted centralized control of all naval forces in the event of war but this was opposed from a number of quarters. In fact the dominions soon set about building up their own forces and Fisher, the First Sea Lord, soon changed his tune from one of complaint about the selfishness of the dominions to enthusiasm. 'It means eventually', he said, 'Canada, Australia, New Zealand, the Cape ... and India running a complete Navy. We manage the job in Europe. They'll manage it against the Yankees, Japs, and Chinese, as occasion requires out there.'[21] Shortly before the outbreak of war Fisher showed that he at least had learned political lessons from his experiences in dealing with these imperial questions: 'the real culprit is A.K. Wilson [Fisher's successor] who will not understand that our great Colonies are practically independent nations and are not going to subscribe to other people's Navies'.[22] But in 1909 it still seemed impossible to reconcile a world-wide strategy of the kind favoured by Britain as a natural complement to a global foreign policy, with the local, and often parochial, strategic and political demands of most of the dominions.

By 1911 the international situation had deteriorated sufficiently for it to be felt necessary to brief the dominion premiers at a special meeting of the CID. This was not a recognition by the British government of the legitimacy of dominion participation in the making of foreign as well as defence policy, though the fact that Borden believed that was what had been conceded shows how unrealistic British attempts to separate defence and foreign policy questions were. The fact was that all the participating governments were anxious to preserve the maximum autonomy for themselves but were usually quite ready to sacrifice the autonomy of other governments in the cause of the general interest. The state of affairs that existed in 1911 (and changed little before the outbreak of war) was succinctly stated by Professor Beloff:

> Where questions of foreign policy directly involving a specific issue of interest to a dominion were concerned, their governments were bound to seek a means of seeing that their influence was felt and of protesting if their opinions were not sought. But on the great issues of European and so of world policy with which Britain was wrestling they neither had specific counsel to offer, nor alternative sources of information with which to support any views they might have, nor was it felt that their actual or presumed contribution to the Empire's fighting strength were such as to give them a prescriptive right to take part in the making of the vital decisions.[23]

The crisis of the summer of 1914 posed a number of problems for the makers of British foreign policy. Not the least of their difficulties was to determine the likely reaction of the dominions to the involvement of Britain in war. The speed at which events moved prevented the British government from consulting with the dominions as had been promised. The recent history of imperial relations lent plausibility to two quite different possible courses of action by the dominions in the event of a declaration of war. On the one hand Britain remembered the unstinting aid given during the Boer War. Against that had to be debited the insistently parochial viewpoints so frequently displayed during the conferences, most consistently by Canada. Furthermore, whereas in 1899 it had been argued that events in South Africa were of interest to several of the dominions the arrangements made by Britain with Japan, France and Russia since that time had not been universally popular in the dominions. Indeed, some statesmen had specifically counselled against British entanglement with the Continental powers. There was thus some uncertainty as to dominion attitudes towards a British declaration of war.

III

In the event the reactions of the dominions made such doubts seem very unrealistic. When war was declared on Germany, New Zealand automatically regarded herself at war with Britain's enemies. There was no separate declaration of war, nor was there a debate in Parliament and, apart from a few socialists, no public dissent. In Australia a general election was in progress, but as the outgoing premier stated on 31 July 'Australia is part of the Empire. When the Empire is at war, so is Australia at war.'[24] In Canada it was likewise assumed that Britain's war was also Canada's war. In South Africa too, though there was some debate and considerable anti-British feeling among some sections of the population, entry into the war was swiftly accepted.

In retrospect it is not hard to find reasons for this display of unity. The claims of kith and kin were by no means negligible, and it is worth noting in this context that it was only in South Africa and Canada – where there were sizeable united groups of non-British but European descent – that voices of any significance were raised against Britain's war. But there were other reasons which pointed to active support for Britain. Statesmen in the dominions knew that if Germany won the war in Europe their countries would not remain immune from the effects of that victory. In English-speaking South Africa there were strong fears of German ambitions in the region; as it turned out the government had to cope with a minor Boer rebellion and it was not until the German colony of South West Africa had fallen to South African forces that fears for future security were banished. In Canada any collapse of the Empire, or the conclusion of a British agreement with Germany on unfavourable terms, risked the effective incorporation of Canada into the sphere of influence, political and economic, of the United States. A decline in British strength threatened the security of Australia and New Zealand; both countries feared Japan and neither had much faith in or liking for the United States. Strategic, economic and political factors thus strongly reinforced the immediate reaction favourable to Britain which made itself manifest in August 1914.

It thus seems clear that the influence of Empire on the key decision of 1914 was at most very limited. It is true that concern about excessive strains on British resources (in part caused by the demands of Empire) had helped change the course of British foreign policy after the turn of the century. But it is equally clear that attempts to produce an integrated imperial defence policy, and thus by implication an integrated foreign policy, had foundered. It is also evident that in 1914 imperial questions played a negligible part in influencing the decision for war; in fact Anglo-German relations outside the European framework were better in the summer of 1914 than they had been for many years. Furthermore, the dominions entered the war in 1914 because of the interplay of emotional, political, strategic and economic factors and not because they felt committed to Britain's cause through any formal or implied arrangements. The CID and its General Staff had undertaken preparatory work in the decade before 1914 which was to prove invaluable during the war of 1914–18 so in this matter the conferences had not been devoid of impact, but it was not possible for Britain to plead to the dominions (as France did to Britain) that there was an obligation to lend her support because certain dispositions had been made which presupposed such support. Foreign policy decisions and imperial questions had necessarily been linked but the hopes of Chamberlain, Seddon and a few others that the Empire might become an integrated political and military unit had been illusory. Yet in 1914 the Empire readily accepted the British decision and backed it with ungrudging support, as in 1897 Reid, Chamberlain's sceptical opponent, had always supposed it would.

Once it became clear that the war was not to be of short duration, however, dominion pressures on the determination of British foreign policy resumed. The despatch of significant numbers of troops from the dominions to Europe compelled dominion politicians to seek to influence Britain. In real terms New Zealand made the greatest contribution, with about 20 per cent of the male population serving abroad. Australia, with a total population of about five million, suffered more fatal casualties than the United States. As Professor Beloff has pointed out: 'it is not surprising that their leaders were unimpressed by American moralizing over the selfishness of their war aims'.[25] Canada, India and South Africa also made notable contributions to the war effort, as the Empire held together much better than some German strategists had supposed was likely. Just as it had been impossible in peacetime to invent a structure through which the dominions could influence policy decisions, so did outbreak of war fail to solve the problem. In fact the appointment of Kitchener as Secretary of State for War seems to have intensified existing difficulties. He was obsessed by the need for centralized control and dominated by a passion for concealing his intentions; these characteristics created problems in Britain and contributed considerably to misunderstanding overseas. By the time of his death on 5 June 1916 a certain strain had crept into relationships with the dominions, not least because imperial war policy had enjoyed only limited success.

During the war opinion in the dominions became more critical of the demands made by Britain on their resources and their goodwill, though there was no threat of a withdrawal of support. As in peacetime British policy-makers were obliged to try to balance the regional demands of some dominions against the requirements of Britain's global strategy. Statesmen in the dominions had to reconcile conflicting local pressures (which grew as the costs of war, in lives and money, mounted) with the obvious necessity of a coherent centralized imperial policy. It is not hard to find examples of conflicting interests and pressures. The entry of Japan into the war against Germany soon created problems. The long-term effect was to encourage Japanese activity in China (as in the case of the Twenty-one Demands of 1915) and hence to promote fears of an expansionist Japan in Britain and the United States. In 1914, however, Japan turned to the congenial task of seizing Germany's Far Eastern and Pacific Empire. Japanese actions were on the whole not well-received in Australia and New Zealand, though in both countries there was relief that the German menace had been removed. Harcourt's opinion that 'it would be impossible at this moment to risk a quarrel with our Ally'[26] was shared by his colleagues in London. In the dominions, however, there were powerful dissentient voices: 'We would feel safer with the Pacific islands under the flag of a white Power than under the emblem of the Rising Sun'[27] trumpeted one newspaper. In the event the views of the dominions were subordinated to the requirements of British policy, though it was always evident that there were limits to such accommodation. The forceful protests of Hughes, Prime Minister of Australia from October 1915 until after the Versailles Conference of 1919, made it plain that concessions to Japan were dictated only by wartime circumstances and did not reflect a change of opinion in Australasia. These views were echoed by the Governor-General of Australia, Ferguson, and his counterpart in New Zealand, Liverpool. In Britain Hughes was not without influential support, for Robertson, the Chief of the Imperial War Staff, noted in 1916 (with reference to the Pacific islands seized by Australia and New Zealand) 'that these islands form a valuable buffer between the mainland and possible Japanese encroachment'.[28]

It should not be imagined that the stridency of dominion demands that their interest not be overlooked steemed solely from parochial notions of strategy. A number of factors caused the dominions to try to influence British foreign policy and the wartime strategy with which it was associated. Primarily, of course, the dominions did have legitimate, identifiably different strategic interests from those of Britain. In the second place the dominions had, in effect, temporarily ceded control of troops and territory to Britain for the duration of the War. Understandably, it was felt that these acts of generosity warranted a sympathetic hearing for their views in London. Finally, just as the prolongation of the war caused political tensions in Britain by making conscription a central issue, so too was the same effect felt in the dominions. But in the dominions the position of the politicians was more vulnerable because it could be argued that Australians or Canadians were dying in defence of British rather than the dominions' interests. The question of conscription split the Labour Party in Australia and promoted a revival of French Canadian nationalism. In New Zealand conscription happily proved to be unnecessary, so the government was subject to much less dramatic pressure.

The British government was compelled by these circumstances to make some gesture towards claims for consultation over matters of high policy. The disastrous Gallipoli campaign of 1915 produced renewed pressure from the dominions, though responsible opinion overseas recognized that detailed consultation on military affairs was implausible at a distance of thousands of miles. The British government responded in two ways. First, the informal arrangement introduced by Asquith by which visiting statesmen from the dominions were invited to attend occasional Cabinet meetings was comprehensively reviewed when Lloyd George became Prime Minister in December 1916. On 20 March 1917 the premiers of the dominions assembled at the first of a series of special meetings of the War Cabinet, renamed for this purpose the Imperial War Cabinet. This experiment was repeated in the summer of 1918. The debates at these meetings seem to have left the majority of participants confused rather than enlightened, but they met the important political point of formal, if irregular, consultation. The more important concession was acknowledgment of the need to consult the dominions regarding peace negotiations and terms. This point was conceded in the first few days of Lloyd George's premiership and represented formal recognition of the fact that the dominions would not only have some distinctive attitudes on important questions but would also expect serious consideration of these opinions.

The importance of dominion influence upon the making of British foreign policy was soon to receive wider recognition. In June 1916 Hughes had attended the economic conference at Paris and had made it plain that he attended with full powers and not as a minor figure in the British delegation. Like all the dominion leaders, Hughes was subject to tremendous domestic pressure (in his case it was to lead to a party and personal re-alignment) which he considered could only be contained by the imposition of harsh terms on the defeated powers. Hughes, to the disgust of Wilson, proceeded in the period 1917–19 to treat Lloyd George in the way Foch behaved towards Clemenceau. Aided and abetted by sections of the press, Hughes whipped up anti-German hysteria in the cause of a vindictive peace. As a leading authority on the economic settlement commented, 'Hughes was partly deaf, easily irritated and seldom afflicted by doubt. Many of his British Empire colleagues regarded him as "l'enfant terrible" to be avoided where possible and accommodated when necessary.'[29] The decision on 26 November 1918 of the Imperial War Cabinet to appoint Hughes as chairman of its Committee on Indemnity confirmed that there would be no moderation in the assessment of war damages. By 10 December the committee had come to the view that Germany owed £24,000 million, which should be paid in annual instalments. This folly, however, paled into insignificance beside Lloyd George's decision to appoint Hughes as one of Britain's delegates to the Peace Conference Commission on Reparation. This action not only prolonged British adherence to a ludicrous over-estimate of Germany's capacity to pay reparations but also led to a near-breakdown of relations with the United States. When Wilson threatened to abandon the conference on 7 April 1919, Lloyd George was compelled to ditch the proposals put forward by Hughes and the other intransigents. The effect on American opinion about the true nature of Allied war aims had, however, been considerable and adverse.

Dominion independence of mind was also reflected in territorial demands which injured relations with both Britain and the United States. In Britain a considerable body of opinion realized that if the peace conference awarded Britain an array of territorial concessions (either in the form of outright cession or of mandates) then it might easily be thought that the war had been fought for the extension of the Empire. Borden, from his Canadian vantage-point, was particularly alive to the poor impression this would create in the United States. Conflict was made more acute by the position taken up by Walter Long, the Colonial Secretary for the last two years of the war, who acted as apologist for even the most extreme demands of the dominions. By the summer of 1918 it was evident that a major breakdown in relations was in the offing. Hughes, Massey, Long and other hardliners were quite determined not to give way to those who favoured some compromise with the United States. The party of compromise, headed by Lloyd George and Balfour, proved, however, quite incapable of formulating a common policy and thus entered the period of negotiations in some disarray. This was to be advantageous to their better-organized and more consistent opponents.

Lloyd George's first priority was to secure some form of Anglo-American colonial concordat. Additionally, he wanted concessions to Britain in the Middle East – an area believed by almost all leading British politicians to be of vital economic and strategic importance. As well as having to balance these needs against the complex requirements of reparation and territorial redistribution in Europe, Lloyd George had also to deal with the demands of the dominions, which were largely annexationist in character. The most difficult imperial question was that of the former German colonies occupied during the war by South Africa, Australia and New Zealand, not least because Wilson had been assured by Lloyd George that the principle of self-determination was applicable to the German colonies. In July 1918, with the aid of Smuts, British politicians tried to find a way out of this dilemma. A form of international control (the Development Board), headed by the United States, was to be set up in Africa. This proposal commanded general assent, particularly when it became clear that it was to deal only with tropical Africa, thus leaving the annexationist ambitions of the dominions untouched. Suggestions that the United States be offered colonial territory were rejected on all sides. Hughes put the matter in a nutshell: 'as regards the Pacific islands ... if anyone wanted to shift Australia from them they would have to come and do it!'[30]

By the time preparations for the peace conference were in hand nothing had been settled. A variety of ideas had been put forward to deal with the question of German East Africa, including the possibility of it becoming a mandate for India. Quite how a country which was not yet self-governing could undertake the duties of a mandate was, understandably enough, a question which was never elucidated. What was clear was that British policy was moving in the direction of acceptance of American proposals that a system of mandates be introduced and authorized by the League of Nations when that body came into existence. If this system were adopted then effective power could be wielded without undue perturbation of Wilson's non-annexationist ideals. It was widely assumed that it would be the wish of the United States to be involved as little as possible in this system; privately it was realized that if the United States were to insist on claiming mandates then the various claims of the dominions could no longer be balanced. In fact several policy-makers argued that the United States was positively unfit to discharge such obligations in areas with complex problems. Amery had referred in uncomplimentary fashion to 'the vigorous but crude ways' of the Americans which 'would be bound to lead to friction'[31] in the Middle East. Curzon had come to a similar conclusion months before when he had argued 'the only civilized Power that is either equipped for the task, or is interested in it, is Great Britain'.[32] On 19 December 1918 Smuts discussed colonial questions at length with Wilson but was unable to reach agreement. He wrote to Lloyd George the following day: 'I need not point out the trouble you are going to have with these Dominions on this matter . . . he [Wilson] must be made to realise your difficulties and assist you to overcome them.'[33] In the absence of a comprehensive agreement it was clear that individual claims would be pursued, even at the risk of imperilling good relations between the United States, Britain and the dominions.

Leaders of the dominions seem to have shown remarkable insouciance in the face of this threat to inter-Allied relationships. Hughes, of course, was at the front of the fray. He regarded, not wholly incorrectly, Wilson's schemes as the product of an impractical mind and the enthusiasm for mandates as 'what a toy was to a child'.[34] The more subtle aim of Lloyd George and Milner of obliging the United States to take on a mandated territory, thus disarming American critics, Hughes treated with scarcely-veiled contempt as a subterfuge that would in the long run deceive nobody but would complicate already difficult problems. On 24 January 1919 the matter was raised in the presence of the dominion leaders at the Council of Ten. Hughes argued that 'Australia would see a potential enemy'[35] in the establishment of a mandatory power in New Guinea. Smuts demanded the annexation of South-West Africa and Massey insisted on Samoa. After their departure Wilson discounted their opinions and argued that annexations would be contrary to the whole conception of the League of Nations. When these tidings reached the dominion leaders they were both amazed and furious, and Lloyd George found himself saddled with the impossible task of trying to square the circle.

The matter was further considered on 27 January when Wilson flatly ruled out the claims of the dominions. Hughes challenged Wilson's views, pointing out inconsistencies between his proposed system of mandates in areas outside Europe and his readiness to recognize the full independence of new authorities in Europe – for example in Alsace-Lorraine. The next day Lloyd George added his pleas to those of the dominions, though he was well aware that this would weaken his argument against the excessive claims of Italy and France. Wilson, however, continued to insist that the League of Nations must allocate the mandates and when Hughes (who had been put under great pressure to accept a modified system of mandates) refused this further concession, deadlock had been reached. Australia and New Zealand were, in Wilson's words, apparently 'prepared to defy the appeal of the whole civilised world'.[36] Dominion recalcitrance was, unsurprisingly, supported behind the scenes by France, Japan and Italy – all of which countries had large territorial ambitions.

Fortunately, during the next few days Lloyd George, Botha and Smuts were able to persuade Hughes not only that Australia would obtain the mandate he desired but that mandates were, in fact, annexation disguised under a different title to enable Wilson to save face. On 30 January the proposals put forward by Lloyd George were reluctantly accepted by the disputants. The matter was not finally settled until the actual allocation of the mandates in May 1919, which when determined conclusively demonstrated the triumph of the dominion annexationists over the idealistic Wilson. Even the final settlement, however, could not conceal the divergent claims on British loyalties.

There was much British sympathy for dominion claims and even for the Australian version of the Monroe Doctrine which Hughes wished to see applied to the Pacific. The very hostile reception given by the press to the system of mandates showed how thin was the ice upon which Lloyd George skated. In particular the press feared the Empire might be disrupted by the attempt to conciliate the United States, and that imperial harmony would be sacrificed on the altar of internationalism – already widely perceived as a false god. On the other hand, leading members of the Imperial War Cabinet had long ago concluded that the only possible way of securing stability in the world was by close and friendly association with the United States. If such co-operation could only be obtained by accepting mandates and sacrificing annexations then this was a price Lloyd George and Balfour were fully prepared to pay. Understandably, the dominions were not. If Britain perforce acceded to dominion demands in 1919 it was nevertheless plain to all parties that dominion security and British security were no longer (if indeed they ever had been) identical in character. It was thus inevitable that in the long term, and perhaps even in the short term, Britain and the dominions would be led to pursue quite different foreign policies.

Although there were important differences on economic and territorial issues it should not be thought that the measure of agreement between Britain and the dominions was negligible. During the course of the discussions preceding signature of the Versailles Treaty Britain frequently relied heavily upon support from the dominions. When France attempted to pursue her claim to the Rhineland (or at the very least to secure its permanent separation from Germany) British resistance was fortified by the opinions of Canada and South Africa. Lloyd George's belief that European security and recovery could only be achieved by treating Germany as reasonably as was possible in the fevered atmosphere of anti-German feeling led him to contest the absurdly inflated claims of Poland; in this he had powerful support from Smuts. The South African saw clearly the dangers likely to arise from a vindictive peace. 'You may strip Germany of her colonies', he said, 'reduce her armaments to a mere police force and her navy to that of a fifth-rate power, all the same, in the end, if she feels that she has been unjustly treated in the peace of 1919 she will find means of exacting retribution from her conquerors.'[37] If other dominion leaders disagreed or felt less strongly on this issue they did agree with another of Smuts' insights: 'Under this Treaty Europe will know no peace, and the undertaking to defend Europe against aggression may at any time bring the British Empire also into the fire.'[38] Even those, like Hughes and Massey, who had been more inclined to take a harsh view of Germany were extremely reluctant to accept any commitment to a long-term defence of the settlement. As Botha put it, it was quite possible to envisage circumstances in which Britain became involved in conflict and one or more dominions remained neutral; it was the inevitable result of 'the status of independent nationhood of the dominions'.[39] Lloyd George was quick to use these opinions and reservations to support his arguments in discussions with Clemenceau and Wilson, though his advocacy of restraint was only intermittently successful.

Within the dominions, as in Britain, there were divided opinions on the creation of the League of Nations. Lord Robert Cecil was the principal British advocate of the creation of an international body and he received strong support from Smuts. Lloyd George's enthusiasm for such a body was distinctly limited because many of his ministerial colleagues were opposed to a League which possessed powers of compulsion. Collective security based upon independent coercive power, as advocated by Wilson, Lloyd George flatly vetoed. Many dominion leaders were prepared to accept the League only as a concession necessary to secure the amiability of Wilson on other issues which they considered more important. As ever, Hughes did not beat about the bush:

> Wilson regards the League of Nations as the great Charter of the World that is to be and sees himself through the roseate cloud of dreams officiating as the High Priest in the Temple in which the Sarcophagus or Ark containing the body or ashes of this amazing gift to Mankind is to rest in majestic seclusion for all time. Give him a League of Nations and he will give us all the rest. Good. He shall have his toy![40]

Hughes clearly spoke for many in Britain who saw the League and the Covenant as tiresome necessities and his robust refusal to regard the League as an international authority authorized to enquire into supposed existing injustices received support at the very highest level. Balfour, for example, was utterly opposed to any right of the League to investigate Irish, Indian or Egyptian demands for independence. Those who had only a faint enthusiasm for the League – and they were many, especially after the refusal of the United States to join – could hardly be blamed for arguing that while all states might be equal it was nevertheless true that some were more equal than others.

The leading enthusiast for the League among the statesmen of the dominions was Smuts, who saw the League as a possible guarantor of security in a reconstructed world. The problem of security, however, was bound to lead to conflict between those who saw the League as the defender of the situation established in 1919 and those who envisaged it acting as a conciliatory body committed in the long term to emendation of the treaties. Furthermore, if dominions were to assume that the League could look after the problems of security in Europe then they might either neglect their own defences (as Canada was ultimately to do) or concentrate upon a robust, and often belligerently nationalist, regional policy (as Australia certainly did under Hughes and his successors). Neither of these attitudes was in the long run likely to assist either the policy of pursuing collective security through the League or that of more tightly-knit imperial defence co-operation. The commitment of the dominions to the League, its principles and its goals was thus formally strong but in practice weak.

Discussions concerning the League highlighted problems in the constitutional relationship between Britain and the dominions. There were those, Hughes and Churchill among them, who feared lest establishment of the League weakened imperial ties. The very establishment of this international body inevitably raised the question of dominion membership. The obvious solution was separate representation for the dominions and this was eventually achieved, despite some opposition from the United States, particularly over the question of Indian membership. There were doubters amongst the imperialists too. Many feared lest multiple membership lead to public discussion of private differences of opinion. Others imagined that international economic obligations might stand in the way of imperial preferences. Those who saw the dominions as part of a British bloc, whether in favour of or against such a body, doubted the wisdom or the propriety of separate representation at any level of international organization. There was, for example, stubborn resistance to dominion representation in the International Labour Organization; the American labour expert Henry Robinson, who was strongly opposed to dominion membership on an individual state basis, being finally over-ruled by the President himself. Membership of the League and its associated organizations thus reawakened old or stimulated new controversies involving the constitutional, economic, and defence relationships between the constituent parts of the Empire.

IV

Thus by the end of 1919 it was clear enough that a new era had dawned in relations between the dominions and Britain. Evolutionary processes which had been set in motion perhaps half a century earlier had accelerated under the pressure of events in the decade preceding the war and during the war itself. The debates concerning important issues of policy immediately after the end of the war had confirmed the simple fact that Britain could not and should not attempt to pursue a foreign policy entirely separate from dominion interests. These discussions had also made it equally plain that Britain could no longer assume dominion consent to her own foreign policy objectives and that the dominions could not individually or collectively expect Britain to underwrite protection of their regional or local interests. In other words Britain and the dominions had come to recognize that imperial unity was a dream and that different states had different interests.

Recognition of these changes has not prevented co-operation in many areas of policy, including foreign affairs, defence and the economy, nor has it meant that the bonds of history, culture and language have been negligible factors in influencing important decisions in London and the dominion capitals. If relations have been formalized by the Balfour Report of 1926 and the Statute of Westminster of 1931 this process of formalization has not actually led to a parting of friends. The behaviour of the dominions in 1939 showed how independence had not necessarily diluted emotional commitment. As recently as 1982 the reaction of the government of New Zealand to the Falklands crisis provided a very modern example of the strength of traditional loyalties.

Yet in the period since 1920 there has also been as much evidence of divergent, and sometimes conflicting interests. Britain and several dominions did not see eye-to-eye over Japanese expansion in the Far East after 1918. In 1954 Australia and New Zealand joined the South East Asia Treaty Organization because they had come to believe that closer co-operation with the United States was essential to the defence of their interests in the Pacific; it was already clear to all parties that any British role in this area would be very limited. The Suez affair divided the dominions deeply, as did the original British declaration of intent concerning entry into the European Community, although by 1973 approval far exceeded hostility. The evolution of a new Commonwealth and the departure of South Africa from it showed that old relationships were not unchanging, even between the predominantly white dominions.

However painful some of these developments were they were accepted because the states involved recognized that a certain price had to be paid for real independence. After the period of peacemaking the realities of independence and the different claims of diverse foreign policy interests could no longer be concealed. Attempts to put together a new imperial framework of co-operation were notably unsuccessful. The influence of Empire upon the foundation of British foreign policy, however strong or weak it might thereafter be, had decisively changed in nature in the few years between 1902 and 1919. Many enthusiasts for imperial unity were undoubtedly dismayed by the increasing evidence of independent policies after the war of 1914–18 but, in truth, the optimism of their predecessors had been based upon unrealistic assumptions. The difficult times through which Britain and the dominions had passed had shown that co-operation was essential but that unity was impossible. Perhaps the notion that imperial considerations ought to be paramount in the determination of British foreign policy had never been realistic. That it was a powerful and attractive idea is unquestionable. If the primacy of imperial questions was ever attainable then the events of the early twentieth century put paid to that possibility. As long as the Empire survived the memories and the dreams lingered on. With the dissolution of the Empire Britain ceased to be a world power and imperial considerations naturally ceased to influence British foreign policy: 'Round the decay of that colossal wreck, boundless and bare, the lone and level sands stretch far away.'[41]

NOTES

1. J. Amery, *Life of Joseph Chamberlain* (London, 1951) Vol. IV, 405. Speech at Birmingham, 16 May 1902.
2. Earl of Cromer, *Modern Egypt* (London, 1908) Vol. II, 75. Salisbury to Baring, 5 Feb. 1892.
3. Cromer, Vol. II, 75fn. Salisbury to Baring, 28 March 1890.
4. J. L. Garvin, *Life of Joseph Chamberlain* (London, 1934) Vol. III, 216.
5. G. E. Buckle (ed.), *The Letters of Queen Victoria* (London, 1928). Second Series, Vol. III, 433. Derby to Ponsonby, 29 June 1883.
6. Viscount Knutsford, *In Black and White* (London, 1926), 217. Salisbury to Holland, 18 April 1887.
7. Knutford, 217. Salisbury to Holland, 27 April 1887.
8. Garvin, Vol. III, 26, *The Times*, 7 Nov. 1895.
9. Garvin, Vol. III, 28.
10. R. Robinson and J. Gallagher, *Africa and the Victorians* (New York, 1967), 404.
11. Garvin, Vol. III, 191.
12. Garvin, Vol. III, 192.
13. G. W. Monger, *The End of Isolation* (London, 1963) 36. Hamilton to Curzon, 25 April 1901.
14. Amery, Vol. IV, 421.
15. Amery, Vol. IV, 417. Speech at the Albert Hall, 7 May 1902.
16. K. Young, *A. J. Balfour* (London, 1963) 224.
17. P. Fraser, *Joseph Chamberlain* (London, 1966) 283. Hewins to Balfour, 18 Feb. 1907.
18. H. Borden (ed.), *Robert Laird Borden: His Memoirs* (London, 1938) 185.
19. G. P. Gooch and H. Temperley (eds.), *British Documents on the Origins of the War, 1898–1914* (London, 1930) Vol. VI, 789. Minutes of the CID, 26 May 1911.
20. F. H. Hinsley (ed.), *British Foreign Policy under Sir Edward Grey* (Cambridge, 1977) 366. Article by I. H. Nish, quoting Nicolson to Ottley, 18 Jan. 1911.
21. A. J. Marder (ed.), *Fear God and Dread Nought* (London, 1956) Vol. II, 266. Fisher to Esher, 13 Sept. 1909.

22. Marder. Vol. II, 266fn. Fisher to Henderson, 10 Feb. 1914.
23. M. Beloff, *Imperial Sunset* (London, 1969), Vol. I, 148.
24. E. A. Benians *et al* (eds.), *The Cambridge History of the British Empire* (Cambridge, 1959) Vol. III, 605.
25. Beloff, 191fn.
26. W. R. Louis, *Germany's lost colonies, 1914–19* (Oxford, 1967) 42. Harcourt to Ferguson, 6 Dec. 1914.
27. Louis, 39; *Southland Times,* 18 Aug. 1914.
28. Louis, 46.
29. R. E. Bunselmeyer, *The Cost of the War, 1914–19: British Economic War Aims and the Origins of Reparation* (Hamden, Connecticut, 1975) 88.
30. Louis, 110.
31. Louis, 112.
32. Earl of Ronaldshay, *Life of Lord Curzon* (London, 1928) Vol. III, 161. Memorandum of 21 Sept. 1917.
33. H. Elcock, *Portrait of a Decision* (London, 1972) 73. Smuts to Lloyd George, 20 Dec. 1918.
34. Louis, 122.
35. Elcock, 74.
36. Elcock, 77.
37. J. C. Smuts, *Jan Christian Smuts* (London, 1952) 227.
38. Ibid., 228.
39. Beloff, 289. Botha to Lloyd George, 15 May 1919.
40. M. L. Dockrill and J. D. Goold, *Peace without Promise* (London, 1981) 59. Hughes to Ferguson, 17 Jan. 1919.
41. P. B. Shelley, *Ozymandias of Egypt.*

# III. Interpreting British Decolonization

# Transfer of Power in India: A 'Re-statement' of an Alternative Approach*

by

Gowher Rizvi

In the lengthening shadows of the imperial sunset, and the availability for the first time of some of the official and personal papers relating to the period of decolonization, numerous monographs and documents on the British Empire have been published. It is natural that India, the 'prima donna' of the scholars, has generated some of the most sophisticated analysis of the workings of Imperial rule. Ever since Anil Seal's *Emergence of Modern Indian Nationalism*, published in 1968, Indian historiography may be said to have come of age. Gone were the days of mere signposting. Simple notions gave way to complex explanations. The history of the British in India was no longer seen as the examplar clash between Imperialism and Nationalism but a much more subtle relationship defined in terms of search for 'collaborators' and the pursuit of power. In the decade and a half since Dr Seal fired his first salvo, a plethora of theses and monographs has emerged so superior in analysis which has considerably altered our understanding of the British rule in India. The explanations are complex and varied. The main thrust of the arguments is that India was far too important – economically and strategically – for the British to contemplate withdrawal;[1] the constitutional innovations and decentralizations are seen as devices to strengthen the stranglehold of imperial control in ever-changing bargains with collaborators; and the growth of self-governing institutions and the devolution of authority is viewed as an exercise in economy by transferring the illusion of power within a system where the controls remained firmly in British hands.[2] The declining military and economic power of Britain only emphasized India's importance to the Empire and consequently the desire to prolong the metropolitan dominion.[3] The British reluctantly agreed to leave India when the collaborators priced themselves out of the bargain and it became no longer profitable to hold on to the country.[4] The arguments are subtle, intellectually exciting and, in an age when Empire is a derogatory concept, they have been so infectiously persuasive as to become the academic orthodoxies of the 1970s and the 1980s. But when one broadens the canvas and looks back over a longer time span, some of these elegant and cynical hypotheses are confronted with uncomfortable facts. The founders and guardians of the Empire had a different vision of their role than that posited by most of their latter-day interpreters.

If history teaches anything it is that it does *not* repeat itself. But this does not give us the liberty to shut our eyes to developments elsewhere. By widening our horizon we learn of the continuities of historical forces and the links between events and ideas. It gives a certain perspective to our inquiry by revealing that an event is after all not so unique, that similar problems and dilemmas have been experienced before and that while in each case the circumstances can never be identical, neither are the solutions necessarily the same; the very knowledge provides a vantage point from which to view an event. The purpose of this paper is not to take issue with the various interpretations of the end of British rule in India. It is much more modest and one merely of approach. It aims to 're-state' the line of analysis so brilliantly put forward by Sir Reginald Coupland some four decades ago.[5] The history of the British in India cannot be studied in isolation and needs to be seen in the larger context of British imperial history. In this article an attempt will be made to show the relevance of the formative influence in Britain's earlier colonial experiences of a decentralized empire and her success, following the loss of the 13 American colonies, in reconciling imperial authority with colonial liberty, in subsequently shaping policies in India and elsewhere. It will be suggested that the decision of the Indian nationalists to discard the well-tried path of gradual devolution in favour of mass agitation and civil disobedience hampered rather than facilitated the transfer of power and probably contributed to the division of India.

Reconciling *imperium et libertas* was a problem: how to secure colonial autonomy and imperial unity, how to adjust independence and interdependence, how far to insist upon uniformity with metropolitan regulations despite distance and differences were questions which had to be resolved. England's experience of her medieval empire provided a useful seedbed of forms for later periods.[6] In 1066 England became a colony of Normandy but soon, with her superior resources and territory, the role was reversed and she became the metropolis of a large empire in Anjou, Acquitaine, Gascony and the Isle of Man and elsewhere. While these 'dominions' remained subject to the King-in-Council (or subsequently King-in-Parliament), they were given substantial autonomy and were allowed to retain their own laws and customs. England thus had some experience of a decentralized empire even before the oceanic discoveries of the sixteenth and seventeenth centuries. It was only natural that when merchant adventurers applied to the King for Charters to trade overseas, the Tudor officials should fall back upon devices most at hand: the Charters were modelled on the old forms in fiefs and guilds. Distance, lack of local knowledge, and the principle of local taxation had made the devolution of imperial authority an imperative. Nor did the powers once delegated to local authorities remain static. The scope of authority was gradually expanded and the 'rights' of Englishmen at home were claimed overseas. In local matters the colonists were virtually autonomous. It was the failure to recognize the dynamics of change that lost Britain an empire. It was also ultimately the successful resolution of the problem of 'sovereign legislature' that gave the second British Empire its distinctive character and proved Turgot's analogy of colonies with ripe fruit as false.

I

The history of the settlement colonies working their way towards responsible government is well known.[7] But the road was halting and only gradually were the imperial statesmen – pushed on by what may retrospectively be termed as colonial nationalism – able to grope their way forward. The silhouette of things to come might be seen in the Royal Instructions to the Peace Commissioners headed by the Earl of Carlyle in 1778.[8] The commissioners were authorized to negotiate a *treaty* with the Americans which would clearly state 'the respective rights of Great Britain and America'. If the Americans agreed not to secede from the British Empire they would be 'given a fixed constitution' with safeguards for American liberties. All official appointments in the 13 colonies would be made from among the Americans and even the office of Governor would be elective and answerable to a colonial electorate, obeying orders from London only to the extent it was acceptable to the local legislature. Britain would remove all commercial restrictions, allow Americans full participation in imperial trade and extend to the colonies the protection of British defence. In return the 13 colonies were required to make a commitment to contribute to imperial defence and keep open the domestic market to British goods. But the Americans, in the euphoria of victory five years later, were unwilling to concede at the conference table what they had won on the battlefield. Nothing short of independence was acceptable.

Even though the attempt to conciliate the Americans failed, the idea of an autonomous state bound to the British imperial association by treaty took a firm hold in the thinking of metropolitan statesmen and provided a basis of imperial policy with respect to Ireland in 1782. Nor were the Irish nationalists slow in recognizing that concessions offered to the Americans could just as well be secured for themselves. Henry Grattan reminded the British in April 1780:

> Take notice that the very constitution which I move you to declare, Great Britain herself offered to America.... In 1778 a Commission went out with powers to cede to the thirteen provinces of America, totally and radically, the legislative authority claimed over by British Parliament.[9]

This was not entirely accurate but nevertheless the demands fell on receptive ears. Like North, Shelburne, Fox and Pitt strove to come to an amicable agreement with Ireland. A memorandum on the Irish government presumably written by Richard Wellesley (Earl of Mornington) in about 1791–2, and sent to Lord Grenville, anticipated many of the arguments of the Colonial Reformers 50 years later. He argued that the proper course was to apply the system of British cabinet responsibility in

Ireland. In other words, he wanted the Lord Lieutenant to hand over responsibility of governance to the chosen representatives of the Irish electorate:

> To convince them that every member of the domestic administration of their country is as truly and legally responsible as persons in similar situation in England, is an object of such material consequence, that it should always be kept in sight. The personal responsibility of Ministers is one of the great securities of the monarchy in England; and the personal responsibility of Ministers in Ireland is the only ground upon which British supremacy can be firmly built.

By removing the Lord Lieutenant from direct responsibility for the administration as in the British constitution, the British Government would be freed from Irish resentment.[10] The idea of a self-governing state within the Empire was a concept not yet formulated. The device of vesting collective responsibility in the hands of colonial ministers could not develop until after the changes brought by the 1832 Reform Act in England had allowed for a comprehensive cabinet responsibility. 'In the eighteenth century the King was still the active head of the executive', wrote Harlow. 'If, therefore, his representative in a colonial government had been withdrawn from a similar participation in and responsibility for executive business, the overseas edition of the British constitution would have diverged from the [then] authorised version at home'.[11] The English ministers therefore continued to insist on a formal treaty whereby the obligations of each party would be explicitly defined and which would bind Ireland to contribute to imperial defence and abide by certain commercial restrictions. Pitt's attempt to establish an autonomous Ireland in partnership with Britain foundered on the twin rocks of commercial reciprocity and defence contributions.[12] And with the outbreak of the French revolutionary wars the question of colonial autonomy was shelved for nearly a generation.

The reconciliation of colonial freedom with the imperial connection had to await the coming of free trade. The inertia of the past was too strong to break the conventions of contemporary thinking. The limitations of mercantilist regulations were evident from the fact that trade with an independent America had multiplied. But a complete break with the past was resisted by merchants who, despite Britain's commercial success, did not have the confidence of a later generation in the ability of the first industrial nation to compete in a free market. The reasons for the shift to free trade need not detain us. Suffice it to say that although Adam Smith, Dean Tucker and other Radicals had questioned the value of colonies and had shown that they were harmful to Britain's political economy and self-interest, it would be naive to believe that Britain owed her conversion entirely to them. The real thrust came from changed factors of international commerce after the dissolution of most rival European empires in the Americas and the establishment of Britain's industrial supremacy. When the whole world was their market, the British manufacturers would have little to gain by confining themselves to the emporia of the colonies. The old mercantilist system was dismantled in the three decades after 1820. In the 1820s Huskisson had removed many of the duties; by 1830 Britain had opened her colonial trade to foreign states on a reciprocal basis; and the Navigation Act was repealed in 1849. In the 1830s the East India Company lost its trading monopoly in India and the trade east of the Cape was thrown open. And after 1846 preferential tariffs and bounties on colonial goods were gradually removed so that by the 1860s Britain received no special economic privileges from the colonies. Thereafter Britain remained free-trading until 1932. The effect of the free trade on the character of the Empire was considerable. Once the economic controls were liberalized, the need for political control became largely obsolete. It was cheap and freed Britain from administrative and defence expenditure. It did not mean the end of Colonial Office control. Nor did it imply that Britain had become anti-imperialist and would abdicate her colonies.[13] Empire in a free-trading era meant, in Gallagher and Robinson's telling phrase, 'trade with informal control if possible; trade with rule when necessary'.[14] In terms of colonial self-government it meant wider devolution of power for those colonies who seemed capable of governing themselves.

The story of the growth of responsible government has been often told but its full significance, as Professor McIntyre pointed out, has been seldom appreciated:

> Possibly because the new system, known as 'responsible government', was, in the main, achieved without violence, it is not often readily recalled to mind even by those who pride themselves on a knowledge of the past. Yet without doubt, it is one of the great achievements of British history. For the subsequent development of the Commonwealth it is the greatest single landmark.[15]

The Colonial Reformers – Durham, Wakefield, Molesworth and Buller amongst others – put their liberal stamp on the Second Empire, and achieved what may be the most successful revolution in the nineteenth century. John Lambton, Earl Durham, the 'Radical Jack' was sent to Canada in 1838 to report on the causes of two rebellions in Upper and Lower Canada. His report in 1839, the importance of which needs no emphasis, became the gospel of the Colonial Reformers. The only way to establish a lasting imperial tie was a relationship based on freedom and equality. What the colonies did in their internal affairs was of little relevance to the metropolis and therefore ought to be left to the colonial ministers responsible to their own legislatures. In a passage reminiscent of Richard Wellesley's memorandum, Durham wrote: 'Follow out consistently the principles of the British constitution, and introduce into the Government of these Great Colonies those wise provisions, by which alone the working of the representative system can in any way be rendered harmonious and effecient...'[16] The measures of self-government he proposed related only to internal or local matters and not to imperial subjects – colonial constitutions, foreign relations, international trade and the disposal of waste lands – which were to be 'reserved' for the British Government.[17] The Report was fortunate in respect of timing – by the fourth decade of the nineteenth century the mercantilist controls were on their way out and the British merchants were much more confident of their ability to hold their own in a free market – and its recommendations were in accord with the spirit of the age. Even so, colonial self-government was at first viewed with suspicion. Only in 1846 when Lord Grey was appointed Secretary of State for Colonies and Lord Elgin, Durham's son-in-law, became the Governor General of Canada, could it at last be shown that responsible government could work safely and indeed itself be a safety valve. In the 28 years that elapsed between the Durham Report and the passage of the British North America Act of 1867, experience in responsible government had been gathered and many of Durham's arbitrary distinctions between colonial and imperial spheres of policy were found unpractical and gradually whittled down. To have tried to prevent the encroachment of the colonial governments in the so-called imperial sphere would have precipitated another crisis like that of 1763. Control over waste land was transferred to colonial governments in the 1850s; commercial tariff policies conceded after 1859; and constitutional amendments could be made by most colonies under the terms of their constitutions. The other settler colonies followed suit and obtained responsible government. By 1914 only one of Durham's 'reserved' subjects – foreign policy – remained in metropolitan hands. But after the war the dominions (so styled since 1907) also secured control of their foreign policy. The fabric of imperial policy had collapsed before the pressure of colonial evolution. Between 1839 and 1931 the dominions had become more like independent states than mere dependencies. The conventions already developed in the period were spelt out in the Balfour Report of 1926.

II

Responsible government, however, was not extended to the tropical dependencies inhabited by non-European populations on the grounds that they were lacking in qualifications thought necessary by Victorian England – property, education and stability. To this one might add the Colonial Office's concern for the colony's ability to defend itself, pay for its administration, protect its minorities, and safeguard the metropolitan strategic and commercial interests through a collaborating elite.[18] Although at the start of the century the British Empire appeared to be divided between the self-governing colonies and other dependencies under metropolitan control, India and Ceylon were already moving slowly along the road to self-government. After 1945 it was accepted that – however distantly in the future – other Asian and African dependencies would follow the same route to self-government within the Commonwealth. The progress would not be automatic but because experience had already been gained in devolving authority the road would be clearer and easier, the stages condensed, abridged and telescoped. It is this which gives the British Empire its distinctive feature compared to other empires. We shall now turn to examine the relevance of the dominion experience to India and seek to explain some of the difficulties of applying this model to a plural society.

Looking back it would seem clear that India was put on the very same road as those which other self-governing colonies had travelled.[19] Autocratic rule had been tempered by a Governor-General's Council; plunder by irresponsible company officials had been checked by parliamentary supervision. The founders of the British Empire in India had never supposed that India would always remain under British tutelage. Burke's vision of Britain's role as a trustee was clear: 'Depend upon it, this business cannot be indifferent to our fame. It will turn out a matter of great disgrace or great glory to the whole British nation. We are on a conspicuous stage, and the world marks our demeanour.'[20] Lord Hastings, Henry Lawrence and Sir Thomas Munro were explicit in prophesying India's emancipation; and Macaulay, in the debate in 1833, had declared that the day when India acquired her self-government would be truly 'the proudest day in English history'.[21] And Henry Thomas defined the aim of British trusteeship:

> We cannot expect to hold India for ever. Let us conduct ourselves in our civil and military relations as, when the connection ceases, it may do so not with convulsions but with mutual esteem and affection: and that England may then have in India a noble ally, enlightened and brought into the scale of nations under her guidance and fostering care.[22]

That the goal of British rule in India was the establishment of ultimate self-government was not in doubt. But there was no overriding sense of urgency to attain that goal. Nor was this surprising. The future of a vast and complex subcontinent was in question. The political problems seemed intractable. The more the British officials became aware of the complexities and divisions of Indian society, the more cautious they became. In time the momentum of a vast administrative system tended to blunt the vision in a day-to-day routine that saw only in the doing of a good job the justification of the British Raj. They settled down to become cautious guardians seeking the welfare of their ward with a parental possessiveness.

The East India Company was left in control of government by Pitt's India Act in 1784 but the supervision permitted by Parliament in the cumbrous system of dual control was infrequently exercised. It was the revolt of 1857 which shocked Parliament into activity. The following year the government of India was transferred to the Crown: the Secretary of State for India took over the functions of the Board of Control and the Court of Directors. The revolt had revealed a deplorable lack of contact between government and the governed with no means of knowing whether legislation was favourable or not save by the litmus test of a rebellion.[23] The process of enlisting Indian opinion began with the Indian Councils Act of 1861. The Governor-General's Council was doubled by the inclusion of non-officials; and the Provincial Councils were enlarged in the same way. These reforms were a characteristically British response to an immediate practical need. But quite unconsciously it had the effect of putting India on to what was destined to be her road to self-government. Indianization and decentralization were going hand in hand following a familiar development in colonial legislative councils: first officials, then non-officials, a few elected and finally an elected majority. This was probably not what the authors of the Act had in mind but the momentum carried through to further reforms.

The early Indian nationalists were aware of the development of the self-governing institutions in the colonies and pitched their demands in familiar terms. The British India Association as early as 1852 petitioned Parliament for 'the legislature of British India to be placed on the footing of those enjoyed by most of the colonies of Her Majesty'.[24] In the second half of the nineteenth century the self-governing colonies inspired India's demand for responsible government:

> If the Canadas could have Parliament, if such small and advanced colonies as Prince Edward Island, Newfoundland, New South Wales, New Zealand, St Christopher's Island and Barbados could have elected Councils, surely British India has a fair claim to similar representation. If taxation and representation go hand in hand in all British colonies, why should this principle be ignored in British India.[25]

In 1880 Surendranath Bannerjee reminded the British of India's anxiety: 'Canada governs itself. Australia governs itself. And surely it is anomalous that the grandest dependency of England should continue to be governed upon wholly different principles'. And in 1906 the Congress demanded that 'the system of government obtaining in self-governing British colonies should be extended to India'.[26] Even the Maharastrian firebrand, B.G. Tilak, proclaimed that self-government on the colonial model was the ideal to work for.[27]

Despite many reservations the British policy seemed to be evolving along those lines. Even though the Indian Councils Act of 1892 failed to provide for the principle of popular representation, it did empower the Governor-General to make regulations with regard to nominations. In time representative bodies, groups and associations were invited to elect representatives and those so elected were habitually accepted. In 1909 John Morley took the reforms a stage further. Official majorities were abolished in the provincial councils and provision was made for the appointment of Indians to the Executive Councils both at the centre and in the provinces. Another important innovation, in marked contrast to the development in the self-governing colonies, was the introduction of communal electorates to deal with the dilemma of a plural society. There was considerable uncertainty whether the dominion model could be applied without modification. The Congress Party welcomed the reform as it fitted in with their demand for the Westminster parliamentary model and a responsible cabinet which had been transplanted successfully in Canada and Australia. But that was the very pattern which British statesmen were sceptical of. Morley denied that he was creating miniature parliaments or was moving towards parliamentary self-government. Every reform was accompanied by declarations that it would be wrong to deduce that parliamentary government was the goal. The *durbar*, not the representative legislature, was the oriental ideal. Morley was emphatic that there was no analogy between Canada and India. It was like arguing, he said, that because a fur coat was suitable for the Canadian winter, it would also be suitable for a winter on the Deccan.[28]

However much the imperial statesmen might protest, was there any alternative? The western-educated Indian elite would not be content to play a *durbari* or a *panchayati* role, even if it were assumed that these instruments were suitable for twentieth-century India. Besides, was it not inevitable that once the first halting steps in the direction of the representative system had been taken, before long the rule of an elected majority was almost inevitable? Say what they might, what other models or system of government were they acquainted with? Professor Low is quite emphatic that 'whenever the *melange* that was the British "centre" was looking around for formulas to offer India, they reached for the only models which they had at hand: those of the white Commonwealth'.[29] Professor Mansergh had earlier come to the same conclusion:

> What did ordinary British administrators in India, or for that matter Indian leaders, know of the working of the American, let alone of the Swiss, constitution? Were they really in a position to adopt something in its detail largely or altogether unfamiliar to them all? The answer was obviously in the negative and so as the years went by and options narrowed, the British, with continuing reservations in many quarters, became reconciled to following the pathway of precedent, and the precedent which was most relevant was the dominion precedent with responsible government as an integral part of it.[30]

While debate on India's future continued, important events were taking place at home and abroad which gave impetus to Indian nationalism and increased Indian impatience for self-government. Just before the turn of the century Italy had been defeated by Abyssinia in 1896; the Boers had given stiff resistance to the imperial forces in the South African war of 1899–1902; while diplomatically Britain stood isolated in Europe. The signing of the Anglo-Japanese alliance in 1902 had shown to discerning eyes the decline of Britain's power in Asia and when two years later Japan defeated Russia, a European power, it sparked a nationalist fervour from India to Indo-China. The United States had set a date for the independence of the Philippines; and Britain had herself conceded responsible government to the two Boer states of Orange Free State and the Transvaal. Nearer to India they had witnessed Britain's anxiety to reach a settlement with the Russians over Afghanistan and Persia in 1907, and with China over Tibet in 1908.[31] And at about the same time Germany was beginning to challenge Britain's naval supremacy. In India itself politics was in ferment. Following the decision to partition Bengal in 1905 – albeit on perfectly rational administrative grounds – the Congress moderates had been pushed aside and the way opened for terrorism, assassination, boycott of British goods and withdrawal from public offices. The movement was ineffective and perhaps largely confined to high caste Hindus. The Muslims, who were the principal beneficiaries of the partition, waited expectantly to see the outcome of this contest. The partition was revoked in 1911. The movement demonstrated the ability of a vested interest to organize agitation and was an indication of things to come. The Muslims were frightened and felt the need to organize themselves to protect their interests.[32]

### III

When the war broke out in 1914, the Indians, far from taking advantage of Britain's difficulties, threw in their lot whole-heartedly with the war effort. Muhandas Karamchand Gandhi, of South African fame, appointed himself as a recruiting agent for the British army. By this outburst of loyalism the Indians won the gratitude of the British and extracted a pledge which bombs and daggers had failed to deliver.

Unlike the practice in the case of the older dominions, the British government decided to make an explicit declaration of the objective of British rule in India. Montagu's declaration of 20 August 1917 provided for the gradual development of self-governing institutions with a view to progressive realization of responsible government in India as an integral part of the British Empire.[33] The declaration was clear and unequivocal: it recognized India as a potential dominion.[34] Despite Sir Malcolm Hailey's attempt to draw a distinction between responsible government and dominion status,[35] there was no doubt in the minds of the contemporary statesmen. Even Curzon, Milner and Sir Valentine Chirol, who had earlier opposed responsible government for India, reluctantly bowed to the prospect of a self-governing India.[36] The Montagu-Chelmsford report set aside any doubts as to the implications of the 1917 declaration when it spoke of 'a completely representative and responsible Government of India on an equal footing with other self-governing Dominions'.[37] Twelve years later Lloyd George, whose government had authorized the declaration, admitted that it was the considered opinion of his government that 'if the experiments were successful ... we would extend it until India ultimately enjoyed full partnership in the Empire on equal terms with our great Dominions'.[38] Professor Mehrotra correctly concluded that this declaration was a definite repudiation of the 'two empires' – the concept that there could be, under the British flag, one form of constitutional evolution for the West and another for the East, or one for the white races and another for the non-white.[39]

Between the declaration of 1917 and the enactment of the 1919 Act, the proposals of Montagu-Chelmsford were watered down. The concessions were timid and tight-fisted. It remodelled the Central Legislature, by enlarging the principle of election and representation, while in the provinces it introduced the novel principle of 'dyarchy'; the Indian ministers were made responsible to the provincial legislatures for certain departments of the government. Despite Congress's disappointment, the Act might well have been acceptable on its own intrinsic merit. But the timing of the Act could not have been less auspicious. Three events in 1919 and 1920 aggravated the Indian political opinion: repressive measures advocated in the Rowlatt Report to curb 'seditious activities'; the 'Jalianwala Bagh massacre' where several hundred unarmed civilians were killed and over a thousand injured as a result of army firing to disperse a political gathering; and the announcement of the terms of the Treaty of Sèvres which threatened to dismember the Ottoman Empire, the integrity of which was an intimate concern for Indian Muslims. Moreover, India was suffering from an influenza epidemic, price rises and the impact of the international post-war recession. Gandhi's response was the launching of the non-violent non-cooperation movement against the British. The result was the opening of a new phase in Anglo-Indian relations. The gradual, measured and leisurely growth of self-governing institutions along the dominion model was challenged and Congress sought to capture power by *tour de force*.[40] Even though Britain had some taste of this in Ireland, the spectacle of mass civil disobedience was unfamiliar and drove the British into their shells. The damage to the cause of India's independence was irreparable. All old suspicions, prejudices and fears reappeared with a renewed vigour. Those in Britain who had opposed devolution of power in India could now say 'I told you so'; and the friends of Indian reforms were thrown on to the defensive.

The 1919 Act was an experiment in training Indians in the art of self-government and it was understood that as Indians gave evidence of shouldering responsibility, more areas would be transferred to ministerial responsibility and that at the end of ten years or sooner a statutory commission would examine the working of the Act and recommend future changes.[41] The moderates (mainly the Liberals) who might have worked the reforms were, in the wake of a mass movement, voted out in the 1923 elections. The Swarajist wing of Congress consisting of many able leaders had it in their power to make the reforms work. But in entering the legislature they had broken from the radicals and were constantly aware that their actions were being scrutinized by those Congressmen who were non-cooperating. They demonstrated their patriotism by playing to the gallery in a manner hardly likely to win the confidence of the British. The experiment in dyarchy was never given a fair trial and all eyes were fixed on the next instalment of reforms. The all-white composition of the Statutory Commission in 1927 was a tactical blunder and consequently boycotted by the majority of the politically articulate Indians. Its report, despite Simon's masterly survey of the Indian scene, was still-born and had been overtaken by events in India. The Viceroy, Lord Irwin, secured the permission of H.M.G. in 1929 to reassure the Indians that the natural issue of India's constitutional progress was the attainment of dominion status and invited the Indian leaders to attend a conference to work out the basis of India's future constitution.

Irwin's declaration was a clear reaffirmation of the 1917 faith. Congress boycotted the first Round Table Conference in 1930 with tragic consequences for India's future. Without the participation of the largest political party the conference could scarcely formulate viable plans for the future. And by the same token Congress, by abstaining, forfeited the opportunity of bringing to bear its opinion on the counsel of the conference. In 1931, however, as a result of the Irwin-Gandhi pact, Congress was prevailed upon to participate in the next conference. Gandhi came to London as the sole representative of the Congress and by his insistent claim to represent all groups and communities, he made little contribution to proceedings apart from exacerbating the fears of the Muslims.[43]

The results of the deliberations of three Round Table Conferences and a Joint Select Committee of Parliament were embodied in the Government of India Act of 1935. The Act established a federation for India and allowed provincial autonomy by giving them a separate legal personality and liberating them almost entirely from the centre. It established a federation for India, reproducing dyarchy at the centre, with foreign affairs and defence 'reserved' in British hands. Parliamentary government was confirmed and extended in the provinces and was introduced at the centre. Communal electorates were retained.

The new constitution was the handiwork of the British and not the product of an Indian constituent assembly. It was a conservative scheme, hedged with numerous safeguards whereby, initially at least, the real powers at the centre were outside the orbit of popular control. Nevertheless it was a remarkable feat of constitutional engineering. The constitution, if it had any hope of passing through an essentially Conservative Parliament, had to appear to safeguard imperial interests, including those of investors, merchants and civil and military personnel in India. In India it had to marry the 'despotic' Indian India with a 'democratic' British India; and not least of all had to satisfy the Muslims that their interests would not be brushed aside. At the same time the new constitution had to be a parliamentary democracy based on the Westminster model to meet Indian demands. It was therefore not surprising that the constitution was cautious and seemingly cumbersome. What is often forgotten is that it was the last great debate on India's future and once the Act had been passed – although it was very nearly defeated – the issue of India's independence was settled. The provisions of the Act were transitional, capable of organic growth and designed through usage and convention to move India towards the freedom and equality of dominion status.

The Congress had been non-cooperating for so long that it could not appreciate the significance of the 1935 Act. It was living in the past and could not grasp the steady progress which India had made towards dominion status since 1917. Indeed by comparison India's progress had been remarkably fast. It took Canada nearly 50 years to move from representative to responsible government in the domestic field. The 1919 Act made Indian ministers 'responsible' for a large number of departments within ten years of the introduction of the representative system. And 16 years later the 1935 Act extended the responsibility to the centre, except for defence and foreign affairs. Canada had to bide for 20 years and Australia for 50 before the scope of responsible government was extended from the provincial to the central sphere. Fiscal authority was achieved by Canada in 1859, some 14 years after obtaining responsible status. In India it came within two years of the 1919 Act. India's progress in the international field was even more spectacular. India was represented at the Imperial Conference in 1917; it was a signatory to the Versailles settlement in 1919; it was one of the original members of the League of Nations and had a seat in the International Labour Organization. In 1920 an Indian High Commissioner took residence in London, and seven years later India appointed an Agent General to represent its interests in South Africa. In 1929 she acquired the right to conclude commercial treaties with other foreign powers.[44] It was, as Sir Keith Hancock wrote, 'a recognition of the fact that self-government was India's destiny. It was, so to speak, a payment in advance which India had earned by her extraordinary services.'[45] The Congress chose to ignore this and continued its policy of confrontation.

The hope that the 1935 Act would in time evolve into dominion status could not materialize. Instead of forging a united platform which removed any obstacles to the transfer of authority to Indians, Congress pursued a policy of confrontation simultaneously with the British, the princes and those Muslims who did not join its ranks. The decade after 1937 was dominated by internal dissension and communal rivalry. In retrospect the bankruptcy of the Congress leadership assumed staggering proportions. 'They passionately desired to preserve the unity of India', wrote Sir Penderel Moon, but they 'consistently acted so as to make its partition inevitable'.[46]

In the elections to the provincial assemblies under the 1935 Act Congress emerged as the dominant party in eight out of the 11 provinces but refused to assume ministerial responsibilities unless the governors could reassure Congress that they would not use their 'special powers' given them under the constitution. The demand resulted from a lack of understanding of British constitutional conventions that powers are held in reserve for emergency and normally not used in practice. A governor could not use his 'special powers' indiscriminately, for in a parliamentary democracy the ultimate arbiters are the voters and no governor would risk the resignation of a popular minister unless it was sure of the backing of the electorate. Of course Congress never got the assurances it sought but in the process it aroused the fears and suspicions of those whom the safeguards were designed to protect.[47]

Even after accepting office in the provinces, Congress continued its opposition to the federal scheme because of its undemocratic features. The federation had been designed to strengthen the conservative elements: the princely representatives nominated by their rulers would constitute 40 per cent in the Upper House and 33 per cent in the Lower. This would mean that as long as the princes acted in concert no popular government at the centre could ignore them. This undemocratic gambit had, nevertheless, a clear logic: to make sure that in transferring controls at the centre imperial interests were not adversely affected. The princes, it was hoped, would provide that safeguard. But when the Congress attempted to 'democratize' the states so that the princely representatives were popularly elected, the princes refused to join the federation. The failure to federate was the first major dent in Indian unity.[48]

## IV

At the outbreak of war in September 1939 the Congress ministries had been in office for over two years during which they had discovered to their surprise that the governors did not use their 'special powers' nor did the British civil servants in any way obstruct their programme. The Congress ministers gained valuable experience in administration and passed many useful laws. It was only in the field of Hindu-Muslim relations that some disturbing signs were visible. Many of the Muslim allegations of their mistreatment at the hand of Congress governments may simply reflect pique at the exclusion of the Muslim League from power. Whether valid or not, however, it was these resentments which were to prove crucial to political events. In fact, the war had provided a convenient moment for the Congress to mend the breach with the Muslims. India was at war and the opportunity might have been used to broaden the Congress ministries to include the Muslim League and play its role in the war against the Axis – after all, Nehru had for long been chastising the British for appeasing Hitler. But contrary to all logical expectations, the Congress made the definition of British war aims in relation to India a precondition for their support. When a satisfactory reply was not given, the Congress high command, despite much opposition from the provincial ministers, secured the resignation of the Congress governments from all eight provinces.[49] It seemed that the Congress had committed political suicide.

There was an unreality about Congress's persistent demands. Few in Britain could be convinced that the 1935 Act needed revision so soon, particularly when the evidence was that it was actually working well if only partially. And when the 'phoney war' ended and Britain was fighting for survival, the question of India was considered an intrusion into the War Cabinet's time.[50] It is probably true that Congress had always been an anathema to the British in India. But when in Britain's darkest hour the Congress cynically adopted a pacifist stance, it is not surprising that many officials came to harbour contempt for Congress and began to consciously promote Muslim power.[51] In August 1940 the British responded to Congress demands by promising dominion status at the end of the war but added a rider giving the Muslims a veto over India's future constitutional progress.[52] This was not seeking to 'divide and rule'; rather acknowledging its gratitude to a community for standing by it. After all, three Muslim ministries were enthusiastically supporting the war and the Muslims made up nearly 40 per cent of the Indian Army.[53] No wonder many officials were reluctant to see Congress back in power.

It was after the fall of Pearl Harbour, with the Japanese on India's frontiers and when from different quarters Sir Tej Bahadur Sapru, Chiang Kai-Shek and F. D. Roosevelt pressed Churchill for a solution to the Indian deadlock, that some members of the War Cabinet were able to persuade their reluctant leader to despatch Cripps to India.[54] 'Lord Durham saved Canada to the British Empire' argued Attlee, 'We need a man to do in India what Durham did in Canada'.[55] The Cripps offer conceded the Congress demand for a constituent assembly to frame India's constitution immediately after the end of the war with the right to secede, and invited the Indian leaders to participate in the government immediately.[56] Congress was perhaps justified in rejecting the offer when Cripps retracted the promise that 'government' would function as a cabinet. But failure of the mission had an unexpected consequence. The Cripps offer, in order that it would be acceptable to the Muslims, contained a 'non-accession' clause: the Muslim majority areas were to have the right to secede. But the process was complicated. It would require over 80 per cent of the Muslim population in Bengal and the Punjab voting for secession. Jinnah rejected the offer because he did not command such massive support in 1942 and realized his bluff would be called. But when Congress opted out of the political scene after the 'Quit India' campaign in August, it left the field open for the Muslim League. Jinnah copied Congress's organizational technique and by a skilful campaign, blessed with official patronage, he brought the majority of the Muslims under his flag.[57] And when, after the war, the constitutional negotiations were resumed, Jinnah was able to remind the British of their 'solemn oath' to the Muslims of their right to a separate homeland.

Gandhi had launched the 'Quit India' movement in desperation against the better judgment of Azad and Nehru.[58] The Government of India could not be expected to tolerate a rebellion in the middle of war. Congress was proscribed and its leaders were incarcerated for the duration of the conflict. At the end of the war when the Congress leaders emerged from prison, the promise of granting immediate dominion status in the Cripps offer remained valid, but now partition had become a reality. The decision to partition India and fix a time-limit for leaving

India had both been taken by the British before the end of Lord Wavell's viceroyalty.[59] It was left for Mountbatten to sound the last retreat.

It has not been possible in this short space to explain the motives of the nationalist leaders or do justice to the pressure under which they were working. That they were fired by patriotic visions to liberate their country is beyond doubt. Nor should one belittle their sacrifices in the quest for freedom.

Cool and rational decisions, so obvious in retrospect, were not options always open to them. The mass campaign has its own logic and once set in motion it has its own momentum. Advocates of moderation are swept away and radicals must outbid each other to hold onto the leadership of the movement. When in 1921 Gandhi promised *Swaraj* within a year and launched his non-cooperation movement, he nailed the coffin of the moderates; and when his campaign failed, Gandhi could not revert to moderation, for fear of being displaced by competing extremists. The aggressive image had to be maintained. It has been suggested above that the strategy of agitation had backfired. It did not bring independence any nearer but made partition a reality by playing up the dissensions in a plural society. The above analysis by suggesting that a well tried-out alternative path of gradual progress was available does not endorse the Whig interpretation of history of judging events in the knowledge that in 1947 the British left India and in little over two decades the bulk of the Empire had been wound up. It would be sterile historiography which saw smooth progress from Burke to Attlee. There were often rude jolts and back-slidings. Nor was there ever a clearcut plan, let alone a theory, along which the dependent territories could reach responsible government. The developments were haphazard and often a pragmatic response to a particular situation. But once an experiment had been successful – for nothing succeeds like success – it was more than likely that the experiment would be repeated in another not too dissimilar situation rather than search *de novo* for a fresh solution. It is in this sense that early imperial experience became relevant to tropical dependencies. It has another advantage. It holds off the temptation to interject present preoccupations and obsessions into the past. In a period when the main concern of governments – whether socialist or capitalist, whether Keynesian or Monetarist – is the state of the economy, historians often forget this was not always so. To a generation brought up to think in terms of balance of payments and gold standards, it has not always been possible to comprehend a generation used to thinking in terms of balance of power and two-power standards. The result is an anachronism: the Whig interpretation of history has been stood on its head.

## NOTES

*The phrase is borrowed from Sir Reginald Coupland. I have drawn heavily from Dr Madden's lecture notes. To him, and to Sir Edgar Williams who commented on this article, I am most grateful.

1. P. S. Gupta, 'The Military Factors in Constitutional Change in India, 1917–1947' (Paper presented at the Institute of Commonwealth Studies, London, 26 Feb. 1980).
2. A. Seal, 'Imperialism and Nationalism in India', *Modern Asian Studies*, 7, 3 (July 1973); B. R. Tomlinson, *The Indian National Congress and the Raj 1929–1942. The Penultimate Phase* (London, 1976).
3. J. Darwin, 'Imperialism in Decline? Tendencies in British Imperial Policy Between the Wars', *The Historical Journal*, 23, 3 (1980).
4. B. R. Tomlinson, *The Political Economy of the Raj* (London, 1979).
5. R. Coupland, *The Indian Problem 1833–1935* (Oxford, 1942), Ch. iv.
6. A. F. Madden, '1066, 1776 and all that: the relevance of English medieval experience of "empire" to later imperial issues' in J. E. Flint and G. Williams, *Perspectives of Empire* London, 1973).
7. W. D. McIntyre, *Colonies into Commonwealth* (London, 1966).
8. V. T. Harlow, *The Founding of the Second British Empire 1763–1793* (London, 1952), I, 496-501.
9. Cited in ibid., 527.
10. V. T. Harlow and F. Madden, *British Colonial Developments 1774–1834: Select Documents* (Oxford, 1953), 183.
11. Harlow, *The Founding of the Second British Empire*, I, 496.
12. Ibid., Ch. xi.
13. A. G. L. Shaw, *Great Britain and the Colonies 1815–1865* (London, 1970) 1.
14. J. Gallagher and R. Robinson, 'Imperialism of Free Trade', *Economic History Review*, vi, 1 (1953).
15. McIntyre, *Colonies into Commonwealth*, 35.
16. Cited in R. Coupland, *The Durham Report* (Oxford, 1945) 141.
17. Ibid., 144.
18. R. Hyam, *Britain's Imperial Century 1815–1914* (London, 1976) 35-36.
19. Coupland, *The Indian Problem*, Ch. ii.
20. Edmund Burke, *Works* (7th edition, 1881), ii, 441.
21. Coupland, *The Indian Problem*, 18-19.
22. Cited in R. Coupland, *The Empire in These Days* (London, 1935) 106-8.
23. Cmd. 9109 (1918) para. 60.
24. Cited in S. R. Mehrotra, *India and the Commonwealth 1885–1929* (London, 1965), 30.
25. Kristo Pal Das in *Hindoo Patriot*, 24 Aug. 1874 cited in ibid., 30-31.
26. D. Chrakrabarty and C. Bhattacharyya, *Congress in Evolution* (Calcutta, 1935) 11.
27. Kesari, 22 Jan. 1907, cited in Mehrotra, *India and the Commonwealth*, 49.
28. Coupland, *The Indian Problem*, 26.
29. D. A. Low, *The Lion Rampant* (London, 1973), 169.
30. P. N. S. Mansergh, 'Some Reflections on the Transfer of Power in Plural Society', in C. H. Philips and M. D. Wainwright (ed.), *The Partition of India. Policies and Perspectives 1935–1947* (London, 1970), 45-46.
31. W. D. McIntyre, *The Commonwealth of Nations. Origins and Impact* (Minnesota, 1977) 90.
32. M. Noman, *Muslim India. The Rise and Growth of All India Muslim League* (Allahabad, 1942).
33. Cmd. 9109 (1918) para. 6.
34. Coupland, *The Indian Problem*, 54.
35. Mehrotra, *Indian and the Commonwealth*, 175.
36. Ibid., 175.
37. Cmd. 9109 (1918) 277.
38. Mehrotra, *Indian and the Commonwealth*, 175.

39. Ibid., 105-6.
40. B. N. Pandey, *The Break Up of British India* (London, 1969) Ch. iv.
41. L. Curtis, *Dyarchy* (Oxford, 1920), part viii.
42. M. Gwyer and A. Appadorai, *Speeches and Documents on the Indian Constitution 1921–47* (Oxford, 1957), i, 228-29.
43. *The Memoirs of Aga Khan* (London, 1954), 221-31.
44. Coupland, *The Empire in These Days*, Ch. viii.
45. W. K. Hancock, *A Survey of Commonwealth Affairs* (Oxford, 1937), I, 169.
46. P. Moon, *Divide and Quit* (London, 1961) 14.
47. G. Rizvi, 'Reluctant Collaboration: Congress Accession to Power in 1937', *Indo-British Review*, viii, 3 & 4.
48. G. Rizvi, 'The Attempt at All-India Federation. A Re-assessment of Lord Linlithgow's Role', *Indo-British Review*, viii, 1 & 2.
49. H. V. Hodson, *The Great Divide. Britain-India-Pakistan* (London, 1969) 78.
50. R. J. Moore, 'The Stopgap Victory', *South Asian Review*, vii, 1 (Oct. 1973).
51. Professor Edward Thompson, 'Report on India' (Submitted to the Rhodes Trustees, Dec. 1939).
52. V. P. Menon, *The Transfer of Power in India* (Calcutta, 1957) Ch. iv.
53. L/PO/6/106b, Note by Maj.-Gen. Lockhart, 'The Indian Army in Relation to Constitutional Policy', 25 Feb. 1942. IOR.
54. Mss. Eur. F.125/124, Sapru to Laithwaite, 2 Jan. 1942, IOL; War Cabinet Conclusions 131 of 1941, PRO; *Foreign Relations of the United States of America* (Washington, D.C., 1959), II, 604-8.
55. L/PO/6/106a Memo. by Attlee, 2 Feb. 1942, IOR.
56. Menon, *The Transfer of Power in India*, Ch. v.
57. Z. H. Zaidi, 'Aspects of the Development of Muslim League Policy, 1937–47' in Philips and Wainwright, *The Partition of India*, 245-75.
58. Maulana A. K. Azad, *Indian Wins Freedom* (Calcutta, 1959), 70-79.
59. P. Moon (ed.), *Wavell: The Viceroy's Journal* (London, 1973), xi.

# The Mediator's Moment: Sir Tej Bahadur Sapru and the Antecedents to the Cripps Mission to India, 1940–42

## by

## D. A. Low

The second item in the first of the 12 volumes of Professor Mansergh's great series of documents on *India. The Transfer of Power* is a letter dated 2 January 1942 from the distinguished Indian 'moderate' figure, Sir Tej Bahadur Sapru, to the Private Secretary to the Viceroy. It enclosed a copy of a telegram Sapru had sent on behalf of himself and a dozen others of his kind – the veteran 'moderate' Sir Srinivasa Sastri, and the subsequent President of India, Radhakrishnan, amongst them – to Winston Churchill, the British Prime Minister, in Washington. Following upon the entry of Japan into the Second World War, and consequently that of the United States, Churchill had gone to Washington to consult with President Roosevelt. Sapru's telegram was thus despatched at a critical moment. It made a careful, urgent appeal to Churchill for some 'boldstroke far-sighted statesmanship ... without delay' so as to transform 'entire spirit and outlook administration India' (*sic*: telegraphese). It called for the immediate establishment of a wholly non-official national government for India 'subject only responsibility to Crown'. It asked for the re-establishment of 'popular governments broadbased on confidence different classes and communities' in those Provinces of British India which were currently 'ruled autocratically' by their British Governors, and it sought agreement with the propositions that India should be represented on all important war and peacemaking bodies at the instance of its own national government, which should be generally treated upon an equality with the other governments of the British Dominions. The telegram quite deliberately stated that detailed questions relating to the ultimate constitution of India should 'wait more propitious times, until after victory achieved in this titanic struggle against forces threatening civilisation'.[1] So far as Sapru was concerned his despatch of this telegram represented the climax to a year's energetic labour. It derived its character from his lifelong involvement in such matters.

Numerous other such missives from the last decades of British rule in India could be catalogued. Sapru and his associates were not the only ones, moreover, who at this tense moment of the war, believed that 'something should be done about India'.[2] He had, however, framed and timed his initiative with exemplary skill. While Churchill's immediate reaction was to fulminate against its very suggestions,[3] it was promptly taken a great deal more seriously in London as soon as it was published there, and before very long became the public peg on which the momentous discussions which now ensued in Britain about 'what should be done about India' were hung. On his return to London later in January, Churchill, for all his initial predilections, not only found he could not ignore it but was soon sending Sapru a conciliatory interim reply; and when he eventually announced that the British Government was sending the Lord Privy Seal, Sir Stafford Cripps, to India to discuss a new draft declaration on British policy with the major Indian political leaders, he sent a quite personal message to Sapru saying he hoped he would take his announcement as obviating the need for a more direct reply to the telegram of 2 January as it was 'in effect the answer to that telegram'.[4]

I

The broader background to these events scarcely now needs retelling. After two and a half decades of greatly enhanced activity, the Indian national movement, principally embodied in the Indian National Congress, and led in a unique manner by Mahatma Gandhi, had become a formidable force.[5] In response to the pressures it had mounted, and after often interminable debate, the British had eventually fashioned the new Government of India Act of 1935 as a further step towards fulfilling their established pledge that India could eventually have 'dominion status' within the British Commonwealth.[6] The 1935 Act provided the legal basis for the Provinces of British India to have full 'responsible government' and made provision too for an all-India Federation containing both these Provinces and the numerous Indian Princely States. In 1936 a new Viceroy, Linlithgow, arrived. Despite the affirmations of the Congress leaders that they would have no part in the provincial governments established under the new Act, Linlithgow was soon being notably successful in easing Congress ministries into office in the seven Provinces where they had won majorities at the elections of 1936. But for all his own personal endeavours, Linlithgow failed to be similarly successful in bringing about the creation of the all-India Federation. Congress, the Muslim League, and the Princely leaders, each for their separate reasons, displayed a marked hostility to the whole idea, and the Viceroy enjoyed only equivocal support for his efforts in London. When war broke out in 1939 the federal proposals were shortly put aside.[7]

Serious divergences then emerged over the implications for India of the Second World War. Upon the Congress side it was affirmed that if India was to support 'the cause of freedom' she needed to have both a much greater, immediate measure of freedom, and an unequivocal undertaking that at the end of the war she would be granted as much freedom as was promised (as the war proceeded) to those countries in Europe that fell under Axis rule during the conflict.[8] The British found themselves quite unable to face these demands. Had they already made up their minds to grant India full independence within the clearly foreseeable future as the Americans had for the Philippines in 1935, or had they, like the Dutch over Indonesia, or the French over Indochina, been quite clear that any such thought was beyond their contemplation, they might not have found themselves at such inextricable cross-purposes.[9] The problem was that, on the one hand, they were now irrevocably committed to granting India full self-government at some stage (and by 1939 numbers of them knew that for all practical political and/or moral reasons their days were already numbered), while on the other hand, there was still considerable determination, especially in ruling Conservative Party circles, to put off that denouement – for some wellnigh endlessly, for others certainly until they could be sure that it would all eventuate to Britain's own liking. Such conflicting strands in Britain's thinking about India during these wartime years increasingly befogged, embittered and finally exploded the political relationship between Britain and India.

The doublethink they entailed upon the British side could be all but endlessly illustrated. On 8 August 1940, for example, on the very day the Viceroy issued his so-called August Offer publicly seeking the cooperation of Congress in the war effort and offering to include some 'representative Indians' in his Executive Council to that end (an 'offer' which in the prevailing circumstances he knew to be quite inadequate), he signed a letter to all the British Governors of Provinces explaining that the unique Revolutionary Movements Ordinance he had been simultaneously preparing as a weapon against the Congress embodied a 'clear determination to crush that organisation as a whole'.[10] Or again, two years later, late in 1942, while Amery, the British Secretary of State for India, was writing to his old friend, the South African Prime Minister, Field Marshal Smuts, denouncing his own Prime Minister, Churchill, for failing to accept that Indian national aspirations had to be given consideration, he was at precisely the same time heavily involved in backing the Viceroy in violently suppressing the largest revolt ever mounted in support of those aspirations.[11] During the first four years or so of the Second World War there were countless fruitless stand-offs in India that turned on the guessed-at inwardness of demands from the Indian side and the curious semantics of declarations from the British side, in relation to what would otherwise seem to be fairly straightforward propositions, such as 'a national government', and 'self-government at the end of the war'.

The palpable absence of any internally consistent policy on the British side meant that it was necessary to adduce some arguable public rationalizations. Two predominated. There was, it could not be forgotten, a war on: indeed, one of the two all-engrossing conflicts of the first half of the twentieth century. There were accordingly all kinds of arguable reasons why its momentous demands had to take precedence over all other considerations. Such was the argument which enjoyed wide support in Britain, and in a good many Indian minds too. It was that held by the Viceroy with total commitment and the utmost sincerity.[12]

During the 1930s the purpose here had principally been served by adducing the problem of the future of the Indian Princely States. Come the war this concern, as embodied in the Federation provisions of the 1935 Act, was (as we have seen) set aside.[13] In its place the natural anxieties of many members of the large Muslim majority in India were called into service instead. These concerns had their justifications. Many Muslims (pre-eminently in religious but also in cultural terms) understandably saw themselves as part of a community which was distinct from that of their fellow Indians who were Hindus. It must be remembered, moreover, that down the years there had been all too many violent Hindu-Muslim clashes; the countrywide scars of that have still to be sufficiently allowed for. Later, elsewhere, the British usually sought to assuage concerns like this.[14] During the Second World War, however, in India they patently used them for their own purposes. Nothing illustrates this better than their elevation of Jinnah, the President of the All-India Muslim League, as the single spokesman of the Muslim minority onto an equality with Gandhi, the leader of the far more substantial Indian National Congress,[15] to the wellnigh total exclusion of the otherwise scarcely less significant Muslim Premiers of the Muslim majority Provinces of Bengal and the Punjab.[16] One can readily extract the reasons for this proceeding from some of the documentation that will be further used below: 'however tiresome Jinnah may be ...', Linlithgow *en passant* wrote to Amery in May 1941, 'I remain unshaken in my view ... that it is desirable if possible to keep the Muslim League together because of the post-war discussions, because it represents the only organised opposition to Congress .... Nor do I want to risk a combination against us of Congress and the Muslim League'.[17] Such contortions in Britain's policy towards India during these wartime years provoked in the Viceroy a persistent preference for 'lying back' and in everyone else a great deal of frustration all around. In those who would essay to change some of this, there would be a call for some quite special skills – as Sir Stafford Cripps was to find to his cost in 1942.

The difficulties began when, despite warnings, but with full constitutional propriety, Linlithgow declared India to be at war in September 1939 before any Indian public body had had an opportunity to consider the matter. There was as a result keen resentment; and soon afterwards Congress was declaring that 'India cannot associate itself in a war said to be for democratic freedom when that very freedom is denied her';[18] and it went on to ask both for a clear statement of the Government's war aims, and an immediate and substantial step towards the ending of the imperial bondage. In reply Linlithgow stated in October 1939 that Britain would 'at the end of the war be prepared to regard the [existing Government of India] Act as open to modification in the light of Indian views'; in the meanwhile, however, he proposed to do nothing more than establish an all-India 'consultative group'. This proposal was brusquely rejected, and Congress ministers in the Provinces were soon resigning in protest.[19]

By July 1940 when, with the fall of France, the war had taken a dramatic turn, Congress returned to the fray to demand the immediate establishment of a national government for India. Linlithgow was already in communication with the new Churchill government, and after a good deal of very confusing telegraphic discussion he came up the next month with the August Offer of 1940. In this he proposed to appoint a majority of Indians to the Viceroy's Executive Council (and it was well understood that these would be mainly drawn from the political parties). The Congress President, Maulana Azad, however, rejected the offer out of hand. Not only was there no mention in it of a national government; the Viceroy had made it clear that he would retain the key portfolios of Finance, Defence and Home in official hands. The Offer contained, it is true, an undertaking that at the end of the war 'with the least possible delay' the British would establish 'a body representative of the principal elements in India's national life' and would 'lend every aid in their power to hasten decisions on all relevant matters to the utmost degree'. But this was scarcely worth the paper it was written on. For not only was there nothing here about the Congress demand for independence; everything was constrained by a clause which made all change 'subject to the due fulfilment of the obligations which Great Britain's long connexion with India has imposed upon her'. Clearly that could be crippling. There was little of substance here for Congress; and it is clear that for Churchill, that was very deliberately so.[20]

The August Offer was chiefly notable because it contained the first major British response to the Muslim League's separation resolution, the Pakistan resolution, of the previous March. With the possibility of independence now beginning to engross everyone's mind, it was natural that increasing numbers of people should be paying as much attention to the distribution of power upon its attainment as to its attainment itself. The matter was felt most acutely by those Muslims from Provinces in which Muslims had for many centuries past enjoyed a politically pre-eminent position, but who with the advent of the ballot box saw those days numbered. Protracted attempts over 25 years to secure agreement about the allocation of Muslim reserved seats in legislatures had eventuated in little general agreement, and following the Government of India Act of 1935 the whole issue had been gravely aggravated by a dispute over the creation of coalition governments in the Hindu-majority Provinces. Because the Muslim League felt itself thwarted here, above all, by Congress, the movement for a separate Pakistan began to attract a following, and in response to it, because, as we have seen, the British were anxious not to alienate the Muslim League when Congress was hostile to it already, the August Offer stated that the British would never transfer power to any government 'whose authority is directly denied by large and powerful elements in India's national life. Nor could they be parties to the coercion of such elements into submission to such a Government.'[21] These sentences promptly became Jinnah's sheet anchor, and in the second half of 1940 it was not merely relations between the British and Congress that were broken off; despite Gandhi's efforts, relations between the Congress leaders and Jinnah came to an end as well. It was not long, moreover, before Amery, the Secretary of State for India, was declaring that until Indians could agree amongst themselves no constitutional progress could be made. Such became his theme song for the next two years. There was soon, indeed, deadlock all along the line. Nine Provinces and the centre were already under autocratic British rule; in October 1940 Gandhi launched his 'individual satyagraha' campaign; and in November the Viceroy formally withdrew the August Offer.[22]

## II

It was at this moment that Sir Jagdish Prasad, a retired Indian Civil Servant and a former member of the Viceroy's Executive Council, who had now become active in non-Congress politics in northern India, called on Sir Tej Bahadur Sapru at his home in Allahabad, and urged him to come out of his political hibernation and take an active part in resolving the prevailing deadlock.[23] Sapru was now 65. He came from the same community and the same city as the Nehru family. As a Kashmiri Pandit he firmly believed that culturally he bridged the Hindu-Muslim divide. He had at the same time been leader of the Allahabad Bar for upwards of two decades and, besides appearing occasionally in both Calcutta and Madras, he was clearly the leading lawyer in all of northern India. There had once been a time when Jawaharlal Nehru had seen him as a possible leader of the Indian National Congress; but, while Sapru had great respect for Gandhi, with his own strong belief in the necessity for the rule of law, he could not go along with him over civil disobedience. In the early 1920s he found himself instead briefly Law Member of the Viceroy's Council. In the decade that followed he turned himself into India's foremost constitutional lawyer, and was a major participant in the so-called Nehru Committee of 1928. When in 1929 he once again broke with the Congress leaders, he became the principal Indian participant through all the three ensuing Round Table Conferences in London in the early 1930s. He became deeply involved, moreover, with his principal associate M. R. Jayakar in intricate negotiations on three or four occasions between successive Viceroys and the Congress leaders, Gandhi especially.[24] Late in 1940 Prasad sought him out not only because he was now widely renowned in India for his contacts, integrity and experience, but because no Indian was held in higher repute in London.

According to his own lights Sapru remained a staunch Indian nationalist. He had, however, for several years been spurned by the Congress leadership, especially in his own United Provinces. He was not impressed, therefore, with Prasad's entreaty that he should once more employ his talents in a public cause. He issued a statement of his views to the press; but he firmly declined the suggestion that he should head a deputation to the Viceroy.[25]

Given the straits of the times his press statement seems, however, to have caught the eye of a number of leading political figures in the country.

When the United Provinces Provincial Muslim League met in Allahabad in Christmas week 1940, both Nawab Mohammed Ismail and Liaqat Ali Khan talked with him, and on the major Hindu-Muslim issue Sapru was left with the impression that although 'the task of settlement would present great difficulties it was by no means hopeless'.[26] As a result a few days later he wrote an article for a political journal for the first time in six years. It appeared under the title 'The Needs of the Hour' in the January number of the monthly review *Twentieth Century*. In it he urged that Gandhi and Jinnah should get together once again. He urged as well that the Viceroy's Executive Council should be fully Indianized, and that on psychological grounds it was especially important that without more ado its Defence portfolio should be put into Indian hands. Using his old connections he was careful to send copies of this article to the editors and correspondents of the quality newspapers both in India and in England – to the latter because on the basis of his long previous experiences he was keenly aware of the need to appeal over the head of the Government of India to Caesar.[27]

Shortly afterwards his old junior at the Allahabad bar, Dr S. N. Katju – long since a staunch Congressman – came to see him to explore whether any practical steps might be taken. He was soon followed by other Congressmen, including Purushottamdas Tandon. From several quarters there was now therefore pressure on Sapru to play a political role once again, and soon quite specifically to act as a mediator between Gandhi and Jinnah. Sapru, however, had a strong aversion to exposing himself in the ways that would be necessary unless he was assured of the definite support of some of those more directly involved. Katju took the point, and sat down to write to Gandhi, giving him a full account of his conversation with Sapru.[28]

For several weeks Gandhi had been encouraging a number of people – like Rajkumari Amrit Kaur, G. D. Birla, and Sir Purshottamdas Thakurdas – to make contact with Jinnah for him; but he had not had much success.[29] He now clutched at another straw and, greatly to Sapru's surprise – they had not communicated with each other for nearly nine years – Gandhi on 25 January 1941 wrote to Sapru a personal letter. 'I have just finished reading your article in the *Twentieth Century*', the Mahatma began. He very much agreed that Jinnah and he should get together again: but 'my impression is', Gandhi declared, that Jinnah 'does not want a settlement till he has consolidated the League position'. Yet, he concluded, 'if you have faith why don't you see him without being asked by anybody'.[30]

Gandhi's letter put Sapru on his mettle. There was, he was careful to note, very little substance to it; but it did contain the Mahatma's blessing for any personal explorations he might make; and in the deadlocked circumstances which prevailed that was of considerable moment. Accordingly, after some further correspondence – and in the end somewhat to Gandhi's alarm – Sapru wrote to Jinnah (with whom he had had an amicable conversation back in the previous August in Bombay) suggesting that he should meet Gandhi again, to see if they could not arrange to hold a conference and settle their differences. At the same time he wrote to the two Muslims, Nawab Mohammed Ismail, and Liaqat Ali Khan, who had spoken to him in Allahabad in December, in the hope that they would use such influence as they had with Jinnah to evoke a favourable response from him.[31]

Within a few days Sapru received a formally courteous reply from Jinnah in which the latter declared that he was always prepared to meet Mr Gandhi, or indeed 'any other Hindu'. To describe Gandhi simply, however, as a 'Hindu' was to deny the whole basis of the Congress position *vis-à-vis* the League, and accordingly the exchange abruptly terminated before it had even begun.[32]

Its outcome, however, was decisive for Sapru. Over the turn of the year he had been pressed to preside over a non-party conference to be held in Bombay. It had been suggested to him that not only his personal friends but the Viceroy and a number of both Congressmen and Muslims were anxious that he should try his hand at resolving the accumulating differences. To begin with he strongly resisted the idea, both because he had no confidence in the associated tactic of sending a deputation to the Viceroy, and because he believed that it was very much more important to get Gandhi and Jinnah together first. But when his own attempt to do this failed, he reluctantly agreed to attend the conference.[33] His resolution was strengthened by a conversation with Gandhi in Allahabad on 28 February 1941 at which the Mahatma told him he would not oppose any settlement which Sapru might effect with the government (and would advise Congress not to do so either);[34] whereupon Sapru threw himself into the Bombay conference very much more fully than he had originally intended, and agreed indeed to become its President.

When the conference met on 13-14 March 1941 in Bombay, only 34 people attended; but they included a number of 'the knights of the round table', those 'prominent' non-Congress figures who had attended the Round Table Conferences in London ten years previously. They also included representatives of a wide array of political groups that did not belong to either the Congress or the Muslim League. Sapru gave the presidential address, and played a major part in composing the conference resolutions. These proposed that the British should make a declaration promising India dominion status within a fixed period after the war, and in the interval that all central government portfolios should be transferred to the hands of non-official Indians (the Sapru programme, that is, of the previous November-December). Sapru deliberately said nothing about the distribution of portfolios between Hindus and Muslims: in his view this did not present insuperable problems (and, surprising as it may seen, post-war experience suggests he was right). Sapru made it clear, however, that in his view the details of any such arrangements should be without prejudice to the future. He also explained that the Bombay proposals, like his own earlier ones, differed from Congress' current proposals in that they proposed that for the duration of the war the central executive should remain responsible *to the Crown* since the existing central legislature to which Congress wished it to be responsible was not, in everyone's view, for the moment, an adequately representative body.[35]

The Bombay conference received wide publicity. It is quite clear that Gandhi's entourage was watching Sapru's moves very closely. Both Rajagopalachari and Mahadev Desai, Gandhi's secretary, were quick to collect the details about it, and when Gandhi was asked whether he would be contributing to the discussion which the conference had set on foot, he replied he was doing so – by keeping quiet.[36] There was then a notable moment in the central legislature shortly afterwards when Jinnah appeared to trim his sails on the Pakistan issue. Some of the other Muslim leaders, particularly those from the Muslim-majority provinces of Bengal and the Punjab (but including Liaqat Ali Khan from the U.P.), took the opportunity to let it be known that they were not fully in sympathy with Jinnah's more uncompromising demands, and were anxious to see them curbed.[37] Laithwaite, however, the Viceroy's influential Private Secretary, was soon saying that London had decided that for the moment nothing could be done until Congress and the Muslim League had composed their differences; while Linlithgow was privately disparaging about the discussions of 'those amiable gentlemen' in Bombay.[38] Nevertheless, it was not long before Sapru was being asked by the Governor of his own United Provinces if he was going to see the Viceroy. He replied that he had no intention of making the first move himself. It was up to the Viceroy.[39]

In the event on 2 April 1941 he duly received an invitation from the Viceroy to visit him. Linlithgow had no illusions concerning Sapru's high standing both in India and in London, and he realized he must treat him with all due courtesy. On 7 April 1941 the two men were thereupon closeted together at the Viceroy's House in New Delhi for nearly five hours. Sapru pressed the Bombay proposals point by point. Linlithgow had made a close study of what Sapru had lately said and written, and had indeed already sent copies of it to London. Upon the dominion status issue he told Sapru he was personally in favour of fixing a post-war time limit, but London, he explained, had rejected the idea. He would not be drawn on the Pakistan issue, to which Sapru expressed his strong opposition. He asked for more information about 'responsibility to the Crown'; and the two men plainly covered a great deal of ground. Sapru's 'approach throughout', Linlithgow later recorded, 'was sketchy and superficial', but this is hardly borne out by a perusal of Sapru's own record (which stretched to 45 detailed paragraphs), and for Linlithgow the difficulty in Sapru's proposals chiefly stemmed, it seems, from the reluctance of the British to transfer what Sapru, not least from his experience 20 years before as Law Member of the Viceroy's Council, saw to be the two key portfolios of Defence and Finance. Nevertheless at the end of their discussions Linlithgow promised to let Sapru know how the ideas he had advanced fared in London.[40]

Following Sapru's visit to Delhi more advanced opinion both in Congress and the League clearly became very worried lest Sapru and his Bombay men should effect a notable political coup. Some Congressmen indeed (both Satyamurti and Vallabbhai Patel were explicitly named) let it be known that they would be exceedingly disconcerted if the Government settled with Sapru and his associates; while the *National Herald*, Jawaharlal Nehru's organ in Lucknow, now proceeded to attack the Bombay proposals with great vigour.[41] More significantly, Jinnah now took deliberate steps both in speeches and in circulars to his lieutenants to denounce the Sapru programme as a Congress plot, and in May there followed an acrimonious public exchange between the two men.[42]

Within a fortnight, however, of his meeting with the Viceroy Sapru received a letter from Linlithgow saying that the Secretary of State saw 'difficulties in the degree of advance represented by the changes advocated by you';[43] and in a speech in the House of Commons on 22 April Amery proceeded to set out his position on the Bombay proposals in some detail. The suggestion they contained that India should be treated for external purposes as if she were already a dominion would not, Amery said, be acceptable to Parliament, although, as Sapru was quick to point out, the principle had been conceded as long ago as 1919 when India had sent special representatives to the Versailles Peace Conference. Upon the demand for dominion status after the war, Amery had nothing of any real consequence to say, and thus by implication rejected the Bombay plea for some much more definite assurance on this. Amery roundly rejected the proposal for transferring all portfolios at the centre to Indian hands as 'certainly something going beyond what we think practicable in the midst of the ever-increasing strain and injury of the war situation'. And, while like Linlithgow he was careful to be courteous to Sapru, he concluded by playing once more his 1941 theme song. The Bombay proposals, he said, had been sent 'to the wrong address'. They had been denounced by Jinnah as a trap by 'Congress wirepullers', and 'my appeal to Sir Tej and his friends would therefore be', he said, 'not to cease from their efforts, but to concentrate, first and foremost, upon bringing the contending elements in India together'. The interesting point about this speech is that in it Amery rejected as impossible a series of items which the Government of which he was still a member was to concede within the next 12 months, and that he laid down as a *sine qua non* of any advance a condition – of communal agreement – which he himself ignored within the next three.[44]

Sapru, of course, was greatly disappointed. He was especially disturbed at what he called Amery's grant of a veto to Jinnah. Whilst the full force of this only lasted for a month or two, there cannot be much doubt that in one quite vital respect Amery's April 1941 speech enabled Jinnah to consolidate his position in India as never before. Sikander Hyat Khan and Fuzul Huq, the Premiers of the Muslim majority provinces of Bengal and the Punjab, were most unhappy with his proceedings. They were both, however, ignored in London and by the Viceroy, even though it was in their Provinces that Pakistan would have to be based. Jinnah alone was given attention; and when the British kow-towing to him reached its climax with Amery's April 1941 speech, he was quick to use the added prestige it brought him to bring both Sikander and Huq to heel.[45] In the latter part of the year they grumbled continuously in private at Jinnah's imperiousness. But as Sapru for one clearly discerned, they were now irredeemably hesitant to question him in public.[46]

For the rest Amery's speech did nothing but widen the breach between Congress and the League; and in all the circumstances his homily to Sapru was at once unctuous and unwarranted. But it was not his last word. Some of the speeches in the debate in the Commons – by, for example, Sir George Schuster, formerly Finance Member of the Viceroy's Council – were far from being in support of Amery's stand, while the British press was clearly very disquieted too, and eventually in July 1941 Linlithgow announced that because of the increased administrative demands of the war, the Viceroy's Executive Council was now to be enlarged by the appointment of three new Indian members, which would for the first time give it an Indian majority.[47] In a further Commons speech, Amery took credit for the quality of the men appointed.[48] Jinnah for his part was clearly affronted when he realized he had not been consulted.[49] The change was due, or so newspaper correspondents in Delhi and existing members of the Viceroy's Council reported, to Sapru's efforts,[50] and to the support he had received from various Members of Parliament who had experience of India and had been stirred into action by the Bombay resolutions earlier in the year. Sapru noted that there had been no transfer of the crucial Finance, Defence and Home portfolios, but so far as he was concerned it was a small step in the right direction, and he hoped the Indian majority in the Council would soon begin to flex its muscles.[51] Encouraged, moreover, by the support he was eliciting in London, he agreed to preside at the end of July over a second session of the Bombay Conference, this time in Poona, at which he vehemently expostulated against the continued shortcomings in the government's stance.[52]

The second half of 1941 was, all the same, a dreary period. In September there was a considerable stir when Churchill appeared to deny that the recently signed Atlantic Charter could have any reference to India.[53] There was a good deal of evidence, moreover, to suggest that the Viceroy was now simply dragging his feet. Hodson, the newly appointed Reforms Commissioner, stayed with Sapru in Allahabad in August, and vigorously defended Amery. The trouble, he kept on saying, was Churchill, who was as diehard over India as he had ever been. However, in November the new Indian members of the Viceroy's Council (with whom Sapru was in very close touch) were instrumental to the dismay of Churchill – who telegraphed his disapproval to the Viceroy – in securing the release of those Congress prisoners whose terms of imprisonment had not yet been completed (of whom the two most prominent were Azad and Nehru).[54] By now, moreover, there was a good deal of talk in Congress about going back into office once again.[55]

## III

There then came December 1941 with both Pearl Harbor and the Japanese invasion of South-East Asia. Together these put India right in the forefront of the war. There is no evidence that either Congress or the Muslim League made any positive move at this stage. From London Nehru's friend Krishna Menon suggested that he should take a 'positive initiative for National ... Government'. 'May I use discretion to see Amery and others?', he telegraphed to Nehru. 'Undesirable your interviewing British official', Nehru tartly replied.[56] The problem was, it seems, that Congress was too engrossed, first, with the problem of the degree to which they should hold to Gandhi's policy of non-violence when the Japanese might soon be at the gates of India, and secondly, over Gandhi's resignation on this issue from all his formal positions within it. The only important initiative came from Sapru. After discussing the question with two of the new members of the Viceroy's Council, he drummed up his chief Bombay following, and sent the long telegram of 2 January 1942 to Churchill in Washington.[57]

With one shot he scored a bull. It looks as if Roosevelt somehow got hold of a copy of the telegram and raised it in one of his meetings with Churchill. Churchill rounded on him with all the vehemence of an unrepentant diehard. Since for Roosevelt an association with Churchill was vital to the future prosecution of the war, and Churchill was clearly being bull-headed about India, Roosevelt thereafter trod carefully; but for the next nine months he kept up the pressure on him even so.[58]

Churchill was clearly worried by the Sapru telegram. Within four days of its receipt he was inveighing against it to his Cabinet colleagues in London. 'The Indian troops are fighting splendidly', he boomed, 'but it must be remembered that their allegiance is to the King-Emperor, and that the rule of the Congress and Hindu priesthood machine would never be tolerated by a fighting race .... I trust we shall not depart from the position we have deliberately taken up'.[59] But upon his return to London later that month he quickly discovered that any such stance was no longer tenable, for Sapru (as had long been his wont) had sent the text of his telegram to the press. It was immediately reported in a number of London newspapers, and as the principal exponent of moderate Indian opinion for the past 20 years his forceful intervention immediately caught the London eye. Soon, in *The Times*, the *Manchester Guardian*, and elsewhere leader writers were making it plain that in their view Sapru should be listened to by the Government.[60] Moreover, in the general debate on the war in the Commons which followed upon the Prime Minister's return from Washington, while Churchill himself said nothing concerning Indian politics, a number of other members did,[61] and by the second half of February the Prime Minister had clearly been forced to change his mind.

Early in February 1942 three provincial meetings – in Calcutta, Madras, and Nagpur – of Sapru's Non-Party conference (as it was now called) were held; and on 21-22 February a third meeting of the full conference (which was fully reported in London) took place in New Delhi. Although sick and unable to read his own presidential speech, Sapru once more reiterated his previous demands.[62] There was still scarcely any move from either Congress or the Muslim League. In January Nehru had sharply rebuked Rajagopalachari for toying with the Sapru approach: 'it is much too late for any real compromise', he wrote.[63] There was now important support, however, from the leader of Britain's new Asian ally, China, in a statement by Chiang Kai-Shek in which he declared that 'the vast majority of the world's opinion is in full sympathy with India's aspirations for freedom';[64] and on the day the Delhi conference met Sapru was able to publish a personal message which had been sent to him through Amery and Linlithgow from Churchill.

Churchill began:

> In the normal course, I should have replied earlier to the telegram which you and your distinguished colleagues sent to me in Washington. The pressure of public business connected with the grave events of recent weeks has however prevented my doing so.... You will be aware that on two of the points ... effect has been given to your views in that an invitation has been issued to the Government of India to be represented ... in the formulation of policy in the War Cabinet in London and on the Pacific War Council. We shall welcome unreservedly ... whoever may be chosen to fulfil these responsible duties.

Then came the boon in the tail. 'The other proposals which you put to me', the Prime Minister concluded, 'are far-reaching issues in regard to which I hope to give you my considered answer before long'. Considering that just a month before he had told the House of Commons that he did not think the raising of Indian constitutional issues when the enemy was at its gates would be advantageous, this represented a considerable *volte face*.[65]

Professor Mansergh's first volume details the story of the Cabinet committee which was then set up in London under Attlee's chairmanship which included three members with considerable Indian experience, together with Sir Stafford Cripps.[66] Churchill was plainly still opposed to any substantial change in the executive government of India, and the London discussions nearly became as unproductive as those which had preceded the August Offer in 1940. But when Cripps, the Labour member whom Churchill had just made Leader of the House of Commons, where there was a predominantly Conservative membership, offered to go out to India to arrange a settlement himself, the Cabinet committee eventually cut through the tangles. The Viceroy (by now acutely aware of the mishandling which had dogged his own attempts at negotiation in 1939 and 1940) suggested that only a draft declaration should be discussed with the Indian leaders so that some room for adjustment could be left before anything was finalized. After a full discussion in Cabinet the outlines of a draft declaration were settled. In the intervening weeks political circles both in Britain and India had become increasingly agog with the Indian issue. On 6 March the *Manchester Guardian* reported that Churchill's statement 'in reply to the Sapru overtures' would be made shortly,[67] and eventually five days later on 11 March 1942 the Prime Minister rose in the House of Commons to reiterate, or so he said, the August 1940 promise of dominion status for India 'as soon as possible after the war' (in fact the August Offer was worded in a critically different manner), and announced that Sir Stafford Cripps had agreed to fly to India.[68] Two days later Sapru received a personal letter from the Private Secretary to the Viceroy. It read:

> His Excellency has been asked by the Prime Minister to convey to you a message relative to your telegram of January 2nd. The Prime Minister observes that as you will no doubt appreciate his statement in Parliament and the mission of Sir Stafford Cripps are in effect the answer to that telegram, and he hopes that you will therefore excuse him from sending a detailed reply at this juncture.[69]

The details of the collapse of the Cripps negotiations in Delhi can be readily ascertained elsewhere.[70] So far as dominion status after the war was concerned the draft declaration was unequivocal. The manner in which the constitution was to be speedily framed was, moreover, set out with none of the potentially debilitating qualifications which had hamstrung previous declarations. These were major steps forward. In addition, the provisions for the immediate reconstruction of the Government of India at last contained proposals for the transfer to Indian hands of the Home and Finance Departments. Furthermore, there was obviously not much disposition to allow the details of communal differences to hold up the change. The stumbling block was Defence. Had Amery and Linlithgow in the previous year seized time by the forelock and transferred Defence before the Japanese had struck at India – and the previous Commander-in-Chief, Auckinleck, had in personal conversations with Sapru and others in March 1941 shown himself quite responsive to this idea[71] – the outcome here could have been critically different. As it was there was something of a case for not conceding control over Defence whilst Japanese planes were already over India. But to the Indian leaders the transfer of the Defence portfolio became the touchstone of British good faith.

Sapru visited Delhi to be one of the numerous people whom Cripps saw. He was in contact with Rajagopalachari (who had written to him in warm appreciation of his earlier efforts) but he did not see the other Congress leaders (he had recently had no more than some limited social contact with Nehru and Azad).[72] He did, however, see Gandhi, and when the conflict over the Defence portfolio came to a head, Sapru, with his old companion-in-arms, M.R. Jayakar, after fully consulting Rajagopalachari, issued a statement saying that a satisfactory division of responsibility between the British C-in-C (Wavell) and an Indian Defence member should be possible. In its aftermath a Cabinet meeting authorized Cripps to attempt something along the lines they proposed.[73] But to no avail. The details could not be agreed, and when the Congress leaders met resistance here they made it plain that in their considered judgment this meant that the British still did not intend to install a national government in India. That was hard on Cripps. But it was a correct discernment of Churchill's mind. He made no attempt to rescue the negotiations, and was greatly relieved when they failed. From the reactions of the British press it is clear, moreover, that at this juncture a really effective transfer of power was not in the mind of any of the circles it represented either.

For present purposes what is significant about the Cripps Offer is not that in the immediate event it fell to the ground, but three or four other sets of considerations.

First, although the chronology suggests very strongly that Sapru's Washington telegram, and more particularly its publication in Britain, was of major importance in precipitating the British Government into sending Cripps to India, there is an interesting contrast between the emphasis it gave and the emphasis in the draft declaration that Cripps carried with him. The main emphasis in the telegram was upon the necessity for some immediate and radical change in the Government of India. The main emphasis in the Cripps Offer was upon procedure for the post-war period. The contrast does not reduce the importance of the telegram or Sapru's initiative. Sapru was clearly right in pointing to the vital importance of immediate changes. Had in fact his telegram been considered in London in its specific and not just in its more general terms, then Cripps could hardly have gone to India with his mind in the confused state it clearly was over what he meant by a national government and a cabinet, and on how he saw responsibilities for Defence being apportioned as between an Indian Defence member and the Commander-in-Chief as War Member. On their side the British were still much preoccupied with the Muslims. They were clearly, however, overdoing this, since whatever Jinnah may have said in the past two years or so, when it came to the climax of the Cripps negotiations, by his action in delaying his reply till the Congress had sent in theirs, he made it plain that he would not – because he could not – hold out for his own terms.[74] British assertions notwithstanding, the crucial negotiations which Cripps conducted in India were with the Congress leaders, and not with Jinnah at all. There was, moreover, very little discussion in India about the post-war situation. The testing issues related to those which Sapru had set out so carefully in his telegram, and if the Cabinet committee had been somewhat less enmeshed in the obfuscating indecisiveness that characterized Britain's wartime policies towards India, and instead of focusing chiefly on still distant eventualities, had really faced the crucial immediacies, Cripps might have gone to India very much better prepared for his task than he proved to be and more effectively positioned to bring the negotiations to a successful conclusion. For they broke down precisely on those issues to which Sapru had principally drawn attention: the national government and the transfer of all portfolios to Indian hands; and in the light of his telegram it is not possible to argue that the British were not warned of their importance.

The fact was, however, that the British as a whole were still having enormous difficulties in actually facing up to the real prospect of Indian independence, however much they had accepted it in principle. This was strikingly illustrated by the abstention of Linlithgow from any constructive part in the negotiations, even though he would have been a crucial figure, had they been successful, in their aftermath. Throughout he never uttered a single word of encouragement to any of the negotiators. The major problem here was aggravated, we can now perhaps see, because the British were still largely operating with the unamended model of the 'white' commonwealth in mind, where the advance towards full self-government took place in three great leaps forward – in the classic progression, from Crown Colony status, to Representative Government, to Responsible Government, to Dominion Status. During the Second World War they were not prepared, it seems, to move forward in India from stage three to stage four: and because this became so patent to most people in India, most Indian leaders denounced any intermediate concessions as worthless. It was only much later – in Africa, and elsewhere in the British Colonial Empire – that a much more sophisticated progression was worked out, in which, in place of one or two final leaps forward, a whole series of small steps forward came to be taken instead.[75] It was to some such new approach to the final stages of empire that Sapru turned his mind in 1941. Incremental advance in the final stages seemed to him a fully acceptable procedure, as his suggestion about the Viceroy's Council continuing to be 'responsible to the Crown' showed. The British gave their minds to the possibilities here, as the 1939, 1940, and 1942 Offers suggest; but, unlike Sapru, they never made in India any real commitment to it, as their regularly promulgated qualifications to their declarations indicated.

It is clear nevertheless, in retrospect, that the Cripps Offer finally registered the fact that the British Government – Churchill and their current hesitations notwithstanding – had now committed itself fully to the creation of independence for India as soon as the war was over, and had committed itself as well to the transfer of all central portfolios, once the crisis had ended, Defence included, to an interim Indian government, whenever that could be formed. With the Cripps declaration, that is, the British had made all the remaining decisions of principle which affected their own position *vis-à-vis* India. In those that remained – pre-eminently concerning Pakistan – their role was secondary, not primary. Sapru's crucial part in the aftermath of the August 1940 debacle in ultimately precipitating them in this direction seems difficult to gainsay.

## IV

One of the most striking features of Sapru's actions between 1940 and

1942 is at the same time that they bear classically the marks of a mediator. He had by this time no personal political ambitions. He never said things privately he would not say publicly. He was widely known for his integrity, and he could gather about him a band of faithful lieutenants, such as the men who originally dragged him back into the political arena in 1941, and not only organized the Non-Party conferences thereafter but kept a secretariat going in the intervals.

We need, however, to distinguish here between two sorts of proceeding. One involved acting as a go-between, an intermediary. Sapru acted as such at the end of 1940 and early in 1941 when, after speaking with Nawab Mohammed Ismail and Liaqat Ali Khan, he spoke to Dr Katju and to Purushottamdas Tandon before communicating with Gandhi on the one hand and Jinnah on the other. He was always cautious about proceeding in this way, as his reluctance to move at this time without positive support from at least one of the parties, and his reluctance a few months later to approach the Viceroy direct after the Bombay Conference, illustrate. His preferred procedure was the other method – the one which involved being the prophet speaking to the people – one which he employed not least at the Bombay Conference itself. In this the major *modus operandi* was the public statement *urbi et orbi*, in which as the patently independent man, renowned at once for his moderation, wisdom and skill, he proclaimed aloud what he believed to be right. He used this method in his press statement and journal article in November 1940 and January 1941, and moved Gandhi, if not Jinnah. He used it again in his Presidential address to the Bombay Conference, and forced Linlithgow into treating him with great personal attention. Above all, he used it in his telegram to Churchill in Washington, and thereby succeeded in moving even Churchill himself, upon some crucial matters at any rate. And in association once more with Jayakar he used it in the midst of the Cripps negotiations as well, not without effect.

It is important nevertheless to note the limitations in the mediator's role. Sapru could not have made much of it in 1937–9 while Congress was in office; nor in 1939 and 1940 while Gandhi was still negotiating with the Government. It later only had limited relevance, moreover, while Cripps was negotiating with the Congress leaders in Delhi in 1942. Equally, when the 'Quit India' campaign erupted in August 1942, Sapru quickly found himself pushed to the wall.[76] When, that is, there was either direct communication between the two sides to a dispute, or direct open conflict, he had no part to play. He could only swing fully into action when an interstitial role opened up. Two preliminary examples of this of a negative kind spring readily to mind. First, given that Congress was still committed in April 1941 to its 'individual satyagraha' campaign, and that neither Churchill, Amery nor Linlithgow saw very much point in embarking at that stage once again on the fruitless negotiations of 1939–40, Sapru's efforts at the Bombay Conference and in his long interview with the Viceroy in April 1941 were unlikely to yield much fruit. In a sense Amery's dismissive April 1941 speech was conditioned by its structural situation: Congress and the Raj were still too far apart at that stage for a mediator to operate effectively. Secondly, in the arguments between Gandhi and Jinnah, Sapru stood intellectually and emotionally with Gandhi: the interstitial position here was accordingly outside his reach, and so his efforts to mediate between the two men collapsed in his own bitter exchange with Jinnah in May 1941. It was only when a clearly demarcated interstitial position opened up that his interventions had any chance of success. Given just a little more leverage Sapru's discussions with his visitors in Allahabad around the new year 1941 might just have led to negotiations between Congress and the League in the weeks that followed. Given, moreover, some skill and flexibility by the Government of India immediately after the first Bombay Conference something of a concordat might then have been effected. But both were only fleeting opportunities, which proved too tenuous to hold.

It was different in January-March 1942. On the one hand the outbreak of the Japanese War and the disquiet in the British press over India, placed Churchill and his Government in a quite new, and politically vulnerable, position. Upon the other side both the Japanese advent and the petering out of 'individual satyagraha' put the leaders of the Congress into a new position of uncertainty too. The situation was thus altered. Given the change in the situation since the previous April, Sapru could this time – with his telegram to Washington – effect a conjuncture which nine months previously had almost certainly been out of the question. A mediator is dependent upon the nature of the situation in which he operates. He needs at the same time some quite special personal attributes. If he then times and fashions his interventions skilfully, he can have a quite remarkably catalytic effect. Sapru was just such a man. In January 1942 he seized the mediator's moment with unerring skill and, despite several major disappointments, India thereupon turned irrevocably on to the road towards independence at the conclusion of the war. It was a crucial moment in the history of India – and of the British Empire.

NOTES

1. Nicolas Mansergh, *Constitutional Relations between Britain and India, The Transfer of Power 1942–7*, Vol. I: *The Cripps Mission January-April 1942* (London 1972) 3-5.
2. R.J. Moore, *Churchill, Cripps, and India 1939–45* (Oxford, 1979) (hereafter Moore) 45-70; *The Times*, 23 Dec. 1941; *Manchester Guardian*, 17, 22, 24 Dec. 1941.
3. Winston S. Churchill, *The Second World War; Vol. III, The Grand Alliance* (London, 1950) 614-5.
4. See Pinnell to Sapru, 14 March 1942, National Library, Calcutta, Sapru Papers, 1st Series, Vol. 13 (hereafter SP).
5. D.A. Low, *Congress and the Raj: Facets of the Indian Struggle, 1917–1947* (London, 1977).
6. R.J. Moore, *The Crisis of Indian Unity 1917–1940* (Oxford, 1974).
7. Gowher Rizvi, *Linlithgow and India. A Study of British Policy and the Political Impasse in India, 1936–43* (London, 1978), Chs. 2-3.
8. Ibid., Ch. 4.

9. D. A. Low, 'Sequence, crux and means: some Asian nationalisms compared', in R. Jeffrey (ed.), *Asia – The Winning of Independence* (London, 1981) 258-79.
10. M. Gwyer and A. Appadorai, *Speeches and Documents on the Indian Constitution 1921–47*, Vol. II (London, 1947) 504-5; Linlithgow to Governors, 8 Aug. 1940, NAI (National Archives of India), H. Poll (I) 6/13/40.
11. Amery to Smuts, 10 Aug., 13 Nov. 1942, Smuts Papers, Vol. 67.
12. Lord Glendevon, *The Viceroy at Bay: Lord Linlithgow in India 1936–43* (London, 1971).
13. Barbara Ramusack, *The Princes of India in the Twilight of Empire* (Columbus, Ohio, 1978); S. R. Aston, *British Policy towards the Indian States 1905–1939* (London, 1982).
14. For example, British Colonial Office (re Nigeria) *Report of the Commission appointed to enquire into the fears of minorities* ... London, Cmnd. 505, 1958; *Report of the Uganda Relationships Committee* (Entebbe, 1961).
15. Glendevon, *Viceroy at Bay*, Ch. 14-15.
16. For example, Sapru to Prasad, 27 Aug. 1941, SP 18; NAI H. Poll 17/4/41.
17. Viceroy to Secretary of State, tel. 22 May 1941 IOL (India Office Library) MSS. Eur. F125/20.
18. Gwyer and Appadorai, *Speeches and Documents*, II, 485.
19. R. J. Moore, 'British Policy and the Indian Problem 1936–40', in C. H. Philips and M. D. Wainwright (eds.), *The Partition of India* (London, 1970) 79-94.
20. Moore, Ch. 2.
21. Gwyer and Appadorai, loc. cit; David Page, *Prelude to Partition* (Delhi, 1982).
22. Moore, Ch. 2; Rizvi, Ch. 3.
23. Sapru to Dalvi, 9 Dec. 1940, SP 15; Shiva Rao to Sapru, 13 Nov. 1940, Sapru to Shiva Rao, 16 Nov. 1940, SP 20.
24. D. A. Low, 'Sir Tej Bahadur Sapru and the first Round Table Conference', in Low (ed.), *Soundings in Modern South Asian History* (London, 1968).
25. Sapru to Shiva Rao, 12 Dec. 1940, SP 20; Sapru to Natesan, 28 Nov. 1940, SP 40; Sapru to Sinha, 9 Dec. 1940, SP 56 and enclosure; Sapru to Roy, 10 Dec. 1940, SP 50.
26. Sapru to Prasad, 27 Dec. 1940, SP 26; Sapru to Bajpai, 27 Dec. 1940, SP 5.
27. Sapru to Low, 3 Jan. 1941, SP (2nd Series) II L90; Sapru to Prasad, 1 Jan. 1941, SP 26; Natesan to Sapru, 20 Jan. 1941, SP 40.
28. Sapru to Prasad, 10 Jan. 1941, SP 26; Sapru to Shiva Rao 10-13 Jan. 1941, SP 20; Sapru to Katju, 20 Jan. 1941, Katju to Sapru, 20 Jan. 1941, SP 32; Sapru to Natesan, 24 Jan. 1941, SP 40.
29. Birla to Thakurdas, 22 Dec. 1940, NMML (Nehru Memorial Museum and Library), Thakurdas Papers 177.
30. Gandhi to Sapru, 25 Jan. 1941, Sapru to Gandhi 28 Jan. 1941, SP 6.
31. Gandhi-Sapru correspondence for this period, SP 6 and *Collected Works of Mahatma Gandhi* (Ahmedabad 1978), Vol. 73, items 372, 393, 413, 331, 455, 484 and Appendices ix, x.
32. Sapru to Prasad, 13-14, 18 Feb. 1941, SP 26.
33. Sapru to Prasad, 29 Jan. 12-13, 16 Feb. 1941; Prasad to Sapru, 8 Feb. 1941 and enclosure, SP 26; Sapru to Shiva Rao, 6 Feb. 1941, SP 20; Jayakar to Sapru, 8 Feb. 1941, Sapru to Jayakar, 11 Feb. 1941, SP 10.
34. Sapru to Gandhi, 2, 10 March 1941, Gandhi to Sapru, 7 March 1941, SP 6; Sapru to Reed, 30 April 1941, SP 50.
35. Sapru to Laithwaite, 24 March 1941, SP 30; 'Report', SP 29, Misc. 31.
36. Sapru to Jogendra Singh, 21 March 1941, SP 24; Desai to Sapru, 23 March 1941, SP 6; Jayakar to Sapru, 1 April 1941, SP 10.
37. Shiva Rao to Sapru, 22, 26 March 1941, Sapru to Shiva Rao, 25 March 1941, SP 20; Prasad to Jayakar, 1 April 1941, NAI. Jayakar Papers (file number) 576.
38. Shiva Rao to Sapru, 19-21, 25 March 1941, SP 20.
39. Shiva Rao to Sapru, 22, 23 March 1941, SP 20.
40. Sapru's 'Summary ...', SP 29, Misc. 32; Note of an interview between HE the Viceroy and Sir Tej Bahadur Sapru, New Delhi, 7 April 1941. IOL (India Office Library) Mss. Eur. F125/136; Linlithgow to Amery, 5, 6 April 1941, ibid. F/125/10 d 20; Shiva Rao to

Srinivasan, 9 April 1941, Jayakar Papers 576; Sapru to Jayakar, 12 April 1941, SP 10.
41. Sapru to Shiva Rao, 18 April 1941, SP 21.
42. Sapru's statement, 4 May 1941, SP 29; Sapru to Shiva Rao, 8 May 1941, SP 21; Sapru to Sinha, 13 June 1941; Sapru to Kodanda Rao, 2 April 1941, SP 22; Prasad to Jayakar, 5 April 1941, Jayakar Papers 576.
43. Linlithgow to Sapru, 20 April 1941, SP 13.
44. 'The Provinces and the Constitution'. House of Commons 22 April 1941, L. S. Amery, *India and Freedom* (Oxford, 1942) 77-89.
45. NAI H. Poll. 17/4/41 I.
46. Sapru to Shiva Rao, 5 Nov. 1941, SP 21.
47. Amery to Linlithgow, tel., 5 May 1941, Mss. Eur. F/125/20; Shiva Rao to Sapru, 12 May 1941, SP 21; Linlithgow to Sapru, 8 July 1941, SP 13.
48. 'Expansion of the Executive Council', House of Commons, 1 Aug. 1941, Amery, op. cit., 90-100.
49. Shiva Rao to Sapru, 4 July 1941, SP 21; Jinnah to Suhrawady, 1 Aug. 1941, NAI H. Poll. 17/1/41; Prasad to Sapru, 22 Aug. 1941, SP 18.
50. Shiva Rao to Sapru, 9 June, 25 Oct. 1941, SP 21.
51. Sapru to Shiva Rao, 16 Aug. 1941, SP 21.
52. Shiva Rao to Sapru, 6 June 1941, SP 21; Sapru to Amery, 16 Aug. 1941, SP I.
53. Churchill, *Grand Alliance*, Ch. XXIV, and ibid. Vol. IV, *The Hinge of Fate* (London, 1951) 786.
54. Churchill, *Grand Alliance*, pp. 748-9; Shiva to Sapru, 21 June 1941, SP 21; Sapru to Prasad, 19 Aug. 1941, SP 18.
55. Nanna to Kamaladevi, 12 Oct. 1941, NAI H. Poll. 4/8/41 I; Birla to Thakurdas, 8 Nov. 1941. NMML Thakurdas Papers 239.
56. NAI H. Poll. 4/5/51.
57. Sapru to various, 27 Dec. 1941, SP 29, Misc. 35; Sapru to Jayakar, 29 Dec. 1941, SP 10; Sapru to Prasad, 29 Dec. 1941, Prasad to Sapru, 12 Jan. 1941, SP 18.
58. Churchill, *Hinge of Fate*, 185-190.
59. Churchill, *Grand Alliance*, 614-5.
60. Shiva Rao to Sapru, 3 Jan. 1942, SP 21; *The Times, Manchester Guardian, Daily Herald, Daily Express, New York Times*, 5 Jan. 1942, etc., Sapru to V. Sastri, 6 Jan. 1942, SP 23; *Manchester Guardian*, 6 Jan., 7 Feb. 1942; *The Times* 8, 23 Jan. 1942.
61. For comment see Shiva Rao to Sapru, 30 Jan. 1942, SP 21.
62. For a summary see *Manchester Guardian*, 10 Feb. 1942 and *The Times*, 23 Feb. 1942.
63. Nehru to Rajagopalachari, 26 Jan. 1942, NMML, Nehru Papers: Rajaji file; Prasad to Sapru, 18-20 Jan. 1942, SP 18.
64. Mansergh, *Transfer*, I, Ch. 2, for the whole story.
65. M. Pinnell to Sapru, 20 Feb. 1942, SP 13; see also *Daily Telegraph*, 21 Jan. 1942.
66. Mansergh, *Transfer*, I. Ch. 3.
67. *Manchester Guardian*, 6 March 1942, and the London press *passim* during the first few days of March 1942.
68. Gwyer and Appadorai, *Speeches and Documents*, II, 519-20.
69. Pinnell to Sapru, 14 March 1942, SP 13.
70. Mansergh, *Transfer*, I, Ch. 4; Moore, Chs. 4 and 5; Rizvi, Ch. 6.
71. See Shiva Rao to Sapru, 25 March 1942, SP 22.
72. Rajagopalachari to Sapru, 26 Feb. 1942, SP II R 32; Sapru to Shiva Rao, 3, 5, 1942, SP 21.
73. NAI, Jayakar Papers, 753.
74. Intelligence Bureau reports, 28 March 1942, NAI H. Poll. 221/42.
75. D. A. Low, *Lion Rampant* (London, 1973) 175-6.
76. Gandhi to Sapru, 4 Aug. 1942, *Collected Works of Mahatma Gandhi*, 76, item 415.

# The Imperial Factor in British Strategies from Attlee to Macmillan, 1945–63*

by

R. F. Holland

Over recent years the study of British decolonization has attained a measure of intellectual rigour. Three contributions can be singled out as examples of how the level of discussion has been raised above the crude, if diverse, simplicities which had previously been dominant. A. G. Hopkins, in his broad survey of West African history, has connected the secular trend from 'open' to 'closed' non-European economies with the sapping of the imperial status quo;[1] B. R. Tomlinson, whilst applying elements of the Hopkins model to India,[2] has elsewhere emphasized that the British Empire was never a reflection of nation-based power, but pre-eminently lent itself as a carrier for international capital and skills, only to find that these institutional arrangements decayed during the twentieth century;[3] whilst Jack Gallagher, in his posthumously-published Ford Lectures, has traced how the UK's imperial role after 1918 was finally destroyed by the triple buffetings of domestic constraints, international pressures and colonial political developments, but not without ups (such as the great colonial mobilization between 1939 and 1945) as well as downs along the way.[4] These studies, however, have their centre of analytical gravity in the pre-1945 period. For the two subsequent decades there are, as yet, few works available which attempt a broad view of metropolitan policy, although a substantial literature exists on particular events. In dealing with this more recent, and climactic, phase the current article seeks to comment on the variables which underlay changing British assessments of the colonial connection.

One qualification in particular, however, must be noted as a preliminary. The attempt to define and divide into periods the stages of metropolitan revision in colonial policy will inevitably fit somewhat awkwardly with the chronologies of change in specific dependencies. Beyond this lies the tangled questions of the relative weights to be assigned metropolitan and peripheral forces, and the nature of their interaction, in the decolonization process. Contemporary answers on these large matters must remain vague and unsatisfying whilst not only the quantity of relevant scholarship remains scant, but its quality often marred by the narrow specialisms endemic to the modern profession. In the context of decolonization, each situation had a time-frame of its own, and any definitive study will face the laborious task of probing the common denominators in these multiple settings. Ultimately, however, the only time-frame which mattered was that in Whitehall, and this was never more true than in the later 1950s, when Macmillan was engaged in drawing the threads of colonial policy into his own hands. The immediate task, then, is to investigate the motives and instincts prevailing in the recesses of British government in the two decades after 1945.

I

The restoration of European colonial empires after the Second World War, whilst planned almost from the moment of their loss by conquest, may understandably appear to the historian as a strange and piquant affair. The French, with a broken domestic economy and a glimmering Soviet threat to the east, shifted manpower and materials to Indo-China, and after May 1947 unleashed a protracted war of pacification against Viet Minh nationalists. Even more astoundingly, the Dutch, with a home population which was still acutely malnourished after the 'Hunger Winter' of 1944/5, similarly planned the re-acquisition of their East Indian possessions, and subsequently expended scarce resources to dislodge Sukarno's breakaway republic from its Javanese heartland. The British did not have to fight their way back into their own empire, although it is worth remembering that it was UK and Indian Army troops who first reoccupied Saigon and Surabaya; but the reimposition of civil authority in the British empire was still a costly and exhausting exercise.[5] These were all hardly examples of European surplus capital resuming its search for profitable outlets overseas; the metropoles were squeezing themselves to the bone in order to regain control of peripheries which were themselves frequently war-shattered to the point of famine.

The high premium which the British attached to colonies after 1945 arose fundamentally from uncertainties as to the ultimate direction of government policies in the United States. It was possible, for example, that, as after 1918, the US administration might shirk the task of reconstructing an international trade system. If protectionist sentiments again came to prevail in the White House, Britain's colonial possessions provided her with the basis for an alternative strategy – as they had in the early 1930s. Nevertheless, it was widely recognized that the US economy had expanded too greatly during the war to turn its back on foreign markets again.[6] The most common fear, then, was that the Americans would sustain their drive towards multilateral trading arrangements, but would do so in ways which paid minimal heed to the adjustment needs of other industrial nations. Thus the gains of post-war recovery would be overwhelmingly appropriated by US producers, leaving other western economies in a state of permanent subordination. One way out of this looming dependency was to enforce industrial efficiency at home; but under conditions of troop demobilization this approach had severe limitations. It was in this context that British business opinion became deeply attracted to the thesis of colonial development, since the boosting of purchasing power in those underdeveloped areas where the UK enjoyed trade preferences and political control could make a vital contribution to the maintenance of the British market-share in international trade.[7]

It was the significance of colonies as commodity-producers, however, which made them especially pertinent to metropolitan needs. Thus, as the US economy continued to grow, it was bound to suck in a swelling volume of colonial commodity imports; and provided these dollar revenues were kept within the Sterling Area 'pool', the post-war disparity between the British and American currencies would become subject to a self-correcting mechanism. Certainly the management of the Sterling Area to this end by the London authorities subsequently provided the key to UK monetary stability; and the Bank of England was able to discriminate against Crown Colonies in its pool operations in order to alleviate the resentments of the more powerful Sterling Area participants, such as India and Egypt.[8] This has been held to be an example of pure colonial exploitation; in other words, a form of appropriation which arose directly from a constitutional inferiority which made the Crown Colonies incapable of independent monetary action. This probably requires some qualification. What allowed the British Government to whip the Sterling Area into line was not its sovereign authority over many of the latter's members, but the UK's position as an exporter of industrial goods which were in very short supply. Some West African states, for example, would have had little option but to accept the discriminatory workings of the Sterling Area, since in the context of a classic sellers' market only the UK was likely to fit West African import needs (for consumption or development) into their allocation programmes. The pattern of British trade gave the UK a unique leverage among commodity producers at a time when raw material demand, too, was rising rapidly; and the exercise of that power held out hope that the commercial hegemony of the United States would prove short-lived.

The ambiguity of the UK's industrial position in 1945/6 derived from this enormous, but transitory, power held by those industrial producers with a surplus for export just at the point when demand for non-military goods roared ahead of supply. This, above all, was to the benefit of the United States; but the other advanced nation well-placed to exploit this passing conjuncture was Great Britain. Hence, whatever the degree of the UK's overhanging paper obligations, at a time when political and economic influence hinged overwhelmingly on physical production, the British could exhibit a certain smug confidence as groups of pleading customers – the Indian industrial delegation in 1945, for example, desperate for capital equipment which might give them some hope of participating in post-war development – perambulated through the factory districts of the Midlands and northern England. But British manufacturers and their bankers knew that world recovery, especially in Europe, would erode these happy circumstances and restore sellers' competition to the market-place. It was, therefore, the ability of the British economy to navigate this transition from a sellers' to a buyers' market, where price and not mere supply would be the criteria of success, which caused apprehension within UK government and business. Thus international recovery, ostensibly so desirable, had a downside when viewed from Birmingham or Bradford, since it entailed a re-engagement with the constraints of costs and efficiency – in some senses, for the first time since 1939. It was in this setting that the colonial connection in general, and the Sterling Area in particular, however significant in British calculations in 1945/6, actually became much more relevant during the course of the newly-elected Labour Government, since it was a counter to the persistent tendency of the UK price-level to rise at a more rapid rate than that of its key competitor, the United States. Now it is at least conceivable that a Churchill-led Cabinet might have corrected this inflationary bias by tacking monetary stringency onto the existing battery of physical controls. But no post-war Labour Government could risk rattling Ramsay MacDonald's skeleton in this manner. Instead, it was forced to cling all the more desperately to the trade and currency network of the Sterling Area as a means of preventing overseas consumers from switching to US suppliers. The colonies and dominions, in other words, were a counter-inflationary cushion at a time when Attlee's economic policies were close to disintegration. The nationalizations, medical provision and expansion of education so magnanimously legislated by Labour Ministers was largely achieved because the Bank of England kept the Sterling Area show on the road. It is not, therefore, surprising that the Labour Party between 1945 and its defeat at the October 1951 General Election omitted to plan in any serious way for political change in the colonies; whilst the conscription of empire to do its duty by British socialism (which had always constituted one strand in Labour tradition) must rank as one of the quainter accidents of the period.

There is a central paradox in Attlee's colonial policies, however, which requires attention: it was his government which pushed Indian decolonization through even at the price of partition, but which also increased the British commitment to colonialism in Africa. The explanation for this lies, partly, in the different stages of indigenous political development in the two areas, and specifically in the variegated effects which the Second World War had wrought within them. But it is equally important to set the Labour Cabinet's imperial decisions in a broader and more shifting framework. The relationship of the disparate crises which bore down upon UK Ministers during 1947 holds the key to this problem. The terms of the US Washington Loan to the UK, finally authorized by President Truman on 15 July 1946 after a long Congressional wrangle, had preordained some break in British policies because they stipulated that within a year of its operation sterling should become freely convertible into dollars.[9] In fact, the UK economy had moved into a phase of acute disequilibrium by late 1946, when the slow recovery of domestic production began to tail off as excess demand destroyed any rational distribution of physical resources. Finding adequate internal adjustments politically unacceptable, Attlee moved to relieve those marginal pressures associated with external commitments: in February 1947 it was announced that British troops would evacuate from Greece where they had been fighting Communists; in mid-July the Indian Viceroy, Lord Louis Mountbatten, announced that India would now receive her independence as early as 15 August; and in September the imminent abandonment of the Palestine Mandate was made public by the Foreign Secretary, Ernest Bevin. Of course, each of these situations possessed a local dynamic of its own; and it might be argued that British policy towards India was never more thoroughly directed from Delhi, and not from London, than under the Mountbatten Viceroyalty. But then India had never possessed a Viceroy whose personal conception of his objectives was so closely conditioned by his sense of what was, and what was not, tolerable to the metropole; this, after all, was why his predecessor, Wavell, had been so peremptorily dismissed and Mountbatten appointed. Thus, amidst all the twists and turns of events 'on the ground', the Attlee administration, locked into a metropolitan crisis concerned with balancing the demands of social reform and economic stabilization, can be discerned cutting adrift from dependencies which were net liabilities, and maintaining a grip on those (largely African) possessions which remained bankable assets.

Amidst this concatenation of financial and imperial diplomacy, the Americans and the British were each attempting to get a head-lock on the other. Thus in forcing sterling through the wringer of convertibility in August (when the pound slumped immediately and controls had to be re-imposed) President Truman was aiming to break the British will to steer an independent course on international economic questions. Meanwhile, the British, by their decisions over Greece, Palestine and (to some extent) over India, sought to signal to Washington that the UK would become more selective in its acceptance of security functions if it did not continue to receive special consideration in the commercial field. British living standards, Indian self-government and Palestinian land rights were, in this context, pawns being moved about in the tactical battle raging between London and Washington. Naturally, no Cabinet minutes will emerge on either side of the Atlantic recording decisions in these lights, since no Cabinet Secretary would be so injudicious as to submit such ministerial *realpolitik* to paper.

In engaging in such a covert struggle with the US during 1947 the British Government was acting in the belief that the Americans would, in the end, baulk at the costs and risks of world leadership and finally accept the UK as a partner-in-dominance. That prospective partnership might not be quite as equal as the often lop-sided relationship which had prevailed between 1941 and 1945;[10] but in Whitehall it was thought likely to be much more equal than at the time of the UK's near-bankruptcy in 1945/6, when the perceived Soviet threat had been decidedly less. This, however, was a gross underestimation of the price the Americans were willing to pay for global pre-eminence. Truman's decision to take up the anti-Communist struggle in Greece where the British had left off was the first sign of this new American adventurism; but it was revealed in its awesome extent by the introduction of the European Recovery Programme in July 1947, or, as it became more commonly called, the Marshall Aid Plan. In the folklore of British austerity this unbuttoning of the American purse is recalled with fond gratitude. It was not, however, greeted in some quarters with unqualified pleasure. Thus it was natural that British industrialists should be anxious about any funding of those continental economies, such as the German, which the war had so happily destroyed.[11] The operation of Marshall Aid became particularly dangerous to UK interests when it emerged that one of the underlying US aims was to nudge the British into integration with western Europe. The implications of this for a socialist Cabinet in London were disturbing: President Truman was setting out to limit the quantity of free spectacles in Pontefract (or better state schooling for Hampstead's golden youth) until similar facilities could be afforded in Lille or Cologne. Thus during the final phase of Labour's rule, the nurturing of colonial links took on yet new significance as one of the several means to fend off American insistence that Britain redefine its identity as a West European power. In short, the reasons why the Attlee Government presided over withdrawal from its Indian and Palestinian commitments, and yet seemed bent on maintaining the colonial presence in Africa, were all of a piece: these contrary policies all ministered to the central theme of British policy after 1945, which was to cut a path towards some meaningful degree of economic and diplomatic independence in a world dominated by the United States.

But if the colonies were intended between 1945 and 1951 to help the UK break out of the dependency trap in which it seemed to be set, their development could not be a sham. The British Government could not simply legislate for increased Colonial Development and Welfare monies; it also had to revise administrative traditions 'on the ground' which were not congruent with new necessities. The Colonial Office did try to promote action along these lines but was defeated by that reconsolidation of pre-war patterns (and the vested interests clustered around them) which affected British life in metropole and periphery. Thus in establishing the Malayan Union in May 1946 the Colonial Office hoped to free Chinese entrepreneurship from some of the constraints long imposed by cautious administrators and fiercely conservative Malay sultans; the opposition of the latter groups, however, managed to force the abandonment of the experiment in January 1948.[12] In Kenya, too, the London authorities recognized that sustainable economic growth in the colony hinged on dislodging the white farmers, with their crippling overheads, from some of the positions of power they had attained during the war, and shifting government resources towards African producers; but the returning Governor, Sir Philip Mitchell, failed to educate the European settlers in the fact that racial exlusivism could contribute nothing to giving colonialism a stable future in East Africa.[13] It was not until the anti-colonial insurgencies in Malaya and Kenya during the early 1950s, involving massive injections of metropolitan military power, that the imperial government was able to impose its will to reform on those local networks for whom the entrenched collaborative arrangements were so amenable.

If colonial administrations were often obstructed by white settler power from instituting political changes in the later 1940s, they did make an enormous effort to improve indigenous land use, above all, in East Africa. Indeed, British administrators seemed to conceive of 'development' as little more than staving off the allegedly imminent ecological crisis after centuries of deleterious farming practices by the *indigenes*. In this way the ruling bureaucracies identified a role ministering to 'African needs' but which did not carry any political implications for settler supremacy. But heightened intervention in the village economy only served to destabilize the administrators' relationships with the peasantry. The cause of this new peasant disaffection was not so much the resentment of the forced labour involved in contour-ridging to reduce soil erosion, since such practices were hardly new. Large sections of the peasantry, however, were beginning to feel 'left behind' after 1945 as the effects of the war in stimulating African cash-crop farming were consolidated; the distinction between those who sported bicycles, watches and 'fashionable' clothes, and those who did not, was becoming increasingly visible. The administrative drive to reconstruct land use, therefore, confirmed the fears of many Africans that times were changing, and not in their favour. British officials thus became suspect as developers in a way that they had never been when their role had been more narrowly conceived. Nationalist politicians in Kenya, Tanganyika, and (to quote a non-African example) Cyprus, were able to garner vital early support in the milieu of peasant fear touched off by rural improvement programmes.[14] In trying to prove themselves capable of meeting the tasks of modern development, the colonial governments only exposed their own institutional bluntness. However much the older and more conservative district officers (in contrast with their usually more liberal juniors) might resent the reforms initiated from London after 1950, the declining relevance of their service once 'politics' replaced 'administration' as the moving force of events, made them, on the whole, putty in Whitehall's hands.

II

The first main phase of the post-war period was capped by the formation of the North Atlantic Treaty Organization in 1949. This can only be represented as a strategic defeat for the UK by those who, at the time and since, failed to perceive any Soviet threat to western European independence. But the UK's participation in NATO was, undoubtedly, a defeat in one important sense: it deepened the constraints within which national decision-making worked. The British Government's room for manoeuvre in foreign and colonial policy was, however, somewhat improved after 1950 by the boom in world trade which accompanied the Korean War. This boom was, in part, the result of US strategic stockpiling; but, more importantly, it sprang from widespread business euphoria (and therefore investment) as the expansionary cycle in the US economy showed no signs of flagging. This was American-led recovery with a vengeance. Under its aegis the Conservative Government, elected in October 1951 and led by Winston Churchill, was able to phase out austerity; German, French and Japanese reconstruction could proceed further without the displacement of British exports in third markets; and political and social change in British colonies could be encouraged under favourable conditions of rising living standards. The stablization of the international trading system in the first half of the 1950s, therefore, eroded the dangerous dependence on the Sterling Area which had previously characterized the British economy; and it is worthwhile to consider how much more contorted subsequent European decolonizations might have been under less beneficent economic circumstances.

It was these relaxed commercial conditions which permitted schemes for western European integration to get under way. Nevertheless, the Churchill Government kept on the outside of these arrangements. This caused some surprise at the time, since Churchill had played a prominent role in the early days of the movement for western European unity.[15] But most British opinion continued to be sceptical of the French ability to sustain open market competition with their German neighbours; at some point, it was believed, the French trade barriers would be put up and the experiment brought to a grinding, and embittered, halt. British industrialists, furthermore, felt much more comfortable with a trading strategy geared to the Sterling Area system; after all, they had spent much of the twentieth century trying to seal themselves off from the full blast of German production, and they had every reason to continue to do so. Furthermore, ever since the late 1930s it had been widely argued that the real slack in the use of world resources lay in Africa and Asia; and after 1950 it seemed that the US-generated boom would see this slack rapidly taken up. In this period British economic interests still seemed to lie in an orientation towards exchange with primary-producing countries, many of them UK colonies and dominions, rather than towards western Europe.

The particular significance which Churchill and his Foreign Secretary, Anthony Eden, ascribed to what was becoming known as the 'underdeveloped world', however, had its roots more in diplomacy than in economics. Both were concerned that, through the operation of NATO, the Americans would manipulate the British into playing the role of front-line guarantor of western Europe against Soviet aggression. Eden, in particular, saw the cultivation of a special relationship between the UK and a broad swathe of underdeveloped countries, in which the UK played the part of an orchestrating and mediating power, as an effective means of remaining a viable extra-NATO entity. This, as we have seen, fitted British economic instincts; it also provided a method for countervailing the political pressures emanating from the US and mainland Europe. Nor, in the context of the mid-1950s, did this amount to illusions of grandeur. Many underdeveloped countries at this juncture were eager for the patronage of a western industrial state, but feared the hegemonic ambitions of the US; the UK, much less forbidding as a partner, and with a more externally-oriented economy than that of France or Germany, was well-placed to offer itself as a medium through which such nations could hope to penetrate the big power system. This explains the subtle bedding-down of Anglo-Indian relations after 1950. For India, continued intimacy with the British helped to off-set the dangers posed by the evident US preference for Pakistan; for Britain, a new-model axis with India was the perfect means of putting its special status in the underdeveloped world on a modern footing. Indeed, the great weight which Nehru's opinion carried in London during these years preceding the Suez crisis is symptomatic; and when President Eisenhower put enormous pressure on the UK to join a security bloc in south-east Asia explicitly directed against Communist aggression, the UK Government refused unless India were also admitted as a founder-member and the pact's aims left undefined.[16]

The reason why US diplomacy in this period was couched in such simplistic anti-Soviet terms was, not least, because it made it more difficult for her western allies to evolve strategies of their own; and the particular resentment felt in Washington towards Britain after 1954 was rooted in the suspicion that Eden (who virtually ran British foreign policy with few intrusions from his ageing Prime Minister) was seeking to prise open some cracks in the ideological mould. Such suspicions were confirmed during the final phases of the Franco-Viet-Minh war in Indo-China. It was Eden who effectively vetoed the plan of the US Secretary of State, John Foster Dulles, for American bomber strikes against the Communist forces besieging the French garrison at Dien Bien Phu, and so ensured that the subsequent peace talks took place with the military initiative very much in the hands of Ho Chi Minh.[17] Even more dramatic was the stance which Eden struck at the Geneva Conference of April 1954, called to discuss, amongst other matters, an Indo-Chinese settlement, and at which the British Foreign Secretary was co-chairman with his Soviet counterpart. Conspicuously failing Dulles' litmus test of anti-Communism, Eden strove to coax into being some new equilibrium between the negotiators, establishing good relations, for example, with the Chinese delegation led by Chou En Lai. Eden's style spoke louder than many communiqués; he was signalling the view that the emerging diplomatic configuration was infinitely complex, and that this complexity (whilst not overshadowing certain fundamental divisions) nonetheless afforded room for independent action by middle powers irrespective of their ideological colouring or stage of economic development. Thus, whereas for the US the Indo-Chinese settlement appeared as a defeat because it put a new Communist state on the map,[18] for the British it was an exemplary case of how the capacity for unilateral decision-making could be nurtured back to life.

Viewed against this background, the UK's changing approach in its colonial dependencies assumes a broader logic. The laborious elaboration of local government structures which had characterized 1940s 'reform' gave way to the construction of national states. Only such modernized polities could play the role of economic partner which the UK's trade strategy required; just as importantly, such state-formation would legitimate the UK as the western power most prepared to play a lead-role in African and Asian development. One of the hallmarks of the period was, therefore, the hammering apart of old colonial particularisms and their re-integration into federal or quasi-federal units. These actions did not follow lines laid down by a new-style inventiveness; they cleaved to the particular amalgamationist traditions which had marked colonial thinking in east and central Africa for much of the century. What was new, however, was the single-mindedness with which the British Government was now prepared to override the moral and tactical considerations which had previously been sufficient to thwart substantive change. Perhaps the most suggestive image of this process was provided by events in Buganda, where the Kabaka's refusal to cooperate in the British plan for a Ugandan federation led to this long-standing ally of local colonial rule being bundled into an aircraft and swept off to a cautionary, if short-lived, exile in London.[19] Initiatives of this sort ( the same year witnessed the bonding of a Central African Federation governed, essentially, from Salisbury, and a Nigerian constitutional conference designed to break the resistant regionalisms of that most diverse society) do not indicate an imperial power clinging, nonplussed, to the status quo, but point to a metropole with a clear sense of how to explore new coalitions capable of underpinning its international influence.

The transmuting of segmented colonial communities into 'steel-framed' national units carried one awkward implication for the metropole: it necessitated a time-tabling of progress towards self-government. Only by thus opening up the prospect of power at the territorial centres could colonial cadres be lured out of their localized frames of reference. In theory these changes risked a scramble for supremacy by demagogues and social groups which would trample over metropolitan interests. But national politics meant elections; and the electoral process, Westminster-style, was the most potent weapon in the metropolitan armoury during the era of decolonization. Wherever national elections were integrated into the colonial system, the British could make or break African politicians. They could make them, for example, by assisting the appropriate party in gearing up its vote-collecting apparatus; they could break them, or at least discipline them, by deciding at what point their popularity should be subjected to the test of the hustings.[20] The crucial moment of decolonization was, in many respects, that at which nationalist leaders tied themselves to a constitutional process supervised by the presiding power. In the Gold Coast this came as early as 13 February 1951 when Kwame Nkrumah accepted the post of Leader of Government Business following elections under the Coussey constitution; whilst in Tanganyika Julius Nyerere strove after 1952 to keep the Tanganyika African National Union a small and law-abiding association, purged of all undisciplined elements, in order to win British confidence in its capacities as a Westminster-type organ.[21] It was African nationalists, much more than colonial authorities, who feared populist disturbances, since such an outspilling of politics would reveal their own organizations as the ramshackle affairs they so frequently were; for Nkrumah and Nyerere, an ordered, and British-supervised, constitutionalism provided a much more reliable route to their desired destination. It was, admittedly, implicit in these arrangements that the British would have to accept whatever leaders the electoral whirligig might throw up; but this was a small price to pay when the British knew their Africa well enough to know how malleable these infant democracies, hemmed in by fancy franchises, would be to the judicious application of customary pressures.

There were instances, however, when the British willingness to control and shape these transformations was tested by violent opposition. The three great colonial revolts with which the UK Government was confronted occurred in Cyprus, Kenya and Malaya. The background to each of these crises was different. Thus in Cyprus it appeared that the imperial authorities had no foreseeable intention of altering the island's subordinate status; in Malaya the position was more fluid. But Mau Mau fighters in Kenya, young Chinese Communists in Malaya and supporters of Enosis (or Union with Greece) in Cyprus all shared one common motive: they were struggling to prevent the metropole mapping a future in which their group interests (as landless peasants, wage-earners or, in the Cypriot case, Orthodox loyalists fearful of a secular politics fostered by a Protestant power) were likely to get scant respect. They were responses, in other words, not to the *stasis* of the colonial presence, but to its dynamic, which now, for the first time, threatened to plough them under. The massive intrusions of metropolitan authority which ensued, however, was evidence of the UK's determination to direct change even at high levels of cost. In Malaya this meant resettling 400,000 Chinese in new villages;[22] in Kenya it meant reforming village patterns in Central Province and encouraging a new class of African small-farm capitalists with a stake in property rights;[23] in Cyprus it meant breaking the Enotists by according Turkey a *locus standi* in any decision about the island's future, blocking any possibility of absorption into the Greek state.[24] Here was metropolitan intervention on a scale that outdid that even of the period of conquest, and a ruthless determination to adopt whatever tactics were necessary to smash nationalist scenarios which did not fit Whitehall's schedule.

There remained, however, the perplexing dilemma of the white settler presence in the British colonies of eastern and central Africa. Was it not inevitable that racial confrontations in these areas would cause more traumatic disjunctures than contemporary British conceptions of decolonization allowed for? If so, British policy in these cases in the mid-1950s simply represented a hopeless playing for time, or a crass inability to feel the pulse of African change. But in this phase it was still logical enough to perceive white settlers as, on balance, metropolitan assets, however awkwardly they resisted even modest concessions to African advancement, since this European ballast promised to make political change more sensitive to internal checks and balances. The curious *sang froid* with which London policy-makers regarded the settler problem really derived from the assumption that economic imperatives would ultimately force accommodations between white and black interests. Thus it was assumed that African capitalists would tailor their political views to their need for access to local European (and Indian) credit; and that European producers would, in the end, prefer the co-optation of an African landlord and trading class than face their unqualified competition in the market-place. The metropolitan thesis of 'multiracialism', usually articulated in flaccid terms of racial good-neighbourliness, was fundamentally grounded in the perceived engagement of African and settler capitalism. The pattern of that engagement would obviously vary from one territory to another, although federations (such as that between the Rhodesias and Nyasaland) could give order and uniformity to the process. In mid-decade, then, with Mau Mau insurgency in Kenya under control, when stubborn particularisms such as that in Buganda had been disciplined, and when, most significantly, the Central African Federation had got off to a reasonably satisfactory start, metropolitan officials could quite justifiably look forward to a protracted and stable evolution in which competing races and ethnic groups accepted long-term compromises arbitrated from London.

### III

At the New Year of 1956, therefore, the Conservative Government led by Anthony Eden (who had succeeded Churchill as Prime Minister in April 1955) could feel reasonably satisfied with the UK's international and imperial position. However bumpy the Anglo-American relationship might be, it was thought unlikely that President Eisenhower would play rough with its one major ally whose resolute response to Soviet aggression within the NATO area could be absolutely relied upon. Whilst the UK was a non-participant in Western European economic integration, its influence on the continent was assured through its continuing military guarantees (four British Army divisions had recently been pledged to the defence of West Germany). In the underdeveloped world, too, Britain seemed to be successful in modulating colonial change and striking a new cooperation with such leaders of the non-aligned world as India. None of these factors made Britain a great power in the contemporary meaning of the term; only a significant nuclear deterrent could do that; and, although Churchill had diverted more cash to the existing nuclear programme, it was very doubtful that the UK could equip itself with such a capacity without American technological assistance on a scale that the latter had shown no propensity for since 1946.[25] But Eden's objective was not to emulate the rival hegemonies of the US or the Soviet Union; had he thought in these terms he would indeed have been a flawed and dangerous visionary. Rather, Eden judged that subtle management of Britain's unique and complex web of relationships in a changing world presented her with opportunities for renewing the capacity for a unilateral diplomacy which (seen through the lens of his occupation, class and generation) was the kernel of the national tradition. The attempt to explore the possibility of restored British independence represented a profoundly appealing challenge to a Prime Minister whose experience and aptitude lay in foreign affairs; and its accomplishment potentially afforded greatness to a premiership which had been kept leashed so long by Churchill's love of office. It was only the unfolding of the Suez crisis in the summer and autumn of 1956 which revealed the extent to which the Americans were prepared to go to crush an ambition which the British establishment had nurtured ever since 1945.

Why, then, did Gamul Abdul Nasser's nationalization of the Suez Canal on 26 July 1956 provoke Eden to collude with the French and Israelis to invade Egyptian territory and depose its leader, with such disastrous results?[26] In 1954 Eden, as Foreign Secretary, had negotiated an Anglo-Egyptian settlement under which British troops would evacuate the Suez Base area; traditional strategic concerns were clearly not the motivating factor in the British Prime Minister's subsequent actions, by which time the last UK troops had left their old Nile haunt. Undoubtedly the security of oil supplies did enter Eden's equation. If Nasser succeeded in excoriating British influence throughout the Middle East, including the Gulf, the UK would be dependent on US help (not least through the latter's Saudi satrapy) for its access to essential fuels. After that any hopes of British unilateralism would be dead. But all existing interpretations of Eden's attitude towards Nasser emphasize that it was ultimately not conditioned by any such discrete calculations; the antipathy felt by the quintessential English diplomat for the Egyptian revolutionary officer (such that reiterated analogies were made with Hitler) arose from a more fundamental and generalized distaste. This distaste had about it the bouquet of personal vendetta; Nasser, by forcing Eden into the 1954 Suez Base agreement, had weakened the latter's standing amongst Tory backbenchers at a vital moment, with the chance of premiership looming. But whatever significance can be ascribed to Eden's piqued vanity, it was filtered through a much larger set of concerns. To the new British Prime Minister, Nasserism was quasi-colonial nationalism of the meanest and most dangerous kind; it sought to work through raising popular Anglophobia to fever pitch; and if it became the dominant mode of mass politics in the Middle East, more amenable nationalisms in the underdeveloped world (such as that of Nkrumah in the Gold Coast) might be infected. This conflict for the soul of politics in underdeveloped societies lay at the heart of Anglo-American differences over Middle East policy. It suited Dulles that Nasser's radical ideology should vent itself in assaults (verbal and otherwise) against British colonialism; the Secretary of State was confident that once this phase was over the Egyptian leader could be guided into an anti-Communist role. In a certain sense, Nasserism served American purposes in weakening the British tendency to play its own game outside the prescribed limits of the formal NATO alliance. It was the recognition of the threat which Nasser posed to British hopes of structuring politics in its traditional spheres of influence, and of the use which others might make of this, which jangled Eden's nerves. The Prime Minister's collusion with France and Israel in a clinical intervention designed to force changes in the Egyptian leadership, then, was not an irrational lapse into adventurism, but a calculated extension of the UK's determination to maintain its leverage in the underdeveloped world, even in the teeth of American resentments.

Is it the case, therefore, that Eden failed to anticipate the economic pressures brought to bear by the US (expressed, as in 1947, by a run on sterling) which forced the whole policy into retreat, even when air-borne and sea-borne British troops had landed and had advanced within striking distance of Cairo? But even if Eden had, incredibly, overlooked this patently obvious consideration, it is impossible that his Chancellor of the Exchequer, Harold Macmillan, who was privy to at least the basic outline of the Anglo-French action in advance, did not bring it to the notice of the Prime Minister. What can be better deduced from events is that Eden and his closest advisers, who included the Foreign Secretary, Selwyn Lloyd, made a clear-eyed calculation that President Eisenhower would shrink from using a reduction in the British standard of living as a lever to impose a withdrawal from the Canal under, inevitably, humiliating conditions. Inherent in this gamble was the idea that the US administration would be deterred from presenting such a choice to its British ally by the fear that the latter *might* accept belt-tightening at home in order to maintain a quasi-imperial role overseas, so cracking the Washington-London axis on which NATO continued to rest. This is, naturally, supposition, and will remain so; but behind the glazed expressions of Presidents and Prime Ministers under pressure it is bluffs and counter-bluffs of this kind which are being weighed in the balance. What was at stake during the Suez affair, apart from Nasser's fate, was the sort of alliance which should prevail in the west: a configuration of capitalist-industrial powers, each pledged to defined actions in the event of Soviet aggression, but free to evolve independent policies in all other circumstances where their interests were perceived to be crucially at stake, or a more disciplined and all-embracing framework within which the lesser partners had always to act in accordance with assumptions prescribed by US Presidents.[27] By stopping the invasion in its tracks at the downward turn of sterling's screw, much to French chagrin, Eden effectively admitted that the Americans were more concerned with imposing their own interpretation of the western alliance than they were with keeping the stopper in the Middle Eastern bottle. The Prime Minister thought this was a mistake as, from a western viewpoint, subsequent events might be said to prove; but under the circumstances it was a *diktat* which the British had little choice but to accept with whatever grace could be mustered.

## IV

The most evident sign of a new American penetration into UK decision-making was, as Eden's most recent biographer has revealed, the degree to which his resignation and Harold Macmillan's succession to the premiership was managed in consultation with Eisenhower's office.[28] It would, of course, be untrue to say that Macmillan was a covert Presidential nominee; but the line between such a statement, and the fact that the US administration privately stressed that they saw Macmillan as the senior Cabinet member whom they could best work with in future, is, under the circumstances of late 1956 and early 1957, a reasonably thin one. Macmillan, therefore, became Prime Minister determined to discharge British interests to the full, but aware that the manner of doing so had to be radically overhauled. Fundamentally, this meant what whereas Eden had tried to explore the workings of British influence outside NATO limits, Macmillan had perforce to operate within that strategic setting to a much more pronounced extent. Power within NATO, however, had little to do with the shifting management of political change in underdeveloped countries, in many of which the UK still carried constitutional responsibility, and a lot to do with contributions towards the outgunning of the Soviet Union. If Britain was to play this game successfully, it was vital to possess a credible nuclear deterrent in a constant state of modernization. In the 1957 Defence Review Macmillan secured a switch of resources from conventional to nuclear programmes on a scale not contemplated by Churchill or Eden. This opened the way to the ending of conscription, finally achieved in 1960. The implication of this was transparent: the UK was not going to fight any large-scale anti-insurgency campaigns of an imperial type in the foreseeable future.

The rub of this revolution in British defence thinking was that its successful implementation depended on American technological (and, by implication, financial) gifts; a new Marshall Aid, but this time for Britain, not western Europe as well, and for bombs, not food. What assurances Macmillan sought and received on this front in the early phase of his premiership we cannot know; but the decisiveness and confidence with which he began to move on colonial issues might imply some guarantees on nuclear assistance. In seeking such US patronage after 1957, indeed, events strengthened Macmillan's negotiating hand. In May 1957 the Soviet Union launched Sputnik I, which made the US land mass vulnerable, for the first time, to Soviet strikes. After that there was a strong (if subsequently very contentious) argument that at least one NATO partner other than the US should have a nuclear arsenal, in order to create uncertainties in Soviet military planning. Nevertheless, the escalating costs and technical complexity of missile development made a compromise between the British and Americans very problematical, and it was necessary for the former to make some credible attempt to evolve a home-made missile capacity; hence the farrago of the abortive Blue Streak project. Suggestively, the critical phase in the establishment of the

British nuclear force between 1957 and 1962 ran parallel with decisive shifts in British colonial policy; and there is little doubt that the UK Cabinet spent more time discussing the former rather than the latter. In the end, President Kennedy, his confidence dented by the Cuban missile crisis, gave in to Macmillan's pressure and the British were gifted (under the Nassau Agreement of 18 December 1962) with a Polaris submarine force which they equipped with their own ('independent') war-heads.[29] This weapon system carried a technical guarantee stretching into the mid-1970s; as such, it represented the high point of British strategic security in the twentieth century, for when else since 1900 had a British Government been able to peer beyond a ten-year period without a multitude of uncertain variables crashing in on the official mind? The almost brazen confidence with which British officials went through the motions of successive decolonizations at Lancaster House undoubtedly bore some relationship to the prospect, and final achievement, of this nuclear apotheosis.

The 'break' in British colonial policy in the aftermath of Suez, however, cannot crudely be attributed to military reorientation, deep-seated in its implications though it was. That reorientation was itself closely related to new financial constraints, since the nuclear argument partly hinged on its cheapness relative to conventional armoury. The underswell of Treasury opposition after 1955 to the grant burdens which Colonial Development was imposing on the UK exchequer was the earliest indication that a sea-change in financial assumptions was occurring. Prior to the mid-1950s it was expected that, after the initial establishment of grant-aided projects, colonial economies would be able to fund their own further development in tandem with commercial lenders. But such optimism regarding self-financing growth in prospectively independent states quickly faded. The Gold Coast experiment was important in this respect, since it became clear that a sovereign Ghana would long remain in the queue for free or cheap loans.[30] Equally perturbing was the Caribbean situation, where metropolitan aid to the smaller islands seemed to have marginal effects in generating development, and where, despite the formation of a loosely-structured Federation in 1956, the larger islands (especially Jamaica and Trinidad) were adamantly opposed to assuming any financial responsibility for their lesser regional partners.[31] In London, therefore, the Treasury took fright at the possibility of the British exchequer becoming the milch-cow for the grant needs of underdeveloped economies, needs which, instead of tapering off, seemed to multiply as populations expanded and interest groups crystallized. Predictably, the Treasury's response was to crack down on colonial loan proposals from whichever quarter they emerged. In addition, that department tried to stimulate the private sector into taking up a larger part of the investment burden, only to find that the financial community in London was becoming less willing to risk funds in underdeveloped areas.[32] As a result of these anxieties the precondition of 'viability' before independence was put on the backburner, since the expenses of such viability would obviously have to be met by the UK Government. Harold Macmillan, during his days as Chancellor of the Exchequer, had been fully exposed to a fiscal critique which easily shaded into a frank anti-colonialism; and it is therefore quite understandable that, on becoming Prime Minister, one of his first acts was to set up a review of colonial commitments on a cost-benefit basis.[33] The effects of these grindings within the Whitehall machine will not be traceable until the records are open. But it can be surmised that the onset of Macmillan's premiership coincided with a new bureaucratic hostility towards the colonial connection.

But the colonial threat to fiscal rectitude must be put in a wider context before the significance of this factor can be properly weighted. The Treasury's attack on development financing was only part of its officials' acceptance of a monetarist analysis of Britain's dilemmas. For an externally oriented trading economy like that of the UK, the constraints within which it worked were ultimately determined by the strength or weakness of its currency, which was why, for example, all its modern imperial crises had coincided with slides in sterling's value. Traditionally such crises had been averted by international funds drawn to London as a commodity entrepot; and after 1945 dollar loans and Commonwealth balances had kept sterling afloat as a reserve currency. But after 1950 financial opinion came to believe that only internal adjustments could underpin a stable equilibrium and, therefore, sustained economic growth. Such an adjustment meant rigid controls on government spending; and so domestic public expenditure became the crux of establishment debate to a degree not seen since the era of high Gladstonianism. The Treasury conviction was that at some point the growth of welfare spending would have to be curtailed; meanwhile the sums meted out to colonial development represented a 'soft', but not insignificant, target. Naturally these monetarist prescriptions appealed to a powerful section of the Conservative Party, and when the first budget of Macmillan's premiership provided only a limited dose of the medicine the (slightly delayed) result was the unprecedented resignation of all three Treasury Ministers.[34] Subsequent moves to excise colonial responsibilities as cleanly as possible, within the limits set by the preservation of 'low level' stability in the territories concerned, was just one way that Macmillan could prove that the reduction of fiscal burdens remained a central objective, even if for the moment the time had not come to freeze the growth in the state's welfare functions. In short, decolonization after 1957 can be related to the return of internal budgetary equilibria as a problem at the heart of British government. Perhaps, too, this helps to explain the curious consensus within UK party politics on late colonial issues; whilst a large number of right-wingers were sympathetic to decolonization because it helped restrain one set of budgetary demands (thereby isolating the die-hard pro-colonialists), left-wingers embraced such policies ostensibly on moral and philosophical grounds, but often because it potentially freed resources for use on social services and other subsidies at home; and although these twains were never likely to meet, they certainly allowed the Government's colonial decisions to go through on the parliamentary nod.[35] It is, therefore, quite logical that after 1963 the most eloquent critic of the UK's East of Suez role, the fag-end of empire, was that lover of the *Raj* and orthodox economy, Enoch Powell.[36]

These British evolutions towards nuclear deterrence and fiscal control marked a more general preoccupation with modernizing British society. This concern with internal renovation was a characteristic of western European nations after 1955. In France, too, there was an explicit connection between social and industrial reform and an emerging prejudice against colonies.[37] The Algerian lobby kept these subterranean movements in check until de Gaulle, for whom the modernization of France and particularly its Army provided the rationale of his quasi-dictatorship after 1958, cut the Gordian knot by dumping *Algerie Francaise* in stages during 1961/2. The decisiveness of Gaullist action on the colonial front between 1958 and 1962, in North and Sub-Saharan Africa, aroused British panic that France was poised for a dynamic role in Europe, and this anxiety lay behind much of Macmillan's thinking. Certainly Roy Welensky, Prime Minister of the Central African Federation, had the impression at the time that the British officials he negotiated with had their minds on Europe, not Africa.[38] For Macmillan, indeed, the UK application to join the Common Market, which he first announced in the House of Commons during July 1961, was intended as a solution for several of Britain's recurrent problems. Thus by yoking British industry into competition with French and German factories, the Market would discipline managements and trade unions into an efficiency they had long evaded, not least under cover of the Sterling Area; it would off-set British dependence on the US implicit in the quest for nuclear status; and it would provide a framework within which the UK's relationship with its current and future ex-colonies could be put on a new basis. Thus when de Gaulle finally vetoed British entry, he did so on grounds (that the UK was not a European power, but one with special responsibilities and duties in the wider world) which were exquisitely chosen to cause the greatest dismay in Whitehall, and which heightened the British belief that decolonization had now to be pushed *a l'outrance*; hence the unseemly bustle with which the most ramshackle dependencies (such as the smaller Caribbean islands, and the High Commission Territories in southern Africa) were pitched into independence during the mid-1960s.

Quite apart from changing bureaucratic assumptions in western Europe, however, decolonization after the late 1950s must be viewed against the backdrop of more general shifts in the contemporary world order. In the mid-1950s the two superpowers had yet to establish an effective condominium; there was 'space' for other systems (such as European metropoles and their colonies) to operate. By 1960 the brashness of President Kennedy and Prime Minister Khruschev expressed a change; the scope for such west European manoeuvre had narrowed and could only be extended, as we have seen, by internal reform and group integration. Meanwhile the centre of gravity of world trade expansion had come to lie between the advanced economies, not between industrial powers and their respective raw material suppliers. This new pattern of commercial growth had been fostered by institutional means (such as the International Monetary Fund and the workings of the General Agreement on Tariffs and Trade) to which non-advanced producers had to accommodate themselves, and which usually accorded them less advantages, in many ways, than the old imperial networks. Within this new milieu of international institutions, with their top-heavy and superbly-salaried bureaucracies, underdeveloped countries were ill-equipped to make their voices heard, however loud they shouted. Even more threatening was the fact that the banking community had revised its risk perspectives in a way that put African and Asian investments well down the pecking order; European financial opinion, too, was becoming conscious of the need to direct a higher percentage of funds to their home economies to match the in-flow of US capital at this time. Whatever the different styles of British, French and Belgian decolonization, therefore, they shared one common characteristic: their prime cause lay not in the inability of declining metropoles to sustain their local rule, but in the fact that new operational modes and challenges had emerged in which the possession of colonies was an expensive (but exciseable) distraction. Thus colonial peoples were accorded sovereign nationhoods so that western Europe should regain some *lebensraum* in a world where the dynamic of Russo-American rivalry was making a mockery of decision-making in London, Paris or Brussels.

V

This article has broken down the working of the imperial factor in British strategies after 1945 into three main phases. The first of these spanned the post-war crisis which lasted until 1949: a crisis of reconstruction, solvency and acute dependency on the United States. In this phase the colonial connection had primarily economic significance in its contribution to monetary stabilization and as a counter-inflationary hedge. The second period (1949–56) was marked by an easing of economic pressures, under the successive impacts of US Marshall Aid spending and the Korean War boom. But the price of American beneficence had been UK participation in NATO, and its exposure to subtle pressures to integrate with western Europe. At this stage the British foreign policy establishment was confronting the fate which it had feared throughout the century: the loss of any credible unilateral capacity through enforced commitment to prescriptive and inflexible alliances. Almost immediately the UK authorities set about trying to work loose from the bonds they felt tightening around them, and the revamping of Britain's relationships with underdeveloped countries in Africa, Asia and the Middle East provided a perfect foil to the US attempts to lock the UK into NATO structures. This meant, among other things, promoting colonial nationalists who fitted into this schema (such as Nkrumah in the Gold Coast) and trying to break those who did not (such as Makarios in Cyprus). The colonial connection continued to be significant in its Sterling Area guise, but its importance primarily lay in this wider political context.

The third phase in British strategy was inaugurated by the Suez debacle of 1956, when the Americans decided to raise the costs of Britain's extra-NATO unilateralism to levels which could not be sustained within the UK political system. Subsequently Macmillan strove, instead, to maximize British influence within the all-embracing parameters of the western alliance, an approach which called, not for complex understandings with clusters of less developed nations, but for a nuclear deterrent and internal reform. Indeed, Macmillan's succession to the premiership coincided with a general re-evaluation of the relationship between British economic growth and the Afro-Asian world, in which an orientation towards the latter threatened to imprison the UK within the most stagnant sector of world commerce; the Sterling Area, for example, came to be seen as an obstacle to coherent UK economic policy.[39] From late 1959 the Conservative Prime Minister commenced a drive towards decolonization which was designed to disencumber the UK of extraneous commitments and so improve her tactical position within the western industrial coalition. In fact decolonizing was much the easiest of metropolitan tasks in this new milieu: screwing nuclear technology out of the US, forcing access to the EEC, damping down the Russo-American rivalries which threatened to crush all who lay between and dumping sterling's reserve currency role were all much tougher. It was not until the early 1970s that the UK slid, as much by luck as by judgement, into the kind of bargaining position envisaged by Macmillan – freed of imperial political and monetary constraints, and less hampered by American hegemony or French intransigence. It was, then, a curious stroke of British misfortune that just at this point the era of post-war economic expansion was ended by another Middle Eastern imbroglio; and if British governments had proved reasonably adept (amidst all the difficulties) at handling the strategic changes of the 1950s and 1960s, they were to prove markedly less successful at presiding over the domestic divisions which dominated the 1970s.

NOTES

*I would like to thank Dr Andrew Porter and Dr Peter Lyon for reading and commenting upon earlier drafts of this paper.

1. A.G. Hopkins, *An Economic History of West Africa* (London, 1973).
2. B.R. Tomlinson, *The Political Economy of the Raj, 1914–47: The Economics of Decolonization in India* (London, 1979).
3. B.R. Tomlinson, 'The Contraction of England: National Decline and Loss of Empire', *Journal of Imperial and Commonwealth History*, Vol. XI, No. 1, Oct. 1982.
4. John Gallagher, *The Decline, Revival and Fall of the British Empire* (Cambridge, 1982).

5. For a study of British colonial reoccupations see F. S. V. Donnison, *The History of the Second World War: British Military Administration in the Far East, 1943–6* (HMSO, 1956).
6. Gabriel Kolko, *The Politics of War: Allied Diplomacy and the World Crisis of 1943–5* (London, 1969) 484-502.
7. British industry's interest in colonial development was prominent from the early phase of post-war planning. See Grand Council Minutes of the Federation of British Industries (FBI) 15 April 1942, FBI Committees January-December 1942, FBI Papers, Modern Records Centre, University of Warwick.
8. N. J. Westcott, 'Sterling and Empire: The British Imperial Economy, 1939–51', Institute of Commonwealth Studies (London) Seminar Paper, Jan. 1983, 6-7.
9. R. Gardner, *Sterling-Dollar Diplomacy: Anglo-American Collaboration in the Reconstruction of Multilateral Trade* (Oxford, 1956) 204.
10. For a narrative of the Anglo-American wartime relationship see Wm. Roger Louis, *Imperialism at Bay: The United States and the Decolonization of the British Empire, 1941–45* (Oxford, 1977).
11. 'Industry and the Dollar Crisis', 20 Aug. 1947, FBI Committees July-Dec. 1947, FBI Papers.
12. For the establishment, and subsequent abandonment, of the Malayan Union, see A. J. Stockwell, *British Policy and Malay Politics during the Malayan Union Experiment 1942–8* (Malaysian Branch of the Royal Asiatic Society, 1979).
13. D. Throup, 'The Origins of Mau Mau', Institute of Commonwealth Studies (London) Seminar Paper, Oct. 1982.
14. For these examples Carl G. Rosberg and John Nottingham, *The Myth of Mau Mau: Nationalism in Kenya* (New York, 1966) 237-241; M. K. Sorrensen, *Land Reform in Kikuyu Country* (London, 1967) 72-93; G. Andrew Maguire, *Towards 'Uhuru' in Tanzania: The Politics of Participation* (Cambridge, 1969) 19-30; Stanley Mayes, *Makarios: A Biography* (London, 1981) 44.
15. Harold Macmillan, *Tides of Fortune, 1945–55* (London, 1969) 151-227.
16. Sir Anthony Eden, *Full Circle* (London, 1960) 97-9.
17. For the classic account of the last phase of French rule in Indo-China see Philippe Devillers and Jean Lacouture, *End of a War: Indo-China, 1954* (London, 1969).
18. Although the Geneva settlement on Indo-China allowed for free elections after a set period, there was never any doubt that Communist rule in North Vietnam was firmly entrenched.
19. A. Low, *Buganda in Modern History* (London, 1971) 102-38.
20. For the usages of national elections in the late colonial setting see Dennis Austin, *Politics in Ghana, 1946–60* (London, 1964).
21. John Iliffe, *A Modern History of Tanganyika* (Cambridge, 1979), 517-18.
22. A. Short, *The Communist Insurrection in Malaya 1948–60* (London, 1965) 173-205, 391-415.
23. For short summaries of this aspect of anti-Mau Mau operations in Kenya see Rosberg and Nottingham, *The Myth of Mau Mau* 303-8; Charles Douglas Home, *Evelyn Baring: The Last Proconsul* (London, 1978) 262-269; M. K. Sorrensen, *Land Reform*, 220-236.
24. S. Mayes, *Makarios*, 62-83.
25. For a general survey of the UK's nuclear policy after 1945 see M. Gowing, *Independence and Deterrence: Vol. I: Policymaking* (London, 1974).
26. The most concise treatment of the Suez affair is in David Carlton, *Anthony Eden: A Biography* (London, 1981) 403-465.
27. For the evolution of this issue see Alfred Grosser, *The Western Alliance: Europe-American Relations Since 1945* (London, 1980).
28. David Carlton, *Eden*, 456-465.
29. Lawrence Freedman, *Britain and Nuclear Weapons* (London, 1980) 15-18.
30. D. J. Morgan, *The Official History of Colonial Development: Volume Three: A Reassessment of British Aid Policy, 1951–65* (London, 1980) 190 and *Volume Four: Changes in British Aid Policy 1951–70* (London, 1980) 121-2.

31. Morgan, *Reassessment of British Aid Policy*, 106-9, 109-139 and Morgan, *Changes in British Aid Policy*, 33-47.
32. Morgan, *Reassessment of British Aid Policy*, 186-191.
33. Morgan, *Reassessment of British Aid Policy*, 13-17.
34. Samuel Brittan, *Steering the Economy* (New York, 1971) 214-19.
35. It is interesting that party political controversy on colonial issues in Britain was, on the whole, more marked during the middle and later 1950s than during the first half of the 1960s. See David Goldsworthy, *Colonial Issues in British Politics* (Oxford, 1971).
36. Phillip Darby, *British Defence Policy East of Suez, 1947–68* (London, 1973) 292.
37. For the anti-colonial theme in Mendésiste thinking, for example, see John Talbot, *The War Without a Name: France in Algeria, 1954–1962* (London, 1981) 31-6.
38. Sir Roy Welensky, *4000 Days: The Life and Death of the Federation of the Rhodesias and Nyasaland* (London, 1964) 345-6.
39. Critiques of Sterling Area operations as they affected the prospects of the domestic British economy became explicit during the course of the 1957 sterling crisis. See A. Shonfield, *British Economic Policy Since the War* (London, 1958) 122-157. Much of the 'observing intelligentsia' had its views coloured by these perspectives, no doubt because the solution it posited for the UK's economic ills seemed relatively painless. See, for example, Susan Strange, *Sterling and British Policy: A Political Study of an International Currency in Decline* (Oxford, 1971).

# British Decolonization since 1945: A Pattern or a Puzzle?

by

## John Darwin

It is scarcely a matter of dispute, or even of serious argument, that by 1945 the British empire was in decline, and British world power ebbing away. The global conditions once so favourable to Britain's colossal empire-on-the-cheap were disappearing one by one with the emergence of the military superpowers, the relative decline of the British economy, the obsolescence of old-style sea-power and the new turbulence of Britain's colonial possessions. It is easy and tempting indeed to regard Britain's international career from 1945 up until her eventual entry into Europe in 1973 as a dismal epilogue to the Second World war, a gloomy saga of lost illusions, lost opportunities and lost causes as the inevitable gradually became the irresistible. From our vantage point in the 1980s we can applaud the realists who grasped the inexorability of declining world status and the futility of resisting it, and regret the wrong-headedness of those who would not read the writing on the wall. From this it has been an easy step to conflate the 25 years after 1945 into a single phase of rapid and predictable decline.

Decline, however, is a treacherously ambiguous phase in the history of empires. The Habsburg empire declined from 1848, or perhaps from 1809, but survived until the last year of the First World War. The Ottoman empire had been in decline since the treaty of Carlowitz in 1699, but survived to inflict 217 years later a series of humiliating defeats on Britain in the Middle East war; the Sick Man of Europe had shown an alarming will to live, perhaps because even sick men will resist being eaten alive. In the same way, though Britain's relative decline as a world and imperial power was a safe bet by 1945, four issues still remained obscure. How rapidly and how completely would British power contract? How swiftly would self-government be conceded to the extremely heterogeneous collection of territories that constituted the imperial system? What would self-government amount to when and if it were granted? And what kind of post-colonial relationship would be established between Britain and her ex-colonies? On each of these questions great uncertainties existed at the end of the war. Yet only by taking these uncertainties into account is it possible to make sense of the calculations of the policy-makers. Unless, that is, we assume that the actual course of British decolonization exactly followed a master plan laid down in Whitehall – an event that would be unique in British post-war history – or that the policy-makers expected or intended that events should fall out as they did. That too strains credulity too far.

I

Of course, from the moment that the British began the transfer of power in their colonial territories after 1945 they set about constructing a rationale for their actions plausible enough and ambiguous enough to satisfy international and especially American opinion, to soothe opinion at home and to flatter the colonial politicians whose goodwill they wanted. The task of fabricating an account that would gratify if not flatter every interested constituency was an heroic one; but it was a challenge that the British official mind was almost uniquely fitted to meet. To extract a set of guiding principles from the raw mass of incoherent political and administrative action, to transform past decisions into the self-evident prelude for future policy (however contrary), to embalm the whole in a paste of consistency with a dash of altruism, these were the tasks for which after all it had been trained and at which the scholar-mandarins excelled.[1] Circumstances required that the policy-makers make myths as fast as they unmade colonies, for the creation of new states and the dissolution of empires was chancy work as the politicians of the French Fourth Republic discovered. Much flannel was needed to prevent combustible elements jarring on each other: the unravelling of empire must appear as an orderly, rational, honourable and, above all, deliberate process – a pattern and not an embarrassing puzzle.

From this necessity was borne what remains perhaps the most influential account of how Britain came to transfer power in her colonial territories after 1945. Its most graceful exponent was Harold Macmillan, a romancer in the tradition of Disraeli. In his memoirs, Macmillan reiterated what had become the orthodox defence of decolonization. 'There is a common illusion', he wrote, 'that this story ... is one of weakness and decay, resulting from the loss of the will to govern inherent in a democratic system. This is an undeserved libel on a people who, twice in my lifetime, demonstrated their courage and tenacity, as well as against its leaders.' He went on:

> It is a vulgar but false jibe that the British people by a series of gestures unique in history abandoned their empire in a fit of frivolity or impatience. They had not lost the will or even the power to rule. But they did not conceive of themselves as having the right to govern in perpetuity. It was rather their duty to spread to other nations those advantages which through the course of centuries they had won for themselves.[2]

In this picturesque version, decolonization became not a symptom of defeat and decline but a crowning achievement of British rule, the goal towards which, Macmillan insisted, colonial rulers had steadily striven.

Implicit in it is the assumption that British colonial policy after 1945 prescribed the steady introduction of phase after phase of constitutional development, carefully graduated to the individual needs of each colony, until at the end of the day a more rapid acceleration became possible and desirable. The road from colonial subordination to sovereign status lay through the corridors of power in a beneficent Whitehall. Empire itself was presented as a white man's burden, a trust honourably discharged and then deliberately and systematically wound up. Here was Whig history large as life and twice as shameless. Just so might we imagine Lord Grey of the Reform bill telling his great grandchildren that his purpose in 1832 had been to pave the way for universal suffrage.

The low-minded alternative to this grandee history has been to see the decolonizing process as an inevitable response to the collapse of British power. One recent Commonwealth historian has discovered in the period 1941–71 an overarching *Pax Americana* and a Britain reduced at the end of the Second World War 'almost to protectorate status'.[3] It is easy in this perspective to see the sloughing off of colonial possessions as the progressive shedding of intolerable burdens at the earliest possible moment. Here decolonization was the conscious recognition that since Britain's days as a great power were numbered, it was essential to speed the transfer of power if disaster was to be avoided. Hence, in rapid succession, representative government, self-government and then independence were offered to grateful colonial politicians, and Britain escaped, as the policy-makers had always intended, unscathed by colonial conflicts that were as futile as they were unwinnable. A modified version of this is represented by those historians who see post-war British colonial policy as a deliberate step-by-step retreat in the face of the floodtide of colonial nationalism, a staged retreat the pace of which was dictated less by British decay than by the rapid growth of political organization and mass politics in the dependencies.[4]

Finally, there are those accounts of post-war British policy which base themselves chiefly upon the memories of civil servants or ministers of the time, or, as in the recent official study of colonial development, upon privileged access to the plans and blueprints of the policy-makers.[5] The result is an uplifting chronicle of sagacity and foresight, of careful adaptation to new circumstances, of enlightened and sympathetic response to the aspirations of colonial populations, of dignified understanding that Britain's role must change with the times. In this version, too, decolonization proceeded in orderly fashion at a pace dictated not so much by the urge to share Britain's democratic heritage, nor by fears of catastrophe, nor by timidity in the face of the nationalist tiger, but rather as a consequence of judicious appraisal, a careful weighing of ends and means, a desire to be helpful and constructive. This, of course, is mandarin history, a version of decolonization of which Sir Humphrey Appleby would approve, and might have written: decolonization as an ordered sequence of memoranda, minutes and masterly inactivity.

Common to all these versions is the assumption that decolonization should be seen as a consecutive sequence, that the British adopted broadly consistent policies across the whole face of their imperial system, and that even if they sometimes changed gear or shifted from the brake to the accelerator and back again, the makers of policy were always moving deliberately in the same direction. The trouble is that the more closely we peer at the actual course of Britain's retreat from empire, the more difficult it is to see any ordered pattern. The notion that post-war decolonization was a long-matured act of benevolence is belied by the record of British rule in much of the pre-war British empire, especially in Africa where the system of indirect rule conserved power precisely in the hands of those whose democratic instincts were least developed.[6] The building of an independent deterrent and the Suez expedition are curious enterprises for a power reduced 'almost to protectorate status'. The onslaught on the Malayan Communist Party, Mau Mau, EOKA or the Front for the Liberation of South Yemen scarcely resemble a staged retreat in the face of nationalism. As for the omniscience of the mandarins, the record of British policy in other spheres, for example, in economic policy or towards Europe, suggests that the predictive powers of the official mind should be measured in hours rather than decades. Moreover, it would have required exceptional clairvoyance to have predicted in the late 1940s that decolonization would follow the course and yield the results that it has.

The fact is, of course, that British foreign and colonial policy after 1945 was riddled with extraordinary and baffling inconsistencies. The independence of India and Pakistan in 1947 took a form precisely contrary to that intended by British policy-makers almost until the last moment. The reluctant concession of self-government to Burma and Ceylon was contrasted with the simultaneous brusque imposition on Malaya and Singapore of a unitary colonial constitution to which local leaders were bitterly opposed and which then had to be abandoned. Colonial withdrawal in South Asia was matched by the uncompromising reassertion of colonial rule in Hong Kong.[7] In 1949 India was admitted to the Commonwealth as a republic. A year earlier, London had refused precisely that concession to Burma which then left the Commonwealth. In Africa between 1948 and 1958 the disparities were no less striking. The Gold Coast and Nigeria were conceded self-government in doses after 1948. But in East Africa African political activity in Kenya was firmly repressed in the 1950s, and an indefinite prolongation of colonial rule envisaged. In Tanganyika, the British tried to impose a multiracial constitution the effect of which was actually to enlarge the influence of immigrant communities – at the expense of Africans – through the new representative institutions. In Central Africa, the centrepiece of British policy was the construction of a white-ruled federation into which the protectorates of Northern Rhodesia and Nyasaland were thrust regardless of the wishes of their African populations. With its telescope clapped firmly to its ear, London declared that opposition could be neither seen nor heard.

Even after 1958, as the scramble out of Africa got under way, British policy remained a jungle of quirks and quiddities. As late as the spring of 1959, the date of Kenya's independence was pencilled in as 1975.[8] The decision to share the benefits of Britain's political tradition with Mr Kenyatta was, to put it mildly, a sudden one. In 1963, the British eventually, and reluctantly, closed down the Rhodesian federation on the grounds that the majority of Africans in the northern territories were opposed to membership. But also in 1963 Aden was gerrymandered into a South Arabian federation after a Legislative Council vote from which most of the elected members (elected anyway by only 10 per cent of the population) were absent.[9] Further east methods were no less proconsular. After a two-month tour of North Borneo and Sarawak in 1962, the Cobbold Commission concluded that although most of the interior population had little idea what the scheme for a Malaysian federation entailed, it could be assumed that the majority favoured it.[10] Plainly, in both cases the wishes or even the interests of the inhabitants were at best a secondary consideration. Nor can it be assumed that even after London became fully committed to the transfer of power in the African colonies and elsewhere, that British policy-makers had quietly resigned themselves to a European destiny or meekly accepted the status to which Britain's relative economic decline condemned her. As late as 1965 the British intended to remain in Aden as the guardians and patrons of a gimcrack South Arabian state, just as they were already of Malaysia, and to use the two great bases. The deployment of the army and navy east of Suez was markedly increased after 1960. As late as 1965 Harold Wilson – that latterday Curzon – made his celebrated assertion that Britain's frontiers were on the Himalayas. (The discovery two years later that they were really on the Rhine was one of the fastest strategic withdrawals in modern times.) Meanwhile, at home, amid a series of financial hurricanes, the Labour Government grimly sought to defend sterling's role as a reserve currency and to preserve the Sterling Area as the economic proof of world power.[11] Not until the dual crisis over devaluation and withdrawal from East of Suez at the end of 1967 did the old imperial reflexes cease to twitch.

Indeed, far from suggesting a staged and deliberate rundown of Britain's overseas commitments and imperial responsibilities, the leaps and lurches of British policy after 1945 form a set of baffling contradictions, indicating neither a gracious manumission of deserving subjects, a headlong retreat in the face of rampant nationalism, nor the cool assessment of Britain's changing interests. What are we to make of it?

During the Second World War, the British had come to recognize that major changes would have to be made in their empire to meet local aspirations, to reflect new social and economic needs and to conciliate American opinion. The necessity for change was most pronounced in Asia where all British colonies had felt the impact of war and conquest. Above all, there was the question of India.

Before 1939 the British had planned to bring India towards dominion status by slow and indefinite stages once the federal constitution laid down in the 1935 India Act had become fully operational.[12] Whatever chances this programme had of success were wrecked by the outbreak of war.[13] Congress denounced India's involuntary participation in an alien conflict and withdrew from government in the provinces. After a series of fruitless negotiations about how much control Indian politicians would be allowed over India's war effort, culminating in the Cripps Mission of 1942, Gandhi launched the abortive 'Quit India' campaign in August 1942. British counter-measures were decisive. The Congress leaders were gaoled and the Congress machine proscribed. But the British remained desperately anxious to secure the support of as many Indians as possible for the Indian war effort and to avoid ruling India by decree. Various politicians were co-opted into office. But the crucial step was to acknowledge the hitherto scouted claim of the Muslim League to be representative of all Indian Muslims, in return for its political cooperation.[14] As a result, by the time the war ended in 1945 Indian politics had undergone a quiet revolution. The Congress leadership, gaoled, bitter and resentful, were determined to reassert their authority. The Muslim League had made hay while the sun shone and captured many Muslims from Congress. Their claim to speak for the Muslim community could not lightly be set aside. Finally, the British were saddled with the promise made by Cripps in the desperate days of 1942 that Britain would give India independence at the war's end.[15]

The Attlee government believed that the prompt fulfilment of this pledge would reap a rich reward in Indian gratitude, and that Congress would respond in a spirit of fraternity.[16] They also intended that Indian independence should follow the formula laid down ten years earlier: an Indian federation that would become the Dominion of India. Their reasons were not merely sentimental. A federal Indian dominion, run by sympathetic Indian politicians would, it was argued fondly in London, respect the long tradition of Anglo-Indian strategic partnership in Asia. India would look to Britain to guarantee her vulnerable northern frontier and in return would share the burdens of the weary titan in South East Asia.[17] But to win this prize, it was essential, as the Chiefs of Staff remarked, for India to be 'stable and contented'.[18] India was anything but that. Congress leaders, now out of gaol, demanded immediate independence and threatened insurrection if it were delayed. They were determined to concede nothing to the Muslim League. Briefly, the Viceroy, Lord Wavell, and London toyed with the idea of a further round of repression to force Congress into a reasonable frame of mind.[19] This was fantasy. In the spring of 1946 the Home Member of the Government of India gloomily remarked 'On the whole I doubt whether a Congress rebellion could be suppressed'.[20] From that moment, British policy in the sub-continent was governed by a sense of frightening impotence. The Raj was over.

Nevertheless, the Attlee cabinet was determined that, come what may, some formula should be found to preserve Indian unity and hold both Muslims and Hindus in a federal state. This was the purpose of the

Cabinet Mission of 1946 which drew up a byzantine scheme for a three-tier federation of India that would reserve external affairs and defence – those aspects of Indian political life which interested Britain most – to a central government, and preserve the unity of India's armed forces. The Mission came, saw and failed.[21] By the end of 1946 Wavell, the Viceroy, was warning that, as waves of communal turbulence washed over the sub-continent, Britain's capacity to keep order was melting away.[22] In desperation Wavell proposed his breakdown plan – to force the Congress and Muslim politicians into compromise. British rule, said Wavell, should be progressively withdrawn from province after province, leaving the local politicians to settle between them the distribution of power, until at last British troops and civilians could be evacuated from the main ports and Indian self-government would become a fact.[23] But the Attlee cabinet would not hear of it.

Their reasons are revealing. Wavell's plan, of course, would fracture the unity of India, probably for ever. But a greater danger worried ministers. To put the plan into effect, it was discovered, would require the repeal or drastic amendment of the 1935 India Act with its obligations and responsibilities.[24] The thought of subjecting their policy to parliamentary debate and public scrutiny at such a moment drove ministers into a panic. They also rejected any idea of setting a time limit on British rule fearing, as the Cabinet minutes record, that it might 'be regarded as the beginnings of the liquidation of the British Empire'.[25] Attlee had not become the King's first minister for that. Instead of changing his policy, Attlee, following a sound political maxim, changed the Viceroy instead.

The new Viceroy, Lord Mountbatten, was shrewd enough to extract from a reluctant Cabinet the promise of a public and precise time-limit,[26] and a virtual free hand to find some way of bringing India to independence. But barren as they were of any idea or policy, the Cabinet's instructions directed the Viceroy to strive for a united India and pay full regard to the defence requirements of the Indian Ocean.[27] Once in India, however, Mountbatten quickly realized that the most for which Britain could hope was to withdraw before British troops and officials were caught up in a vast civil war. But every effort to break down Muslim insistence on Pakistan, or find a formula acceptable to both Congress and the League, seemed doomed to fail until at the last moment Nehru and the Congress reluctantly agreed that partition was preferable to the chaos that threatened.[28] Once Congress accepted partition, Mountbatten set out to terminate British rule at breakneck speed. Before even their new boundaries had been published,[29] two new sub-continental states were declared independent in August 1947.

The course of Cabinet discussion right up to the last phase of the Indian problem disposes of any idea that the end of the Raj represented the triumphant reward for long and careful planning. Relief at Britain's fortuitous escape from a disastrous civil conflict which would have had far-flung repercussions on policy and prestige elsewhere disguised the extent to which India's independence was a humiliating reversal of the hopes and intentions of pre-war and wartime policy-makers. The outcome in India had been dictated not by the blueprint laid down in London nor even by negotiation between British officials and Indian politicians. It was the consequence, above all, of local circumstances, while the policy-makers in London were largely reduced to impatient and nervous onlookers. Even the crucial decision to divide and quit had waited on the conversion of Congress and could not have been done without its consent. The same hasty unplanned retreat occurred in Burma where the British had originally intended to restore their authority and introduce a phased approach to self-government.[30] By December 1946 the Governor reported that the means to resist the principal nationalist party, Aung San's Anti-Fascist People's Freedom League, were lacking.[31] London agreed on immediate independence.[32] To add insult to injury, nothing could persuade the Burmese not to adopt a republican constitution incompatible with the prevailing conventions of Commonwealth membership.[33] Even in placid Ceylon, demands for parity with India's status, British fear of growing communist support, and anxiety to preserve the great naval base at Trincomalee resulted in a dramatic acceleration of the island's hitherto leisurely progress towards self-government.[34] By 1948, Ceylon, like Burma, India and Pakistan, had cast off British rule.

## II

On the face of it, the great bulk of Britain's Asian Empire, once the envy of her rivals, had collapsed like a mud fort in a monsoon. What an Indian historian called the 'Vasco da Gama epoch' in Asian history had come to an end. But the British were curiously reluctant to see the events of 1945–8 in this light. Their strategic thinking, as Phillip Darby has pointed out, showed little sign of being influenced by the loss of India.[35] Indeed, London persisted in thinking that once the excitement of independence had worn off, Indian politicians would recognize how natural it still was to collaborate diplomatically and strategically with their former rulers. In early 1949 Sir William Strang toured South East Asia and the Far East to assess the chances of containing Soviet influence in the region. He reported:

> In all this [that is, Soviet containment] the Indian sub-continent has a special importance.... India in particular has an important role to play in peripheral politics – as a Great Asian Power; as a possible member of the Commonwealth; as a country with whom the United Kingdom now has an opportunity to develop relations on a new basis; as a country with political, cultural and economic interests in South West Asia which we should try to carry with us in the framing of policies and the development of action in that region.[36]

Arguments of this kind, not zeal for the democratic re-definition of the Commonwealth, led the Attlee government to bow to Nehru's demand to stay in the Commonwealth with a republican constitution, although Attlee told Nehru, with Churchillian assurance, that a republic was alien to India's traditions.[37] Agreement was grudging and India was clearly treated as a special case. Much the same pragmatic optimism coloured official attitudes to Ceylon. Patrick Gordon Walker, then junior Commonwealth Minister, visited there soon after independence. British policy, he reported, had been a great success. Local politicians 'are extremely friendly and want to maintain and deepen the British connexion'. If the British had only the sense to be tactful, nothing of substance would change. 'It is hardly too much to say', concluded this future champion of the Commonwealth ideal, 'that if we treat them strictly as a Dominion, they will behave very like a loyal colony: whereas if we treat them as a Colony, we may end in driving them out of the Commonwealth'.[38] Elsewhere in Asia, however, London had no hesitation in treating its colonies exactly like colonies. Hong Kong, as we have seen, was triumphantly reclaimed from a fate worse than death, as a Chinese city.[39] And in Malaya, the Colonial Office was determined to build a strong centralized colonial state, embracing Singapore, as a far more effective bastion of British rule and influence than the ramshackle colony that had collapsed ignominiously in 1942.[40] Even after the Malayan Sultans had successfully repudiated the Colonial Office's brainchild – the Malayan Union – a new federal structure imposed closer unity than ever before without any indication of early self-government.[41] Indeed, London's response to the breakdown of control in 1948 was to declare an emergency and accept a growing military burden in the struggle against the Chinese Communist guerillas.

These dispositions in Asia scarcely look like a master plan for imperial withdrawal, let alone the progressive application of a graduated programme in self-rule. This impression is confirmed by events further west, in the Middle East.

Superficially, Britain's position in the Middle East was much less disrupted by the war which had swept across the colonies in the East. The war ended with British armies in firm control of Egypt and the principal Arab states. British prestige had suffered no such catastrophe as Singapore. Yet turbulence rapidly broke the surface. In Egypt and Iraq, the war had rekindled local nationalism, and in Egypt the end of the war saw renewed efforts by the Egyptian government to persuade the British to give up the giant Suez base and withdraw the garrison which had arrived with the so-called Temporary Occupation in 1882. In Palestine, a far more painful dilemma was in the making. For here British policy was to limit strictly the inflow of Jewish refugees, to reassure the Arab inhabitants and their sympathizers among the Arab States. Yet the flow of Jewish immigration, with the end of Nazi rule in Europe, was swelling to a torrent, while the American government regarded British efforts to check the inrush as inhumane and anti-semitic.[42]

This would have mattered much less had not Bevin and the government's military advisers been determined to create a new and durable

Anglo-Arab relationship which would give Britain's dominance of the Middle East region since 1918 a new and more attractive look. In pursuit of this, Bevin sought new treaties with Iraq and Egypt, and was ready to withdraw British troops from the latter, provided suitable arrangements could be made for the reoccupation of the Suez base in an emergency.[43] But all these plans had come to nothing. The Egyptians demanded a share in the government of the Sudan – which London would not concede – and Iraqi popular feeling led to the collapse of a new defence treaty with Baghdad in 1948. Worst of all, the Palestine Mandate was by now in flames. This tragedy had a two-fold importance for British strategy. In the first place, while Britain remained responsible for the Palestine Mandate, it was likely that Arab opinion everywhere in the Middle East would hold Britain responsible for the political outcome of the Arab-Jewish political struggle. But secondly, the British had assumed all along that the tactical withdrawal from Egypt would be possible because in any sub-division of the Palestine Mandate they would retain control of a zone for military purposes, as a new *place d'armes* in the Middle East.[44]

By the spring of 1947, the futile struggle to find a formula for the partition or self-government of Palestine which would satisfy both Jews and Arabs, concern at growing differences with the United States, anxiety about Arab relations if Britain should seem responsible for an Arab fiasco, as well as irritation at the financial and military burden of acting the policeman in Palestine, had already converted Bevin to the desirability of surrendering the Mandate and repudiating further British responsibility for the territory.[45] In September 1947 the Cabinet decided that this course was inevitable and necessary. Withdrawal was of course partly a gesture of despair and impotence. But it was also calculated and tactical. Britain, argued Bevin, could not remain behind to administer a partition under United Nations' auspices: 'We should be engaged in suppressing Arab resistance ... and antagonising the independent Arab states at a time when our whole political and strategic system in the Middle East must be founded on cooperation with those states....'[46] To remain in Palestine had become incompatible with imperial strategy. And evacuation *was* possible because the Cabinet, far from being intimidated by Egyptian intransigence, had decided to stand pat in Egypt and keep the Canal base. Nor, having abandoned Palestine, was Bevin slow to seek compensation elsewhere. The British had had their eye on Cyrenaica since the end of the war. Now, Bevin told his colleagues in February 1948, the need for strategic facilities was 'paramount'.[47] Indeed, the British set out to promote a united Libya under their client Idris just as they had promoted a unitary Iraq under Faisal 25 years before.

British determination to retain a dominant position in the Middle East, come hell or Harry Truman, was sharpened by their perception of it as a weak and disorderly zone, by fears of Soviet expansion, by a corresponding desire to retain air bases giving access to southern Russia, and by the Middle East's rapidly growing importance as an oil producer.[48] But as the language of the policy-makers conveys, behind these rationalizations lay an instinct or habit of mind. Regardless of what was happening in South or East Asia, regardless of the growth of the superpowers, regardless of Britain's self-evident economic weakness, the old assumptions about what Leo Amery had once called the 'Southern British World' still held good. Britain's spheres of influence had been shaken and stirred – but in the late 1940s they still seemed tenable and defensible.

Paradoxically, it was Britain's very economic weakness after 1945 which reinforced the tendency to think imperially. When the war ended Britain's export economy was in ruins, her supplies of foreign exchange meagre, her debts – especially to sterling and dollar countries – colossal, while her requirement for food, raw materials and other supplies to aid economic recovery was necessarily enormous. The attempt in 1947 to honour the terms of the Anglo-American loan by making sterling convertible, was a fiasco and produced a huge sterling crisis. The Labour Government's reaction was to revert to a highly insulated imperial economy, in which the countries of the Sterling Area (the dominions excluding Canada, the colonies and certain associated states) traded freely with each other but rigorously controlled purchases from outside, especially dollar goods.[49] From a British point of view this system, constructed by Cripps, had three great merits. It preserved sterling as a world currency. It allowed Britain's sterling debts to be discounted by exports, and it secured markets and supplies for Britain which might otherwise have been lost. More completely than ever before, economics and empire had come together, and as colonies like the Gold Coast or Malaya earned precious dollars with their cocoa, tin or rubber, the White Man's burden had come full circle.[50] The poet of empire, had he lived, might well have penned a new imperial ditty:

> Take up the Dollar problem
> Send forth the best ye make
> Preserve the Sterling Balances
> The Yank is at the gate.

This imperial economic solidarity was accompanied by a marked new emphasis upon colonial economic development – to earn more dollars for London's dollar pool. Urging prompt action in Malaya upon his colleagues in July 1948, the Colonial Secretary reminded them:

> [Malaya] is by far the most important source of dollars in the Colonial Empire and it would gravely worsen the whole dollar balance of the Sterling Area if there were serious interference with Malayan exports.[51]

Economic development was also intended to alleviate social unrest and to supply Britain with urgently needed commodities that could be paid for in sterling and on tick. This was the motive behind the disastrous Ground Nuts Scheme in Tanganyika, which inspired the famous slogan 'Give us the job and we will finish the tools'.

For all the drama of Britain's hasty exit from India, Burma, Ceylon and

Palestine, her evident inferiority in economic resources and potential military power to the United States and Russia, it is doubtful if the late 1940s should be seen as a period in which the long-standing assumptions about Britain's position as a world and colonial power were decisively repudiated. Plainly, no intelligent policy-maker could doubt that the scope and shape of British power and influence would have to be remodelled; that in certain theatres preponderance must be yielded to the United States;[52] that prudence required no headlong confrontation with American opinion; and that, in the disturbed aftermath of the war, political opinion in Britain's colonies and client states would need careful handling. What was at work could best be described as the selective shrugging off of commitments, the enforced retreat from exposed positions, coupled with the hope, more perhaps than the expectation, that the heart of the system was still sound. How little even the abandonment of the *raj* was expected to presage the disintegration of British power may be gauged from the almost instinctive decision that Britain must acquire an independent nuclear deterrent – because a great power *must have* the most advanced weapons.[53]

## III

No less than in the early post-war years, British policy towards the colonial dependencies and the spheres of British influence in the 1950s revealed a series of apparently conflicting aims and objects. On one level, the 1950s saw the continuation of the transfer of power begun in India in 1947. The Gold Coast became self-governing in 1951 under the premiership of Kwame Nkrumah – 'Iron Boy', 'Great Leader of Streetboys', as his admirers called him – and fully independent in 1957. The Sudan became independent in 1956. By the late 1950s, too, Nigerian independence was merely a question of time-tabling: at the 1957 Nigerian constitutional conference the British promised that as soon as the new federal government was working properly independence would be given.[54] Malaya too became independent in 1957. Elsewhere in the colonial empire the 1950s saw the steady introduction of new constitutions with wider representation and increasing provision for local participation in the machinery of government. In Kenya, a council of ministers was created in 1954 with some African and Asian membership. Further changes in 1956 and 1958 enlarged African representation in the legislature.[55] Tanganyika was granted a legislative council and then a system of direct election. The old system of 'native authorities' was democratized by the introduction of elected district councils.[56] In Uganda, the Legislative Council was steadily conceded wider powers: an African majority was created among the unofficial members; then a ministerial form of government with five African Ministers; then, in 1958, direct election to the legislature was laid down.[57] In West and East Africa alike, London seemed committed to steady constitutional progress. The emancipation of Africa was in hand. The 1960s would see the completion of the task. And to parallel the forward constitutional moves in Africa, the same steady attenuation of colonial rule could be observed in the West Indies, in the concession of more internal autonomy in Singapore, in the decision to abandon British rule in Cyprus.

But if we are tempted to see in the 1950s a conscious preparation for the great imperial discard of the 1960s, and the recognition of a sharply reduced international status, a number of tiresome inconsistencies have to be explained away. Certainly the British shied away from a struggle with the 'Great Leader of Streetboys' on the Gold Coast. But their willingness to accommodate him may have had much to do with the enthusiasm of the Convention People's Party leaders for a unitary state, a centralizing government and encouraging economic development.[58] Ghana, on independence, remained firmly in the Sterling Area,[59] and it was difficult to see what British interests were damaged by her constitutional progress. In Nigeria the British were obsessed above all with promoting the unification of this vast, valuable but ill-coordinated colony.[60] Although the pressure for more self-government was largely confined to the southern regions, the British energetically promoted constitutional advancement in all as the only way to keep the different parts of the colony in step and offered independence as a bait to persuade the regionally-minded political parties to agree upon the construction of a federal government.[61] Here independence was the horse and unity the cart; the one was meant to pull the other. And as in Ghana, it was hard to see what damage independent Nigeria, bound to the Sterling Area, reliant upon British markets, British capital and British expertise, could possibly inflict on British interests, and easy to see the benefits.[62] In Uganda, the British smiled sweetly upon the representative aspirations of African members in the Legislative Council. But in Buganda where internal self-rule was a living force, and particularist nationalism had growing appeal, the British harassed the Kabaka ruthlessly.[63] Indeed, it is hard not to conclude that the deliberate promotion of the Uganda Legislative Council was not deliberately and chiefly intended to destroy Buganda's Lukiko. Here again, unification and centralization, not self-rule for its own sake, was the centrepiece of British thinking.

The reservations of British policy about the universal desirability of self-government and independence can be easily seen behind the facade of constitutional progress in East Africa. African representation in the Kenya legislature may have been enlarged, but from 1954 until 1960 no African political organization above the level of the district was permitted. Meanwhile, the suppression of Mau Mau and the 'rehabilitation' of its supporters was vigorously prosecuted. The real aim of British policy was to devise a constitution in which the three communities would be obliged to share power, and in which the rules of the electoral game would throw up moderates and throw *out* extremists - of whatever race.[64] Far from swimming with a tide of African nationalism, this was an ambitious effort to outflank and outmaneouvre any demand for universal suffrage and Kenya's independence as a 'black man's country'. Even in April

1959, the success of this bold experiment seemed to require an indefinite British presence. 'I cannot now foresee a date', the Colonial Secretary told the House of Commons, 'when it will be possible for any British government to surrender their ultimate responsibilities for the destiny and well-being of Kenya.'[65] In Tanganyika, a parallel course was followed. As in Kenya, political evolution was to be 'multi-racial'. Thus in the legislature, parity of representation was laid down in a territory where for every European there were four Asians and 430 Africans. Nor was the democratization of local government all that it appeared. The old native authorities had been purely African in membership: the new elected bodies were to have European and Asian members whose influence was, in the nature of things, likely to be considerably greater than their African counterparts.[66] When African opposition to these changes manifested itself it was harassed by government: speakers were banned; branches prohibited. And government itself encouraged the formation of a multi-racial party, the United Tanganyika Party.[67] That this did not flourish may have been partly because its acronym when pronounced meant (approximately) in Swahili 'no bloody good'.

Thus, in East Africa, as opposed to West, London was determined not to concede the principle of independence, nor to recognize Kenya and Tanganyika as 'black man's countries'. The strategic value of Kenya,[68] the size of the settler community and London's belief that, unlike West Africa, economic advancement depended upon immigrant communities, lay behind this resolve. But the supreme example of this highly discriminating attitude to political advancement was to be found in Central Africa.

Until after the Second World War the British had resolutely turned their face against any scheme for the unification of the two Rhodesias and Nyasaland, arguing that their uneven political development ruled out amalgamation or federation.[69] But in the late 1940s, just as the acceleration of constitutional progress in West Africa was accepted, there was a sharp change of approach. A Labour Government blessed, and a Conservative government implemented, a scheme for the federalization of the three territories, two of them British protectorates, the other a self-governing white-ruled colony. The Federation of Rhodesia and Nyasaland was an exotic constitutional beast. The Federal Government was elected on a mainly white franchise and enjoyed wide powers, particularly in the economic field. But internal security in the two protectorates, as well as their constitutional evolution, remained ultimately in the hands of the Colonial Office. And the federation was self-governing but not independent. Here London essayed its most ambitious experiment in multiracial government, for Central Africa was to be the counter-poise to Afrikaner republicanism in South Africa, and an important and dynamic trading partner for Britain. Against such pressing imperial requirements the opposition of African politicians could make, as we have seen, little headway. Moreover, it is clear that the expectation of Conservative Governments in the 1950s was that, when the question was re-examined at the end of a decade of federation, the case for independence would be unanswerable, even if the political life of the federation remained overwhelmingly in European hands.[70] In 1957 London overrode the objections of the local constitutional watchdog, the African Affairs Board, and approved a constitutional amendment which, while prescribing the same proportion of African members in the Federal legislature, made it easier to obtain a two-thirds majority for constitutional change.[71] Under settler pressure, Colonial Office control over Northern Rhodesia was to be reduced by a new territorial constitution, though in an effort to check the surge of *settler* nationalism an elaborate multiracial franchise was devised.[72]

In Central Africa in the 1950s, British policy was in fact far more concerned with taming the aggression of white settler nationalism, while dissuading it from looking South, than with the promotion of African political development, which appeared painstakingly slow. A multiracial dominion in Central Africa under white leadership, not three independent African states, was London's object – and, apparently, the most likely outcome. Further east, the independence of Malaya in 1957 caused barely a ripple. Under the Anglo-Malayan Defence Agreement in 1957, Malaya could continue to call on British military assistance against internal subversion and external attack. In return Malaya consented to remain in the Sterling Area, and to keep its commodity earnings in London's dollar pool.[73] Singapore, meanwhile, remained a great British base, and colonial rule remained in North Borneo and Sarawak. Here too, as in West Africa, independence signalled a new phase of cooperation, not the end of empire.

Against this background of orderly devolution, the Suez crisis stands out like Ayers Rock. It is easy and tempting to treat the operation as a freakish event in post-war British policy, a wild and irrational response to Nasser's urchin impudence, quite out of keeping with the smooth and elegant progression from empire, red in tooth and claw, to commonwealth, fraternal sweetness and light. But there was more to the Suez Crisis than Eden's liver. Like Sarajevo, the crisis over the Canal was the climax to a long period of tension and rivalry – in this case between Britain and Egypt.[74] The British had remained embattled in the Suez base until 1954, as every effort to persuade successive Egyptian governments to sign a treaty permitting re-entry in an emergency came to nothing. Eventually in 1952 the volatile politics of Egypt had erupted and the military regime under first Neguib and then Nasser came to power. With this regime, the British hoped to do business. In 1954 Eden at last concluded with Nasser an agreement to end British occupation of the base provided that re-entry was assured in the event of an external threat to Turkey or any Arab state.[75] Undoubtedly the British hoped by this to improve their Arab relationships; they still had, after all, other bases in the Middle East. Very likely also, they hoped that Nasser would be an Egyptian Ataturk, content to concern himself with the internal transformation of Egypt without challenging Britain's regional influence. Such hopes were ill-founded. By early 1956 it was clear that Nasser was determined to challenge British influence and especially the pretensions of the Hashemite Kingdoms of Iraq and Jordan, Britain's closest Arab allies.[76]

Eden's policy was to try to isolate Nasser in the Arab world.[77] But Nasser was too daring. In 1955 he began buying arms from the Eastern bloc. His nationalization of the Canal was the last straw – but also a golden opportunity to cut him down to size. Undoubtedly, British protests about the breach of international law were genuine; and the claims that Nasser could not be trusted with what was still, even in 1956, an arterial waterway of considerable strategic value was genuinely felt. But it is likely that, certainly in the early stages of the crisis, the British aim was to score a decisive diplomatic victory over Nasser, deflating his growing influence in the Arab world and also, a not unimportant consideration, serving notice that the Base Agreement of 1954 was not a dead letter. From David Carlton's recent and persuasive account we can see how Eden, in the struggle to reconcile these Middle East objectives with Britain's great power dignity as a founding member of the United Nations and the post-war order, was driven eventually to the hollow charade of 'separating' the local combatants.[78] But if we admit that the original plan of publicly disciplining Nasser through concerted international pressure was *not* doomed to failure from the outset, then the Suez episode loses some of its craziness. It loses still more if we accept further that British leaders of both parties wished and expected Britain to remain a global power;[79] and if we recognize that even in the mid-1950s superpower dominance was far from complete and that in Africa, the Middle East and the Indian Ocean, Britain seemed likely to retain much of her old position, at least for some time.

Suez, its aftermath, and the reaction of British leaders revealed not so much the abrupt collapse of British power, or even of British nerve, although the domestic repercussions must have forcibly impressed on subsequent British Cabinets the very considerable risks attached to such overseas intervention on a major scale. What it did show was that the Middle East was much too rough a region, and British control of it far too vulnerable to the interference of *both* superpowers for indirect methods of dominance to work successfully. But whether the policy-makers deduced from this anything more than that one more region – one which they had briefly contemplated abandoning in 1945 – was lost to British influence is, at least, doubtful.

IV

As a phase in the post-war history of British decolonization the 1960s appear much less enigmatic than the 1950s. The decade opened, after all, with Mr Macmillan's reference to a zephyr of mild adjustment in Africa, and ended with Britain's renunciation of all military power East of Suez, and a third and final application to the EEC. After 1960 the retreat from empire seems too consistent to be accidental, too purposeful to disguise ulterior imperialism. The four major decisions of the 1960s – the accelerated withdrawal from East Africa, especially Kenya; the acceptance of majority rule in Zambia and Malawi and the dissolution of the Central African Federation; the application to Europe in 1961, and again in 1967; and the decision to terminate in 1971 all military commitments East of Suez, suggest an agonizing reappraisal of Britain's place in world politics.

Notoriously there was from the autumn of 1959 onwards a markedly more flexible attitude in London towards the political advancement of Britain's colonial territories in East and Central Africa. Various explanations have been put forward for this: the freedom which electoral victory gave to a naturally liberal Mr Macmillan to pursue his policy free from obstreperousness on the backbenches or in Cabinet;[80] Mr Macmillan's own argument that the appropriate moment for transfer of power had arrived; and Ian Macleod's claim that the alternative to prompt withdrawal was a series of bloody colonial conflicts.[81] Doubtless some grain of truth may be found in each of these: but the background to British policy in Africa after 1959 was provided by three events which the policy-makers in London could hardly ignore. The first was the wave of disorder in many different African territories in 1959–60, culminating in the disturbances of Sharpeville. The second was the impact of France's decision to concede independence to her African colonies in 1959, and their triumphant entry into the United Nations in 1960.[82] The third was the devastating prospect opened up in 1960 of anarchy and international conflict in the Congo.[83] These events in turn had to be related to the intensifying rivalry between East and West over the future of the Third World to which Macmillan in particular attached enormous importance.[84] In short, a concatenation of events, mostly external, profoundly altered from 1959 the political landscape of the colonial world: the clockwork schedules of the Colonial Office acquired a curiously pre-Newtonian air.

The constitution-makers now lurched into action with greater urgency than before. At breakneck speed first Tanganyika and then Uganda were advanced to self government followed by independence. Both bordered the Congo, and were exposed to its anarchic fall-out. In Tanganyika, the British made no semblance of resistance to TANU and Julius Nyerere. In Uganda, they abandoned the effort to coerce Buganda into a unitary state and rammed through a new federal constitution, a patchwork quilt of local autonomies whose subsequent history is ample comment on the durability of the arrangements made.[85] Kenya, however, presented a much more complicated problem than either Uganda or Tanganyika where white settlers were far less numerous and powerful. London's tactics in Kenya were, moreover, far from pellucid. The Lancaster House Conference of January 1960 at which Kenya's accelerated advance to majority rule was announced was, it seems likely, the product of London's calculation that, with timely encouragement, Michael Blundell's liberal New Kenya Group would attract support from all three races in Kenya and outflank settler nationalism and black nationalism together.[86] Kenya's new constitution in 1961 was deliberately intended to promote this.[87] Kenyatta was kept in gaol until August 1961, while the British bent over backwards to enhance the prestige first of NKG and then of the anti-Kenyatta Kenya African Democratic Union into which the NKG merged.[88] In 1962, Kenya's constitution was decentralized through the institution of regional assemblies, as a reward to KADU.[89] As it turned out, however, KADU with its tribal divisions was no match for the Kenya African National Union and Kenyatta, once universal suffrage elections were introduced: and Kenyatta in power rapidly lost his demonic quality. But it is at very best uncertain that the British originally intended their constitutional reforms in Kenya to lead to independence under Kenyatta in December 1963; much more likely that they hoped that a moderate multiracial party would be the beneficiary of their constitution-making, with a successor-state bound closely to Britain. Compared with the constitutional problem in Central Africa, Kenya was child's play.

In Central Africa, the British Government had begun by readily endorsing the coercion of anti-federation African political movements in Northern Rhodesia and Nyasaland in February-March 1959.[91] In Nyasaland this policy backfired badly and created widespread disorder with the result that London felt constrained to appoint a commission of enquiry under Sir Patrick Devlin. This report was the most violent castigation of a colonial administration perhaps since 1900, and an explicit testimonial to the depth of African hostility to the white-ruled federation.[92] It was in these unfortunate circumstances that the British were obliged to despatch the Monckton Review Commission to consider whether the Federation was now ready for independence and what adjustments should be made in its working – a review laid down in the Federal Constitution. The Review Commission, far from being remote, technical and implicitly sympathetic to the federation, was forced to adjudicate on its popularity among Africans and concluded that it had none.[93] But far from recognizing the inevitability of the federation's collapse, the Commission recommended a series of sweeping reforms designed to make it palatable to African opinion.[94] The British Government eagerly followed this line.[95] In the course of 1961 the white politicians of Southern Rhodesia were persuaded to liberalize their constitution – 15 of the 65 seats were to be available to Africans – so as to mollify African mistrust of white federal domination. Nyasaland could not be saved from majority rule but its right to secede from the federation was not admitted.[96] The crucial decision was over what kind of constitution would be introduced in the Northern Rhodesia Protectorate, with its small but vociferous white community and its mining industry – whose complementarity with Southern Rhodesian coal and foodstuffs was the economic rationale of federation. If Northern Rhodesia were granted African majority rule, the Federation was dead.

In 1960–61, London agonized over this problem. Enormous ingenuity was expended devising fancy franchises that would just ensure a pro-federation majority – but not blatantly. The Cabinet could not agree upon African majority rule.[97] Then in June 1961 a constitutional scheme was put forward by the Colonial Office which seemed likely to yield a white majority in the Lusaka legislature.[98] The whites were overjoyed. Violent African disturbances broke out in Northern Rhodesia in the latter part of 1961. London changed its tune, mindful perhaps of Katanga and aware that with the Kuwait operation, few troops were spare to keep order. The sums were done once more. This time an African majority was on the cards.[99] But even now, hope was not abandoned. Butler, as Central African Secretary, struggled unavailingly to prolong the federation.[100] But its fate was sealed not in London but by the electoral triumph in both Rhodesias of parties opposed to its continuation. In March 1963, the British Cabinet merely switched off the life support. Nyasaland and Northern Rhodesia proceeded out of federation and into independence. By London's criteria, the outcome of decolonization here, as in India, was a disastrous reversal of British policy.

Britain's decolonizing policy in Africa in the crucial phase of the transfer of power from 1960–64 was unquestionably influenced by the long tradition of trusteeship in colonial administration and respect for certain political maxims. But it was also the victim of unpredicted circumstances. Above all, it was meant as a vehicle for preserving British influence in a period of rapid political and international change on the continent. Fearful of Soviet blandishments, nervous of unfavourable comparisons with the generosity of French policy, anxious to construct amenable successor regimes, the British found themselves sliding far more rapidly than they had expected towards majority rule almost everywhere.

But this remarkable flexibility in Africa was accompanied by striking new dispositions East of Suez. Successive defence white papers from 1961–65 stressed the importance of Britain's role in the Indian Ocean.[101] At London's insistence the South Arabian Federation was cellotaped together with the promise of independence and a defensive guarantee from Britain. The Malaysian federation was formed, with a similar British promise, and as at Aden, the use of a military base of great regional importance. These commitments were undertaken at a time when British military manpower, with the end of National Service, was contracting and costs rising.[102] As has sometimes been suggested, British policy was a welcome reinforcement to Washington as America's effort to contain communism in Vietnam grew more and more strenuous. But this East of Suez role conformed well with the instinct, common to politicians of both major parties, to retain Britain's great-power spheres of influence – for just a little longer. Even after the decision in 1966 that Britain could not afford the new aircraft carrier to make her eastern naval position viable, the Cabinet, in Richard Crossman's account, turned hither and thither for some means to keep the Indian Ocean a British lake.[103] As his diaries show, it required the devaluation crisis of November 1967, the unlikely alliance of Jenkinsite Europeanists and the Left and the timely defection of Wilson to overcome the last ditch resistance of what Crossman tartly called the 'Great Britain' school in the Cabinet, and to extract the final avowal that the last vestiges of the imperial role were at an end.[104]

## V

Much of Britain's experience of decolonization, it might be concluded, confirms the usefulness of Herbert Spencer's law of unintended consequences. Nothing stimulated political mobilization in the British colonies more than London's efforts to encourage economic development. Careful constitutional compromises invariably carried the seeds of their own destruction.[105] Self-government and independence turned out in most cases to be far more real than the British expected; the influence which the British hoped to exercise over their former colonies faded away as their economic fortunes declined.[106] In retrospect, as we have seen, British leaders liked to see their demission of empire as the actions of an enlightened father, wisely conferring responsibility on his boisterous, but essentially good-natured, offspring. In fact, a better image might be that of an impoverished grandee whose hereditary mansion becomes slowly uninhabitable room by room as, in apparently random sequence, the floors give way, the plumbing fails, the ceilings fall in. But however dilapidated the mansion became, it was not to be given up because no other mode of life was tolerable and an address is, after all, an address.

In short, far from there being a planned withdrawal, a considered transformation from empire to commonwealth, what actually occurred from 1945 until the late 1960s was the unpredictable erosion of position after position, foothold after foothold, followed on each occasion by further efforts to hold together the remnants of world power and influence, by one means or another.

Thus, if we search for any logic in the process of Britain's decolonization we may be disappointed. To that extent, the transfer of power and the retreat of British influence followed a baffling wayward course that had little to do with any of the criteria for imperial withdrawal to which British leaders appealed. To that extent it was a puzzle. But a deeper pattern may perhaps be discerned. The pragmatic ingenious adaptation of British policy was geared, above all, to the preservation of British world power in increasingly adverse circumstances. This is neither puzzling nor surprising. It would have made sense to Metternich or Buol. The old equation of world power, independence and prosperity could not be unlearned so easily. Until the end of the 1950s the limits on superpower dominance still seemed to leave much scope for British power. The burdens seemed manageable and the likely benefits substantial. And, who are we, the Falklands generation, to find imperial fantasies so puzzling?

### NOTES

1. See W. R. Louis, *Imperialism at Bay 1941–1945* (Oxford, 1977) 140-46; 188ff; 224.
2. H. Macmillan, *Pointing the Way* (London, 1972) 116-17.
3. W. D. McIntyre, *Commonwealth of Nations: Origins and Impact* (Minneapolis, 1977) 341.

4. For example, S.C. Easton, *The Rise and Fall of Western Colonialism* (London, 1964) 370.
5. See D.J. Morgan, *The Official History of Colonial Development*, Vol.5: *Guidance Towards Self-government in British colonies 1941–70* (London, 1980) 183.
6. P. Gifford, 'Indirect rule: touchstone or tombstone for colonial policy' in P. Gifford and W.R. Louis, *Britain and Germany in Africa* (New Haven, 1967) 351-91.
7. C. Thorne, *Allies of a Kind* (pbk edn. Oxford, 1979) 551, 557-8; G.B. Endacott, *Hong Kong Eclipse* (Hong Kong, 1978) 258-80; D.C. Wolf, ' "To secure a convenience": Britain recognises China – 1950', *Journal of Contemporary History* 18, 2 (1983), 299-326.
8. C. Douglas-Home, *Evelyn Baring: The Last Proconsul* (London, 1978) 283.
9. F. Halliday, *Arabia Without Sultans* (Harmondsworth, 1974) 186-7.
10. *Report of the Commission of Enquiry, North Borneo and Sarawak 1962*, Cmnd. 1794 (1962) 30, 42.
11. Susan Strange, *Sterling and British Policy* (London, 1971).
12. A. Seal, 'Imperialism and nationalism in India', *Modern Asian Studies* 7, 3 (1973), 321-47; B.R. Tomlinson, *The Indian National Congress and the Raj* (London, 1976) 30-1; R.J. Moore, *The Crisis of Indian Unity* (Oxford, 1974) 297-8.
13. 'Hitler has rather overset our Indian politics', remarked the Viceroy in March 1940. Linlithgow to Baldwin, 22 March 1940, Baldwin papers box 107, Cambridge University Library.
14. G. Rizvi, *Linlithgow and India* (London, 1978) 206-7, 237-9.
15. R. Coupland, *The Constitutional Problem in India* (Madras, 1944), Part II, 335-7, 273; R.J. Moore, *Churchill, Cripps and India* (Oxford, 1979).
16. Cabinet India and Burma committee 1st meeting, 17 Aug. 1945. N. Mansergh (ed.), *Constitutional Relations Between Britain and India: Transfer of Power 1942–7* (hereafter *TP*) VI, 79. Cabinet 24 (45) 20 Aug. 1945. CAB[inet] 128/1 P.R.O.
17. Cabinet Far East civil planning unit, report 14 Jan. 1946. *TP* VI. 780; Note by Secretary of State for India on proposed contents of Anglo-Indian treaty. 23 Feb. 1946, *TP* VI. 1051-52; Hollis to Monteath, 13 March 1946, *TP* VI. 1167-73.
18. Ibid.
19. Wavell to Pethick-Lawrence (encl.) 6 Nov. 1945, *TP* VI, 451-4; memo. by Secretary of State for India, 14 Nov. 1945, *TP* VI, 482-3.
20. Thorne to Abell, 5 April 1946, *TP* VII, 151.
21. R.J. Moore, *Escape from Empire* (Oxford, 1983).
22. P. Moon (ed.), *Wavell: The Viceroy's Journal* (London, 1973), 367-75; Wavell to Sec. of State for India, 11 Nov. 1946, *TP* IX, 41.
23. *Viceroy's Journal*, 386ff.
24. *TP* IX, 68; *TP* IX, 332, 358.
25. *TP* IX, 427-31.
26. See K. Harris, *Attlee* (London, 1982) 378-9; *TP* IX, 748-52.
27. *TP* IX, 972-4.
28. S. Gopal, *Jawaharlal Nehru*, 1 (London, 1975), 342-3.
29. *TP* XII, 257-76.
30. See N. Mansergh, *Documents and Speeches on British Commonwealth Affairs 1931–52* Vol. II (London, 1953) 762-5.
31. Governor of Burma to Sec. of State for Burma, 7 Dec. 1946, Prime Minister's papers [PREM] 8/412, PRO.
32. Cabinet 9 (47) 17 Jan. 1947, PREM 8/412.
33. Governor of Burma to Sec. of State for Burma, 9 June 1947; Governor-General, Malaya, to Colonial Secretary, 27 June 1947, both in PREM 8/412.
34. Cabinet 44 (47) 6 May 1947, CAB 128/9.
35. P. Darby, *British Defence Policy East of Suez 1947–68* (London, 1973) Chap. 1.
36. Strang's report, 27 Feb. 1949, C.P. (49) 67, 17 March 1949, CAB 129/33. See also Cabinet Committee on Commonwealth Relations C.R. (49) 2nd conclusions, 8 Feb. 1949, PREM 8/950.
37. Attlee to Nehru, 20 March 1949, PREM 8/950.

38. Memo. by P.C. Gordon-Walker, C.P. (48) 91, March 1948, CAB 129/26.
39. See above Note 7.
40. See A.J. Stockwell, 'Colonial planning during World War II: The case of Malaya', *Journal of Imperial and Commonwealth History* 2, 3 (1974), 337; memo. by Colonial Secretary, C.P. (45) 133, 20 Aug. 1945, CAB 129/1.
41. B. Simandjuntak, *Malayan Federalism 1945–63* (London, 1969).
42. M.J. Cohen, *Palestine and the Great Powers 1945–48* (Princeton, 1982).
43. See Cabinet 57 (46) 6 June 1946; 58 (46) 7 June 1946, CAB 128/5. For Iraq, memo by Foreign Secretary, 3 Oct. 1947, C.P. (47) 277, CAB 129/21.
44. Cabinet Defence Committee memoranda, D.O. (47) 3, 6 Jan. 1947, CAB 131/4; and gloomy report of chiefs of staff dated 7 March 1947, ibid.; also Cohen, *Palestine*, 37-41.
45. Cohen, *Palestine*, 222-23.
46. Memo. by Foreign Secretary, 18 Sept. 1947, C.P. (47) 259, CAB 129/21.
47. Memo. by Foreign Secretary, 4 Feb. 1948, C.P. (48) 43, CAB 129/24.
48. In 1939 the Middle East produced about five per cent of the world's oil. By 1949 this had risen to around 15 per cent. S.H. Longrigg, *Oil in the Middle East* (London, 1954), App.II(b).
49. See P.W. Bell, *The Sterling Area in the Post-war World* (Oxford, 1956).
50. Ibid., 56-7.
51. Memo. by Colonial Secretary, 1 July 1948, C.P. (48) 171, CAB 129/25.
52. B. Rubin, *The Great Powers in the Middle East 1941–47* (London, 1980) 47, 64.
53. M. Gowing, *Independence and Deterrence, 1: Policymaking* (London, 1974) Chap. 6.
54. *Report by Nigerian Constitutional Conference May-June 1957* Cmnd. 207 (1957), 26.
55. *Kenya: Proposals for New Constitutional Arrangements* Cmnd. 309 (1957).
56. J. Iliffe, *A Modern History of Tanganyika* (Cambridge, 1979); G.A. Maguire, *Towards 'Uhuru' in Tanzania* (Cambridge, 1969); R.C. Pratt, *The Critical Phase in Tanzania 1945–68* (Cambridge, 1976).
57. D.A. Low and R.C. Pratt, *Buganda and British Overrule 1900–1955: Two Studies* (London, 1960); D.A. Low and A. Smith (ed.), *A History of East Africa* 3 (Oxford, 1976).
58. The Convention People's Party government eagerly taxed the farmers to provide development finance. G.B. Kay (ed.), *The Political Economy of Colonialism in Ghana* (Cambridge, 1973) 47.
59. For Nkrumah's assurances on this to a former Labour Colonial Secretary, Nkrumah to James Griffiths, 14 Dec. 1956, A. Creech-Jones papers 18/4, Rhodes House, Oxford.
60. See memo. by Colonial Secretary, 3 May 1950, C.P. (50) 94, CAB 129/39.
61. See Note 54.
62. For the early post-independence relationship, O. Ojedokun, 'The Anglo-Nigerian entente and its demise 1960–62', *Journal of Commonwealth Political Studies* IX, 3 (1971).
63. Low and Pratt, *Buganda*.
64. Through such devices as parity of representation and the Council of State.
65. *H.C. Deb.* 5s, 604, col. 563.
66. Maguire, 203.
67. Ibid., 179; Iliffe, *Tanganyika*, 521-2, 535.
68. For London's growing interest in Kenya as a main base in the 1950s, Darby, *Defence Policy*, 124, 125, 175, 203-6.
69. The conclusion of the Bledisloe report in 1939.
70. D.C. Mulford, *Zambia: The Politics of Independence 1957–64* (London, 1967) 51; R. Welensky, *4000 Days* (London, 1964) 77.
71. *H.C. Deb.* 5s 578, cols. 808ff.
72. Mulford, *Zambia*, 50-54, 58-60.
73. *Report by Federation of Malaya Constitutional Conference* Cmnd. 9714 (1956) 8-9.
74. See P.J. Vatikiotis, *Nasser and his Generation* (London, 1978); Patrick Seale, *The Struggle for Syria* (London, 1964); Royal Institute of International Affairs, *Great Britain and Egypt 1914–51* (London, 1952); P. Woodward, *Condominium and Sudanese Nationalism* (London, 1979).

75. D. Carlton, *Anthony Eden* (London, 1981) 356-58; A. Eden, *Full Circle* (London, 1960) 259-61; Selwyn Lloyd, *Suez 1956: A Personal Account* (London, 1978) 21-3.
76. Lloyd, *Suez*, 59; Seale, *Syria*, 247-50.
77. Lloyd, *Suez*, 60; Carlton, *Eden*, 403.
78. Carlton, *Eden*, esp. 427-29.
79. Robert Skidelsky, 'Lessons of Suez' in R. Skidelsky and V. Bogdanor, *The Age of Affluence* (London, 1970).
80. D.J. Goldsworthy, *Colonial Issues in British Politics 1945–61* (Oxford, 1971) 365-66.
81. N. Fisher, *Iain Macleod* (London, 1973) 142.
82. W.J. Foltz, *From French West Africa to the Mali Federation* (New Haven, 1965) 68-70; G. Barraclough (ed.), *Survey of International Affairs 1959–60* (London, 1964) Chap. VII.
83. The summer of 1960, mused Macmillan, bore a disturbing similarity to that of 1914: 'Now Congo may play the role of Serbia' (Diary, 4 July 1960), Macmillan, *Pointing the Way*, 264.
84. Ibid., 47, 116-17, 266, 431.
85. D.A. Low, *Political Parties in Uganda 1949–62* (London, 1962); Low and Smith (ed.), *History of East Africa* Vol. 3, 90-105.
86. Perhaps significantly Macleod's brother was a leading figure in the NKG.
87. G. Wasserman, *The Politics of Decolonisation: Kenya Europeans and the Land Issue 1960–65* (Cambridge, 1976) 46ff; G. Bennett and C.G. Rosberg, *The Kenyatta Election: Kenya 1960–61* (London, 1961) 18ff.
88. Wasserman, *Decolonisation*, 85 for Macleod's jubilation at the electoral victory of the NKG and KADU in 1961.
89. *Report of the Kenya Constitutional Conference 1962*, Cmnd. 1700 (1962) Appendix.
91. Benson to Colonial Office in Mulford, *Zambia*, 104-5.
92. *Report of the Nyasaland Commission of Enquiry*, Cmnd. 814 (1959), paras. 42, 43.
93. *Report of the Advisory Commission on the Review of the Constitution of Rhodesia and Nyasaland*, Cmnd. 1148 (1960), para. 27.
94. Ibid., paras. 100, 114, 123, 221.
95. Lord Home, *The Way the Wind Blows: An Autobiography* (London, 1976) 129-31; Lord Butler, *The Art of the Possible* (London, 1971) 210.
96. Not until December 1962 was Nyasaland's right to secede from the federation acknowledged by HMG.
97. Macmillan, *Pointing the Way* (Diary, 4 Feb. 1961) 309.
98. Mulford, *Zambia*, 194-96.
99. Ibid., 210.
100. Butler, *Art of the Possible*, Chap. X.
101. Darby, *British Defence Policy East of Suez, 1947–68* (London, 1973) 192, 218, 276, 283.
102. Army manpower was more than halved between 1956 and 1966. Ibid., 328.
103. R. Crossman, *The Diaries of a Cabinet Minister*, Vol. 2 (London, 1976) 155-6 (9 Dec. 1966).
104. Ibid., Vol. 2, 634-5, 645-7, 649ff.
105. Iliffe, *Tanganyika*; D.A. Washbrook, 'Law, state and agrarian society in colonial India', *Modern Asian Studies* 15, 3 (1981), 649-721.
106. M. Lipton and J. Firn, *The Erosion of a Relationship: Britain and India since 1960* (London, 1975).

# Notes on the Contributors

**Michael Brock** succeeded Sir Norman Chester as Warden of Nuffield College in 1978, was awarded the CBE in 1981, and holds Honorary Fellowships of Corpus Christi and Wolfson Colleges, Oxford, and an Honorary D.Litt. of Exeter University. He is the author of *The Great Reform Act* (1973), and co-editor, with his wife, of *H. H. Asquith: Letters to Venetia Stanley* (1982).

**David Fieldhouse**, now Vere Harmsworth Professor of Imperial and Naval History and Fellow of Jesus College in Cambridge, succeeded Freddie Madden as Beit Lecturer in Commonwealth History in Oxford in 1958 and was his colleague and collaborator there until 1981, when he moved to Cambridge. His publications include *The Colonial Empire* (1966; 2nd. ed. 1982), *Economics and Empire 1830–1914* (1973) and *Unilever Overseas* (1978).

**Kenneth Robinson**, after serving at the Colonial Office and as a Fellow of Nuffield and Reader in Colonial Administration, became in 1957 Professor of Commonwealth Affairs and Director of the Institute of Commonwealth Studies in the University of London, which he left in 1965 when appointed Vice-Chancellor of the University of Hong Kong. A substantial contributor to the revised *African Survey* published by Lord Hailey in 1956, he also edited with Freddie Madden *Essays in Imperial Government* (Oxford, 1963), a *Festschrift* for Margery Perham. With Professor Bruce Miller he founded in 1961 the *Journal of Commonwealth Political Studies* (now the *Journal of Commonwealth and Comparative Politics*) and continued to edit it until his departure for Hong Kong. His Reid Lectures at Acadia University in 1963 were published as *The Dilemmas of Trusteeship* (Oxford, 1965), and his 1979 Callander Lectures at Aberdeen University, entitled *Memoirs of a Colonialist*, are to be published soon.

**Ronald Robinson**, Beit Professor of Commonwealth History and Fellow of Balliol College, Oxford since 1971, was formerly scholar and Fellow of St John's College, Cambridge, Lecturer in the Expansion of Europe, and Smuts Reader in Commonwealth Studies there. He has written variously on British imperialism of the nineteenth and twentieth centuries, especially in Africa, often with his friend the late Professor Jack Gallagher. With Freddie Madden he contributed several chapters on general imperial issues in the *Cambridge History of the British Empire* (Vol. III).

**Paul Langford** is Fellow and Tutor in History at Lincoln College, Oxford. He is General Editor of *The Writings and Speeches of Edmund Burke* and has recently edited a volume in the series covering Burke's career between 1766 and 1774. His articles have covered a range of domestic and imperial themes in eighteenth-century British history, and his publications include *The First Rockingham Administration 1765–1766* and *The Excise Crisis: Society and Politics in the Age of Walpole*.

**Colin Newbury** is Senior Lecturer in Commonwealth History and Fellow of Linacre College, Oxford. A New Zealander, he has taught History at the University of Ibadan and has been Visiting Professor at Duke University and the University of Hawaii. His publications include editions and monographs on West Africa and the Pacific and articles on imperial labour and economic history.

**Paul Hayes** read Modern History at St John's College, Oxford and then completed his doctorate at Nuffield College. He has also studied at the Universities of Dijon, Marburg, Lausanne and Oslo, and is the author of four books and numerous articles. Since 1965 he has been Fellow and Tutor in Modern History and Politics at Keble College, Oxford, and continued his association with Freddie Madden through a number of specialized courses.

**Gowher Rizvi**, Lecturer in International Studies at the University of Warwick, came to Oxford in 1976 as a Rhodes Scholar from Bangladesh and worked on his D.Phil. under the supervision of Freddie Madden; later he was appointed Beit Junior Lecturer in Commonwealth Studies. The author of *Linlithgow and India: A Study of Constitutional and Political Impasse in India 1936–1943*, he has contributed several articles on themes in imperial policies, the problems of Muslim minorities and the institutionalization of military regimes in Bangladesh. He is currently writing a history of the British Empire-Commonwealth, 1760–1970.

**Anthony Low**, Smuts Professor of the History of the British Commonwealth and Fellow of Churchill College, Cambridge, has been a domiciled resident in four Commonwealth countries. As Professor of History and founding Dean of the School of African and Asian Studies at the University of Sussex, he helped with the foundation of the Institute of Development Studies there. In 1973 he returned to Canberra to be Director of the Research School of Pacific Studies at the Australian National University, and was later appointed Vice-Chancellor. He is the author of three books on the modern history of Buganda, and has contributed to all three volumes of the *Oxford History of East Africa*, the last of which he edited with Alison Smith. His work on modern Indian history includes the editing of two volumes of research essays, compiling a guide on India's archives, writing additional papers and publishing a collection of essays, *Lion Rampant*.

**Robert Holland** was an Open Scholar in Modern History at Jesus College, Oxford and later a Research Scholar at St Antony's College. His doctoral dissertation, later published as *Britain and the Commonwealth Alliance, 1918–39*, was produced under the supervision of Freddie Madden. He was Beit Junior Lecturer in Commonwealth Studies at Oxford and in 1977 became Lecturer in History at the Institute of Commonwealth Studies in London University. He has published various articles on British imperial economic interests in the twentieth century.

**John Darwin** was a research student at Nuffield College, Oxford from 1969 until 1972, and is now Lecturer in History at the University of Reading. His main interests lie in the disintegration of British imperial power after 1914. He is the author of *Britain, Egypt and the Middle East: Imperial Policy in the Aftermath of War 1918–22* (1981), and of a forthcoming study of Britain's retreat from empire after 1945.

For Product Safety Concerns and Information please contact our EU
representative GPSR@taylorandfrancis.com
Taylor & Francis Verlag GmbH, Kaufingerstraße 24, 80331 München, Germany

www.ingramcontent.com/pod-product-compliance
Lightning Source LLC
Chambersburg PA
CBHW061444300426
44114CB00014B/1822